taste of home

EVERYDAY slow cooker

& ONE DISH RECIPES

EDITORIAL
EDITOR-IN-CHIEF Catherine Cassidy

EXECUTIVE EDITOR/PRINT & DIGITAL BOOKS Stephen C. George
CREATIVE DIRECTOR Howard Greenberg
EDITORIAL SERVICES MANAGER Kerri Balliet

SENIOR EDITOR/PRINT & DIGITAL BOOKS Mark Hagen
EDITOR Krista Lanphier
ASSOCIATE CREATIVE DIRECTOR Edwin Robles Jr.
ART DIRECTOR Gretchen Trautman
CONTENT PRODUCTION MANAGER Julie Wagner
LAYOUT DESIGNER Nancy Novak
COPY CHIEF Deb Warlaumont Mulvey
COPY EDITOR Alysse Gear
RECIPE EDITOR Mary King
CONTRIBUTING COPY EDITOR Valerie Phillips

RECIPE CONTENT MANAGER Colleen King
RECIPE TESTING Taste of Home Test Kitchen
FOOD PHOTOGRAPHY Taste of Home Photo Studio
EDITORIAL ASSISTANT Marilyn Iczkowski

BUSINESS
VICE PRESIDENT, PUBLISHER Jan Studin, jan_studin@rd.com
REGIONAL ACCOUNT DIRECTOR Donna Lindskog, donna_lindskog@rd.com
EASTERN ACCOUNT DIRECTOR Joanne Carrara
EASTERN ACCOUNT MANAGER Kari Nestor
ACCOUNT MANAGER Gina Minerbi
MIDWEST & WESTERN ACCOUNT DIRECTOR Jackie Fallon
MIDWEST ACCOUNT MANAGER Lorna Phillips
WESTERN ACCOUNT MANAGER Joel Millikin
MICHIGAN SALES REPRESENTATIVE Linda C. Donaldson
SOUTHWESTERN ACCOUNT REPRESENTATIVE Summer Nilsson

CORPORATE INTEGRATED SALES DIRECTOR Steve Sottile
DIGITAL SALES PLANNER Tim Baarda

GENERAL MANAGER, TASTE OF HOME COOKING SCHOOLS Erin Puariea

DIRECT RESPONSE ADVERTISING Katherine Zito, David Geller Associates

VICE PRESIDENT, CREATIVE DIRECTOR Paul Livornese
EXECUTIVE DIRECTOR, BRAND MARKETING Leah West
SENIOR MARKETING MANAGER Vanessa Bailey
ASSOCIATE MARKETING MANAGER Betsy Connors

VICE PRESIDENT, MAGAZINE MARKETING Dave Fiegel

READER'S DIGEST NORTH AMERICA
PRESIDENT Dan Lagani

VICE PRESIDENT, BUSINESS DEVELOPMENT Jonathan Bigham
PRESIDENT, BOOKS AND HOME ENTERTAINING Harold Clarke
CHIEF FINANCIAL OFFICER Howard Halligan
VICE PRESIDENT, GENERAL MANAGER, READER'S DIGEST MEDIA Marilynn Jacobs
CHIEF CONTENT OFFICER, MILWAUKEE Mark Jannot
CHIEF MARKETING OFFICER Renee Jordan
VICE PRESIDENT, CHIEF SALES OFFICER Mark Josephson
VICE PRESIDENT, CHIEF STRATEGY OFFICER Jacqueline Majers Lachman
VICE PRESIDENT, MARKETING AND CREATIVE SERVICES Elizabeth Tighe
VICE PRESIDENT, CHIEF CONTENT OFFICER Liz Vaccariello

THE READER'S DIGEST ASSOCIATION, INC.
PRESIDENT AND CHIEF EXECUTIVE OFFICER Robert E. Guth

COVER PHOTOGRAPHY
PHOTOGRAPHER Jim Wieland
FOOD STYLIST Kathryn Conrad
SET STYLIST Dee Dee Jacq

@2012 REIMAN MEDIA GROUP, LLC
5400 S. 60TH ST. GREENDALE, WI 53129

INTERNATIONAL STANDARD BOOK NUMBER (13): 978-61765-108-3

LIBRARY OF CONGRESS CONTROL NUMBER: APPLIED FOR

PICTURED ON THE FRONT COVER: SWEET CHILI SHORT RIBS (P. 13).

PICTURED ON THE TITLE PAGE: HOT FRUIT SALAD (P. 89).

PICTURED ON THE TABLE OF CONTENTS PAGE: GYRO SOUP (P. 65), POMEGRANATE PORK TENDERLOIN (P. 141)
& PECAN CHICKEN WITH BLUE CHEESE SAUCE (P. 188).

Table of Contents

Slow Cooker

Beef & Ground Beef 12

Poultry 28

Pork, Ham & More 44

Soups, Sides
& Sandwiches 58

Snacks & Sweets 80

Stovetop Suppers

Beef & Ground Beef 96

Poultry 112

Pork 128

Fish & Seafood 144

Oven Entrees

Beef & Ground Beef 158

Poultry 176

Pork 194

Fish & Seafood 212

Bonus Chapter:

Breads & Salads 226

Slow Cooking 101

The original slow cooker, called a Crock-Pot®, was introduced in 1971 by Rival®. Today, the term "slow cooker" and the name Crock-Pot® are often used interchangeably; however, Crock-Pot® is a brand, and a slow cooker is the appliance.

Most slow cookers have two or more settings. Food cooks faster on the high setting, but the low setting is ideal for all-day cooking or for less tender cuts of meat. Use the "warm" setting to keep food hot until it's ready to serve. The slow cooker recipes in this book refer to cooking on either "high" or "low" settings.

Some newer slow cookers seem to heat up faster than older ones. If you have an older model and a recipe directs to cook on low, you may want to set the slow cooker on the highest setting for the first hour of cooking to be sure the food is thoroughly cooked.

ADVANTAGES of Slow Cooking

CONVENIENCE. Slow cookers provide people with the ability to safely prepare tasty meals while away from home. The appliances are both readily available and budget-friendly.

HEALTH BENEFITS. As more people make better food choices to improve their overall health, slow cooking gains popularity. Low-temperature cooking retains more vitamins in foods, and healthier cuts of lean meat become sumptuously tender in the slow cooker without using extra fats. Many slow cooker recipes call for condensed soups, but lower-sodium and lower-fat versions can work, too. And, for many busy folks, knowing that a healthy meal is waiting at home helps cooks avoid less-healthy "fast-food" meals after work.

The recipes below are just a sample of light recipes in this cookbook that include Nutritional Facts and Diabetic Exchanges. It's easy to see how much fat, sodium, fiber, protein and other important food factors are in each serving of these dishes, helping you and your family maintain a healthier diet.

SLOW COOKER FAJITAS

➡➡ **NUTRITION FACTS:** 1 fajita equals 335 calories, 10 g fat (3 g saturated fat), 69 mg cholesterol, 564 mg sodium, 32 g carbohydrate, 2 g fiber, 29 g protein. **DIABETIC EXCHANGES:** 3 lean meat, 2 starch, 1 vegetable.

SLOW-COOKED SWEET 'N SOUR PORK

➡➡ **NUTRITION FACTS:** 1 cup pork mixture (calculated without rice) equals 312 calories, 10 g fat (3 g saturated fat), 73 mg cholesterol, 592 mg sodium, 28 g carbohydrate, 2 g fiber, 27 g protein. **DIABETIC EXCHANGES:** 3 lean meat, 1 fruit, 1/2 starch, 1/2 fat.

FINANCIAL SAVINGS. A slow cooker uses very little electricity because of its low wattage. For instance, it would cost roughly 21 cents to operate a slow cooker for a total of 10 hours. If you roast a pork roast for 2 hours in the oven instead of using the slow cooker for 10 hours, you would spend $2.51 to operate an electric oven or $1.49 to operate a gas oven. Plus, slow cookers do not heat the home as ovens do, providing summertime savings in home-cooling costs.

TIPS FOR TASTY OUTCOMES

■ No peeking! Refrain from lifting the lid while food cooks in the slow cooker, unless you're instructed in a recipe to stir or add ingredients. The loss of steam can mean an extra 20 to 30 minutes of cooking time each time you lift the lid.

■ Be sure the lid is well-placed over the ceramic insert, not tilted or askew. The steam during cooking creates a seal.

■ When food is finished cooking, remove it from the slow cooker within 1 hour and promptly refrigerate any leftovers.

■ Slow cooking may take longer at higher altitudes.

■ Don't forget your slow cooker when you go camping, if electricity is available. When space is limited and you want "set-it-and-forget-it" meals, it's a handy appliance.

■ Reheating food in a slow cooker isn't recommended. Cooked food can be heated on the stovetop or in the microwave and then put into a slow cooker to keep hot for serving.

■ Use a slow cooker on a buffet table to keep soup, stew, savory dips or mashed potatoes hot.

SLOW COOKER...

know when it's DONE!

145°F

- Medium-rare beef and lamb roasts
- Fish

160°F

- Medium beef and lamb roasts
- Pork
- Egg Dishes

165°F

- Ground chicken and turkey

170°F

- Well-done beef and lamb roasts
- Chicken and turkey that is whole or in pieces

■ Slow cookers come in a range of sizes, from 1-1/2 to 7 quarts. It's important to use the right size for the amount of food you're making. To serve a dip from a buffet, the smallest slow cookers are ideal. For entertaining or potluck dinners, the larger sizes work best. Check the chart below to find a useful size for your household.

■ To cook properly and safely, manufacturers and the USDA recommend slow cookers be filled at least half full but no more than two-thirds full.

■ With many slow cooker recipes, the ingredients are added at once and are cooked all day. For make-ahead convenience, place the food items in the crock the night before, cover and refrigerate overnight (the removable stoneware insert makes this an easy task). In the morning, place the crock in the slow cooker and select the temperature.

■ Do not preheat your slow cooker. An insert that has been in the refrigerator overnight should always be put into a cold base unit. Stoneware is sensitive to dramatic temperature changes, and cracking or breakage could occur if the base is preheated.

■ After the recipe is finished cooking, if there are any leftovers, allow them to cool, then refrigerate. Slow cookers should not be used to reheat leftovers. Instead, use a microwave, stovetop burner or oven to reheat foods to 165°. This ensures that the food has been thoroughly heated and it is safe to eat.

■ Following a power outage of less than two hours, you can finish cooking food from your slow cooker on the stovetop or microwave. If it's been more than two hours or you are unsure how long the power has been out, discard the food for your safety.

SLOW COOKER SIZE

HOUSEHOLD SIZE	SLOW COOKER CAPACITY
1 person	1-1/2 quarts
2 people	2 to 3-1/2 quarts
3 or 4 people	3-1/2 to 4-1/2 quarts
4 or 5 people	4-1/2 to 5 quarts
6 or more people	5 to 7 quarts

A **MELTING POT** OF INGREDIENTS

BEANS. Minerals in water and variations in voltage affect different types of dried beans in different ways; therefore, dried beans can be tricky to work with in the slow cooker. As a result, dried beans should always be soaked before adding to a slow cooker recipe. To soak beans, place them in a Dutch oven or stockpot and add water to cover by 2 inches. Bring to a boil, and boil for 2 minutes. Remove from the heat, cover and let stand for 1 hour. Drain and rinse the beans, discarding the liquid. Sugar, salt and acidic ingredients, such as vinegar, have a hardening effect on beans and prevent them from becoming soft and tender. It's best not to cook beans with these flavorings, but to add them only after the beans are fully cooked. Lentils and split peas do not need to be soaked.

COUSCOUS. For the best results when preparing couscous, cook on a stovetop instead of in a slow cooker.

DAIRY. Milk-based products tend to break down during slow cooking. Add items like milk, sour cream, cream cheese or cream during the last hour of cooking unless the recipe instructs otherwise. Cheeses don't generally hold up over extended periods of cooking, so they should be added near the end of cooking. Condensed cream soups can be cooked in slow cookers for extended periods of time with minimal curdling concerns.

FISH & SEAFOOD. Since fish and seafood cook quickly in a slow cooker and can break down if cooked too long, they are often added toward the end of the cooking time.

MEATS. For enhanced flavor and appearance, meat may be browned before going into the slow cooker. Browning, although not vital, may improve the color and flavor of meat. When cooking a roast over 3 pounds, be sure to cut it in half before placing it in the slow cooker to ensure that it thoroughly cooks. Frozen meats should be completely thawed before being placed in a slow cooker. Trim excess fat from meat or poultry before placing in a slow cooker. A slow cooker retains heat, and large amounts of fat could raise the temperature of the cooking liquid, causing the meat to overcook and become tough.

OATS. Quick-cooking and old-fashioned oats are often interchangeable in recipes. However, old-fashioned oats hold up better in a slow cooker.

PASTA. If added to a slow cooker when dry, pasta tends to become very sticky. It's best to cook it according to the package directions and stir it into the slow cooker just before serving. Small types of pasta, like orzo and ditalini, may be cooked in the slow cooker. To keep them from becoming mushy, add during the last hour of cooking.

RICE. Converted rice is ideal for all-day cooking. If using instant rice, add it during the last 30 minutes of cooking.

VEGETABLES. Vegetables, especially potatoes and root vegetables (such as carrots), tend to cook slower than meat. Place these vegetables on the bottom and around the sides of the slow cooker, and put meat on top of the vegetables. Add tender vegetables, like peas and zucchini, or those you'd prefer to be crisp-tender, during the last 50 to 60 minutes.

COOK TIMES

CONVENTIONAL OVEN
15 to 30 minutes

Slow Cooker
Low: 4 to 6 hours
High: 1-1/2 to 2 hours

CONVENTIONAL OVEN
35 to 45 minutes

Slow Cooker
Low: 6 to 8 hours
High: 3 to 4 hours

CONVENTIONAL OVEN
50 minutes or more

Slow Cooker
Low: 8 to 10 hours
High: 4 to 6 hours

When a range in cooking time is provided, this accounts for variables such as thickness of meat, how full the slow cooker is and the temperature of the food going into the cooker. As you become used to **how your slow cooker works,** you'll be better able to judge which end of the range to use.

CONVERTING RECIPES FOR THE
SLOW COOKER

Almost any recipe that bakes in the oven or simmers on the stovetop can be easily converted for the slow cooker. Here are some guidelines.

■ Before converting recipes, check the manufacturer's guidelines for your particular slow cooker. Find a recipe that is similar to the one you want to convert and use it as a guide. Note the amount and size of meat and vegetables, heat setting, cooking time and liquid.

■ Since there is no evaporation, adjusting the amount of liquid in your recipe may be necessary. If a recipe calls for 6 to 8 cups of water, try starting with 5 cups. Conversely, recipes should include at least a little liquid. If a recipe does not include liquid, add 1/2 cup of water or broth.

■ In general, 1 hour of simmering on the range or baking at 350°F in the oven is equal to 8-10 hours on low or 4-6 hours on high in a slow cooker. Check the chart, top left.

■ Flour and cornstarch are often used to thicken soups, stews and sauces that are cooked in a slow cooker.

Useful Handles for Lifting Food

Layered dishes or meat loaves are easier to get out of the slow cooker using foil handles. Here's how to make and use them:

1. For a 3-qt. slow cooker, cut three 20- x 3-inch strips of heavy-duty foil (or 25- x 3-inch strips for large slow cookers). Or cut 6-inch wide strips from regular foil and fold in half lengthwise. Criss-cross the strips to resemble spokes of a wheel.

2. Place the foil strips on the bottom and up the sides of the ceramic insert. Let the strips hang over the edge. To prevent food from sticking to the foil, coat the foil strips with cooking spray.

3. Place the food in the order suggested by the recipe in center of the foil strips and lower until the food rests on the bottom of the slow cooker.

4. After the food is cooked, grasp the foil strips together and carefully lift the food from the crock. Remove the strips from the food before serving.

- Removable stoneware inserts make cleanup a breeze. Be sure to cool the insert before rinsing or cleaning with water to avoid cracking. Do not immerse the metal base unit in water. Clean it with a damp sponge.

- Wash the insert in the dishwasher or in warm soapy water. Avoid using abrasive cleansers since they may scratch the stoneware.

- To remove mineral stains on a ceramic insert, fill the cooker with hot water and 1 cup white vinegar; cover. Set the control to high and allow to "cook" for 2 hours. Discard liquid, and when cool, wash with hot, sudsy water. Rinse well and dry.

- To remove water marks from a highly glazed crockery insert, rub the surface with vegetable oil and allow to stand for 2 hours before washing with hot, sudsy water.

> "This traditional stew from the Louisiana Bayou is a natural fit for the slow cooker. The recipe skips the hard-to-find spices usually called for but still delivers true seafood flavor."
>
> —**WOLFGANG HANAU** WEST PALM BEACH, FLORIDA

slow**cooker**

Beef & Ground Beef

One of **the greatest things about a slow cooker** is that it turns affordable cuts of beef, such as top round and chuck roast, into tender, scrumptious meals. From hearty brisket to succulent short ribs, there's no better way to **enjoy beef's full-bodied flavor** than with the recipes in this chapter!

- In a large resealable plastic bag, combine the flour, salt and pepper. Add ribs, a few at a time, and shake to coat. In a large skillet, brown ribs in oil in batches on all sides. Transfer to a 5-qt. slow cooker. Add the mushrooms, carrots, onions and celery.

- In a small bowl, combine the tomato sauce, preserves, taco seasoning and brown sugar; pour over vegetables. Cover and cook on low for 6-8 hours or until meat is tender. Serve with rice or potatoes.

Folks may not be able to resist licking their fingers after they try these sassy beef ribs. Thanks to the long cooking time, the veggies take on some of those sweet and savory flavors, too.

—**MICHELLE O'CONNELL** SALT LAKE CITY, UTAH

Sweet Chili Short Ribs

PREP: 30 MIN. ■ **COOK:** 6 HOURS ■ **YIELD:** 5 SERVINGS

1/4 cup all-purpose flour	1 can (15 ounces) tomato sauce
1/2 teaspoon salt	1 jar (12 ounces) apricot preserves
1/4 teaspoon pepper	1 jar (12 ounces) pineapple preserves
1-1/2 pounds boneless beef short ribs	2 envelopes taco seasoning
2 tablespoons olive oil	1/4 cup packed dark brown sugar
1/2 pound sliced fresh mushrooms	Hot cooked rice *or* mashed potatoes
4 medium carrots, sliced	
2 cups frozen pearl onions	
2 celery ribs, chopped	

Olive oil can be stored tightly capped at room temperature or in the refrigerator for up to 1 year. **When chilled, the oil turns cloudy** and thick. Chilled olive oil will return to its original consistency when left at room temperature for a short time.

- Place peppers and onion in a 5-qt. slow cooker. Top with beef. Combine the water, vinegar, lime juice and seasonings; pour over meat. Cover and cook on low for 8-10 hours or until the meat is tender.

- Using a slotted spoon, place about 3/4 cup meat mixture down the center of each tortilla. Top with 1 tablespoon salsa, 1 tablespoon cheese and 1 teaspoon cilantro; roll up.

➡ **NUTRITION FACTS:** 1 fajita equals 335 calories, 10 g fat (3 g saturated fat), 69 mg cholesterol, 564 mg sodium, 32 g carbohydrate, 2 g fiber, 29 g protein. **DIABETIC EXCHANGES:** 3 lean meat, 2 starch, 1 vegetable.

I love fajitas served in Mexican restaurants, but when I prepared them at home, the meat was always chewy. Then I tried this recipe in my slow cooker, and my husband and I savored every last bite.

—**KATIE URSO** SENECA, ILLINOIS

Slow Cooker Fajitas

PREP: 25 MIN. ■ COOK: 8 HOURS ■ YIELD: 8 SERVINGS

- 1 *each* medium green, sweet red and yellow pepper, cut into 1/2-inch strips
- 1 sweet onion, cut into 1/2-inch strips
- 2 pounds beef top sirloin steaks, cut into thin strips
- 3/4 cup water
- 2 tablespoons red wine vinegar
- 1 tablespoon lime juice
- 1 teaspoon ground cumin

- 1 teaspoon chili powder
- 1/2 teaspoon salt
- 1/2 teaspoon garlic powder
- 1/2 teaspoon pepper
- 1/2 teaspoon cayenne pepper
- 8 flour tortillas (8 inches), warmed
- 1/2 cup salsa
- 1/2 cup shredded reduced-fat cheddar cheese
- 8 teaspoons minced fresh cilantro

Vidalias and other sweet onions are mild-flavored and high in sugar and water content but low in tear-inducing sulfur compounds. Sweet onions are **not suited for long-term storage** and should be used within several weeks of purchase.

When I serve California Tamale Pie, I know I'll see smiles on the faces of everyone at the table. With this recipe, you'll enjoy the taste and texture of classic tamales without the time and hassle.

—**PATRICIA NIEH** PORTOLA VALLEY, CALIFORNIA

CALIFORNIA TAMALE PIE

California Tamale Pie

PREP: 15 MIN. ■ COOK: 6 HOURS ■ YIELD: 5 SERVINGS

1 cup beef broth	1 can (15 ounces) black beans, rinsed and drained
3/4 cup cornmeal	1/4 cup sliced ripe olives
1 pound ground beef	1/2 cup shredded Monterey Jack cheese
1 teaspoon chili powder	
1/2 teaspoon ground cumin	Optional toppings: sour cream and fresh jalapeno slices
1 jar (16 ounces) chunky salsa	
1 can (15-1/4 ounces) whole kernel corn, drained	

■ In a 3-qt. slow cooker, combine broth and cornmeal. Let stand for 5 minutes. In a large skillet, cook beef over medium heat until no longer pink; drain. Stir in chili powder and cumin. Transfer to slow cooker. Stir in the salsa, corn, beans and olives. Cover and cook on low for 6-8 hours or until heated through.

■ Sprinkle with cheese. Cover and cook 5-10 minutes longer or until cheese is melted. Top with sour cream and jalapeno slices if desired.

Cornmeal can be white, yellow or blue. It all depends on the strain of corn. Traditionally, white cornmeal is used in the South and yellow in the North. Blue cornmeal can be found in specialty stores. **All three can be used interchangeably.**

Hearty Hash Brown Dinner

At my house, this meal-in-one is frequent fare. It is great for potlucks, too. French-fried onions sprinkled on after cooking create a crispy topping.

—**MARGE BERG** GIBBON, MINNESOTA

PREP: 15 MIN.
COOK: 4-1/2 HOURS
YIELD: 4 SERVINGS

3 cups frozen shredded hash brown potatoes, thawed

1/2 teaspoon salt

1/4 teaspoon pepper

1 pound ground beef

1/2 cup chopped onion

1 package (16 ounces) frozen California-blend vegetables

1 can (10-3/4 ounces) condensed cream of chicken soup, undiluted

1 cup whole milk

12 ounces process cheese (Velveeta), cubed

1 can (2.8 ounces) french-fried onions

■ Place potatoes in a lightly greased 5-qt. slow cooker; sprinkle with salt and pepper. In a large skillet, cook beef and onion over medium heat until meat is no longer pink; drain. Spoon over potatoes. Top with vegetables. Combine soup and milk; pour over vegetables. Cover and cook on low for 4 to 4-1/2 hours.

■ Top with cheese; cover and cook 30 minutes longer or until cheese is melted. Just before serving, sprinkle with french-fried onions.

Zesty Orange Beef

I put this recipe together in the morning before I leave for work. In the evening, the aroma hits me as soon as I open the door. All I have to do is quickly cook some rice, and dinner is served!

—**DEBORAH PUETTE** LILBURN, GEORGIA

PREP: 15 MIN. ■ **COOK:** 5 HOURS ■ **YIELD:** 5 SERVINGS

1	beef top sirloin steak (1-1/2 pounds), cut into 1/4-inch strips		3	tablespoons cider vinegar
2-1/2	cups sliced fresh shiitake mushrooms		1	tablespoon cornstarch
1	medium onion, cut into wedges		1	tablespoon minced fresh gingerroot
3	dried hot chilies		1	tablespoon sesame oil
1/4	cup packed brown sugar		2	garlic cloves, minced
1/4	cup orange juice		1-3/4	cups fresh snow peas
1/4	cup reduced-sodium soy sauce		1	tablespoon grated orange peel
				Hot cooked rice

■ Place beef in a 4-qt. slow cooker. Add the mushrooms, onion, and chilies. In a small bowl, combine the brown sugar, orange juice, soy sauce, vinegar, cornstarch, ginger, oil and garlic. Pour over meat.

■ Cover and cook on high for 5-6 hours or until meat is tender, adding snow peas during the last 30 minutes of cooking. Stir in orange peel. Serve with rice.

➤➤ **NUTRITION FACTS:** 1 cup (calculated without rice) equals 310 calories, 8 g fat (3 g saturated fat), 55 mg cholesterol, 554 mg sodium, 24 g carbohydrate, 3 g fiber, 33 g protein. **DIABETIC EXCHANGES:** 4 lean meat, 1-1/2 starch, 1/2 fat.

Ground Beef Stew

Since I work all day, it's great to come home knowing I have a homey meal simmering in the slow cooker. I like to serve generous helpings of the stew with corn bread muffins.

—**MARY JO WALKER** JASPER, TENNESSEE

PREP: 15 MIN. ■ **COOK:** 6 HOURS ■ **YIELD:** 6 SERVINGS

2	large potatoes, sliced		1-1/2	pounds ground beef, cooked and drained
2	medium carrots, sliced		1	can (10-3/4 ounces) condensed tomato soup, undiluted
1	can (15 ounces) peas, drained		1-1/3	cups water
3	medium onions, sliced			
2	celery ribs, sliced			

■ In a 5-qt. slow cooker, layer the first six ingredients in the order listed. In a small bowl, combine soup and water. Pour over beef.

■ Cover and cook on low for 6-8 hours or until vegetables are tender.

Swiss Steak Supper

To save a step on my slow-cooked specialty, I always keep peppered seasoned salt on hand to use instead of the seasoned salt and pepper called for.

—**KATHLEEN ROMANIUK** CHOMEDEY, QUEBEC

PREP: 20 MIN.
COOK: 5-1/2 HOURS
YIELD: 6 SERVINGS

1-1/2	pounds beef top round steak
1/2	teaspoon seasoned salt
1/4	teaspoon coarsely ground pepper
1	tablespoon canola oil
3	medium potatoes
1-1/2	cups fresh baby carrots
1	medium onion, sliced
1	can (14-1/2 ounces) Italian diced tomatoes
1	jar (12 ounces) home-style beef gravy
1	tablespoon minced fresh parsley

■ Cut steak into six serving-size pieces; flatten to 1/4-in. thickness. Rub with seasoned salt and pepper. In a large skillet, brown beef in oil on both sides; drain.

■ Cut each potato into eight wedges. In a 5-qt. slow cooker, layer the potatoes, carrots, beef and onion. Combine tomatoes and gravy; pour over the top.

■ Cover and cook on low for 5-6 hours or until meat and vegetables are tender. Sprinkle with parsley.

COFFEE-FLAVORED BEEF ROAST

- Place potatoes and carrots in a 5-qt. slow cooker. Sprinkle beef with half of the salt and pepper. In a large skillet, brown beef in oil on all sides. Transfer to slow cooker.

- In the same skillet, saute onion and mushrooms in the drippings for 2 minutes. Add garlic; cook 1 minute longer. Stir in the coffee, chili powder and remaining salt and pepper. Pour over meat. Cover and cook on low for 6-8 hours or until meat is tender.

- Remove meat and vegetables to a serving platter; keep warm. Skim fat from cooking juices; transfer to a small saucepan. Bring liquid to a boil.

- Combine cornstarch and water until smooth; gradually stir into the pan. Bring to a boil; cook and stir for 2 minutes or until thickened. Serve sauce with the meat and vegetables.

Coming home to a complete meal is so wonderful. My roast takes very little preparation but the results are delicious. A hunk of crusty bread completes the meal.

—JEAN COLLIER HANFORD, CALIFORNIA

Coffee-Flavored Beef Roast

PREP: 35 MIN. ■ COOK: 6 HOURS ■ YIELD: 8 SERVINGS (2 CUPS GRAVY)

- 6 medium red potatoes, cut into wedges
- 6 medium carrots, cut into 1-inch lengths
- 2 beef sirloin tip roasts (2 to 3 pounds *each*)
- 1 teaspoon salt, *divided*
- 1/2 teaspoon pepper, *divided*
- 2 teaspoons canola oil

- 1 medium onion, halved and sliced
- 2 cups whole fresh mushrooms, quartered
- 2 garlic cloves, minced
- 1-1/2 cups brewed coffee
- 1 teaspoon chili powder
- 3 tablespoons cornstarch
- 1/4 cup cold water

Browning cuts of beef before putting them in a slow cooker is an important step in the recipe method because it **will add flavor and color** to the finished dish.

Feeding a hungry crowd? Turn to these mouthwatering chimichangas, which feature tender, slow-roasted beef and melted cheese inside a crispy tortilla. For convenience, you can make the beef filling ahead and assemble the chimichangas when you're ready. Everyone will want the recipe!

—JUDY SANCHEZ RACINE, WISCONSIN

Favorite Beef Chimichangas

PREP: 1 HOUR ■ **COOK:** 7-1/2 HOURS ■ **YIELD:** 16 SERVINGS

1	boneless beef chuck roast (3-1/2 pounds)
2	cups chopped peeled potatoes
1-1/2	cups water
1	tablespoon reduced-sodium soy sauce
2	teaspoons garlic salt with parsley
3/4	teaspoon pepper
2	cans (4 ounces *each*) chopped green chilies
2	tablespoons all-purpose flour
2	tablespoons taco seasoning
16	flour tortillas (10 inches), warmed
4	cups (16 ounces) shredded cheddar cheese
1/3	cup canola oil

Optional toppings: guacamole, salsa *or* sour cream

■ Cut roast in half; place in a 4- or 5-qt. slow cooker. Arrange potatoes around the roast; pour water over potatoes. Drizzle meat with soy sauce. Sprinkle with garlic salt and pepper. Top with green chilies. Cover and cook on low for 7-9 hours or until meat is very tender.

■ Remove the roast to a platter. Shred meat with two forks and return meat to the slow cooker. Combine the flour and taco seasoning; stir into meat mixture. Cover and cook 30 minutes longer or until juices are thickened.

■ To assemble chimichangas, using a slotted spoon, spoon 1/2 cup meat mixture off-center on each tortilla. Sprinkle with 1/4 cup cheese. Fold up edge nearest filling; fold in both sides and roll up.

■ In a large skillet, fry chimichangas, folded side down, in oil in batches for 2-3 minutes on each side or until golden brown. Drain on paper towels. Serve with toppings if desired.

The **chuck section comes from the shoulder** and neck and yields some of the **most flavorful and economical cuts of beef available.** These cuts tend to be tough and fatty, so it's best to cook them slowly while partially covered in liquid.

Gone-All-Day Goulash

With this recipe, you can put in a full day's work, run some errands and still get dinner on the table in no time. Make it extra-special by serving the hearty meat sauce over some spaetzle.

—**CYNDY GERKEN** NAPLES, FLORIDA

PREP: 25 MIN.
COOK: 8-1/2 HOURS
YIELD: 4 SERVINGS

2	pounds beef stew meat
2	tablespoons olive oil
1	can (14-1/2 ounces) beef broth
1	large onion, chopped
1/2	cup ketchup
2	tablespoons Worcestershire sauce
1	tablespoon brown sugar
1	tablespoon paprika
1/2	teaspoon ground mustard
2	tablespoons all-purpose flour
1/4	cup water

Hot cooked egg noodles *or* spaetzle

■ In a large skillet, brown beef in oil; drain. Transfer to a 3-qt. slow cooker. Combine the broth, onion, ketchup, Worcestershire sauce, brown sugar, paprika and mustard. Pour over beef. Cover and cook on low for 8-10 hours or until meat is tender.

■ In a small bowl, combine the flour and water until smooth. Gradually stir into beef mixture. Cover and cook on high 30 minutes longer or until thickened. Serve with noodles.

This flavorful meal is a must for St. Patrick's Day—but truly welcome any time of the year. While it usually cooks on the stovetop, a slow cooker makes it even easier. The recipe serves four nicely with enough leftover meat for Reuben sandwiches.

—MICHELLE RHODES
FORT BLISS, TEXAS

CORNED BEEF DINNER

Corned Beef Dinner

PREP: 10 MIN. ■ COOK: 9 HOURS ■ YIELD: 8 SERVINGS

4 to 5 medium red potatoes, quartered

2 cups fresh baby carrots, halved lengthwise

3 cups chopped cabbage

1 corned beef brisket with spice packet (3-1/2 pounds)

3 cups water

1 tablespoon caraway seeds

■ Place the potatoes, carrots and cabbage in a 5-qt. slow cooker. Cut brisket in half; place over vegetables. Add the water, caraway seeds and contents of spice packet. Cover and cook on low for 8-10 hours or until the meat and vegetables are tender.

The word **"corn" derives from Old English,** and was used to decribe any small, hard particles or grains. So "corned beef" **refers to coarse, granular salts** used to cure the beef.

Easy-Does-It Spaghetti

My savory spaghetti sauce is a nice change from some of the sweeter store-bought varieties. With fresh bread and a green salad, you have a complete meal.

—GENEVIEVE HRABE
PLAINVILLE, KANSAS

PREP: 10 MIN. ■ COOK: 4 HOURS
YIELD: 8-10 SERVINGS

2 pounds ground beef, cooked and drained

1 can (46 ounces) tomato juice

1 can (15 ounces) tomato sauce

1 can (8 ounces) mushroom stems and pieces, drained

2 tablespoons dried minced onion

2 teaspoons salt

1 teaspoon garlic powder

1 teaspoon ground mustard

1/2 teaspoon *each* ground allspice, mace and pepper

1 package (7 ounces) spaghetti, broken in half

■ In a 5-qt. slow cooker, combine the beef, tomato juice, tomato sauce, mushrooms and seasonings. Cover and cook on high for 4-5 hours.

■ Stir in spaghetti. Cover and cook on high 1 hour longer or until spaghetti is tender.

HEARTY BEANS WITH BEEF

My husband raved about these beans after tasting them at a party, so I had to get the recipe. Perfect for get-togethers, you can prep the recipe a day early and toss it all in the slow cooker before your guests arrive.

—**JAN BIEHL** LEESBURG, INDIANA

Hearty Beans with Beef

PREP: 5 MIN. ■ COOK: 3 HOURS ■ YIELD: 8-10 SERVINGS

1 pound ground beef	1/2 cup ketchup
1 medium onion, chopped	1/3 cup packed brown sugar
1 can (16 ounces) baked beans, undrained	1 tablespoon barbecue sauce
1 can (15-1/2 ounces) butter beans, rinsed and drained	1/4 teaspoon Worcestershire sauce

- In a large skillet, cook beef and onion over medium heat until meat is no longer pink; drain.

- Transfer to a 5-qt. slow cooker. Stir in the remaining ingredients. Cover and cook on high for 3-4 hours or until heated through.

Barbecued Beef Brisket

I enjoy fixing a sit-down meal for my husband and myself every evening, so this entree is often on the menu. It's fairly inexpensive and takes little effort to prepare. The tender beef tastes wonderful.

—**ANITA KEPPINGER**
PHILOMATH, OREGON

PREP: 10 MIN. ■ COOK: 4 HOURS
YIELD: 8 SERVINGS

- 1 teaspoon salt
- 1 teaspoon chili powder
- 1/2 teaspoon garlic powder
- 1/4 teaspoon onion powder
- 1/4 teaspoon celery seed
- 1/4 teaspoon pepper
- 1 fresh beef brisket (2-1/2 pounds), trimmed

SAUCE:

- 1/2 cup ketchup
- 1/2 cup chili sauce
- 1/4 cup packed brown sugar
- 2 tablespoons cider vinegar
- 2 tablespoons Worcestershire sauce
- 1 to 1-1/2 teaspoons Liquid Smoke, optional
- 1/2 teaspoon ground mustard

- In a small bowl, combine the first six ingredients; rub over the brisket. Place in a 3-qt. slow cooker.

- In a large bowl, combine the sauce ingredients. Pour half over the brisket; set the remaining sauce aside.

- Cover and cook on high for 4-5 hours or until meat is tender. Serve with the reserved sauce.

EDITOR'S NOTE: This is a fresh beef brisket, not corned beef.

TANGY BEEF AND VEGETABLE STEW

- Place the potatoes, carrots and cubed onions in a 6-qt. slow cooker.

- In a large skillet, brown the beef in oil in batches; place over the vegetables. Sprinkle with flour.

- Dissolve bouillon in boiling water. Stir in the vinegar, ketchup, horseradish, mustard and sugar; pour over meat and vegetables. Cover and cook on high for 5 hours.

- Add the peas, corn and mushrooms. Cover and cook on high for 45 minutes longer or until meat and vegetables are tender.

How much does my husband like this stew? So much that he'll eat it *cold*! The ingredient list may look overwhelming, but all of the items are quite common. The final results are well worth the effort. Try it and see for yourself!

—AMBERLEAH HOMLBERG CALGARY, ALBERTA

Tangy Beef and Vegetable Stew

PREP: 25 MIN. ■ **COOK:** 5-3/4 HOURS ■ **YIELD:** 12-16 SERVINGS

- 6 cups cubed peeled potatoes (1/2-inch pieces)
- 8 medium carrots, cut into 1/2-inch pieces
- 2 medium onions, cubed
- 4 pounds beef stew meat, cut into 1-inch pieces
- 1/3 cup canola oil
- 1/3 cup all-purpose flour
- 4 teaspoons beef bouillon granules

- 3 cups boiling water
- 1/3 cup white vinegar
- 1/3 cup ketchup
- 3 tablespoons prepared horseradish
- 3 tablespoons prepared mustard
- 2 tablespoons sugar
- 2 cups *each* frozen peas and corn
- 2 cups sliced fresh mushrooms

Any dish prepared by stewing—**simmering food in liquid for a long period** of time in a covered pot—can be considered stew. Stew most often refers to **a main dish that contains meat, vegetables** and a thick broth made from the stewing juices.

Grandma's Cabbage Rolls

Hearty and heartwarming, these traditional cabbage rolls are nothing short of delicious. Toasted rye bread and polenta make lovely accompaniments.

—TEODORA COSAC OTTAWA, ONTARIO

PREP: 45 MIN. ■ COOK: 6 HOURS ■ YIELD: 12 SERVINGS

1	large head cabbage, cored	1/2	teaspoon pepper
1	egg	1-1/2	pounds lean ground beef (90% lean)
1	medium onion, finely chopped		
1/2	cup uncooked converted rice	2	cups sauerkraut, rinsed, well drained and chopped
1	tablespoon snipped fresh dill or 1 teaspoon dill weed	2	cups canned crushed tomatoes
1	teaspoon paprika	6	bacon strips, chopped
1	teaspoon dried savory or thyme	1	can (14-1/2 ounces) vegetable broth
1/2	teaspoon salt		

■ Cook cabbage in boiling water just until outer leaves pull away easily from head. Set aside 12 large leaves for rolls. Refrigerate remaining cabbage for another use. Cut out the thick vein from the bottom of each leaf, making a V-shaped cut.

■ In a large bowl, combine the egg, onion, rice, dill, paprika, savory, salt and pepper. Crumble beef over mixture and mix well. Place 1/3 cup meat mixture on a cabbage leaf; overlap cut ends of leaf. Fold in sides. Beginning from cut end, roll up. Repeat with remaining cabbage leaves and filling.

■ Combine the sauerkraut, tomatoes and bacon. Spoon half into a 6-qt. slow cooker. Arrange six cabbage rolls, seam side down, over sauerkraut mixture. Top with remaining sauerkraut mixture and rolls. Add broth to slow cooker. Cover and cook on low for 6-8 hours or until a thermometer inserted in rolls reads 160°.

Ground beef is labeled according to the fat content of the ground mixture or the percentage of lean meat to fat, such as 90% lean. **The higher the percentage, the leaner the meat.**

Simple Swedish Meatballs

My slow cooker meatballs are easy to reheat in the microwave, so when my husband packed some of the leftovers in his lunch one day, all his work buddies wished they had their own!

—CHRISTINA LOGAN GUN BARREL CITY, TEXAS

PREP: 15 MIN.
COOK: 5-1/4 HOURS
YIELD: 10 SERVINGS

1/2	pound sliced fresh mushrooms
1	tablespoon butter
3	cups beef broth
1	can (10-3/4 ounces) condensed cream of chicken soup, undiluted
1	envelope beefy onion soup mix
1	teaspoon dried parsley flakes
1	package (32 ounces) frozen fully cooked Swedish meatballs
3/4	cup sour cream

Hot cooked noodles or mashed potatoes, optional

■ In a large skillet, saute mushrooms in butter until tender. Transfer to a 4-qt. slow cooker. Stir in the broth, cream of chicken soup, soup mix and parsley. Add meatballs; toss to coat. Cover and cook on low for 5-6 hours or until the meatballs are heated through.

■ Stir in the sour cream. Cover and cook 15 minutes longer or until heated through. Serve with noodles or potatoes if desired.

Family-Style Meat Loaf Dinner

To me, no food is as comforting as meat loaf. I love it even more when I can make my whole dinner in the slow cooker, including the meat, potatoes, carrots—and even the gravy!

—BARBIE MILLER OAKDALE, MINNESOTA

PREP: 35 MIN. ■ COOK: 5 HOURS ■ YIELD: 6 SERVINGS

- 2 eggs
- 1 cup crushed saltines
- 1 medium onion, chopped
- 1/2 cup old-fashioned oats
- 1/2 cup heavy whipping cream
- 2 tablespoons Worcestershire sauce
- 2-1/2 teaspoons Montreal steak seasoning
- 1/2 teaspoon coarse ground pepper
- 2-1/2 pounds ground beef

- 4 medium potatoes, peeled and cubed
- 2 cups fresh baby carrots
- 1/3 cup finely chopped onion
- 2 cans (10-3/4 ounces each) condensed cream of mushroom soup, undiluted
- 2 cans (4 ounces each) mushroom stems and pieces, drained
- 1 envelope pork gravy mix

- Cut three 25-in. x 3-in. strips of heavy-duty foil; crisscross so they resemble spokes of a wheel. Place strips on the bottom and up the sides of a 6-qt. slow cooker. Coat strips with cooking spray.

- In a large bowl, combine the eggs, cracker crumbs, onion, oats, cream, Worcestershire sauce, steak seasoning and pepper. Crumble beef over mixture and mix well. Shape into a loaf; place in the center of the strips. Arrange the potatoes, carrots and onion around meat.

- In a small bowl, combine the soup, mushrooms and gravy mix; spread over meat and vegetables. Cover and cook on low for 5-6 hours or until no pink remains and a thermometer reads 160°. Transfer vegetables and gravy to a serving bowl. Using foil strips as handles, remove meat loaf to a platter; cut into 12 slices.

When making meat loaf, first combine all of the ingredients except the ground beef. This way, the **seasonings will be more evenly distributed** without much effort.

Italian Pot Roast

PREP: 20 MIN. ■ COOK: 5 HOURS
YIELD: 8 SERVINGS

- 1 boneless beef chuck roast (3 to 4 pounds)
- 1 can (28 ounces) diced tomatoes, drained
- 3/4 cup chopped onion
- 3/4 cup burgundy wine or beef broth
- 1-1/2 teaspoons salt
- 1 teaspoon dried basil
- 1/2 teaspoon dried oregano
- 1 garlic clove, minced
- 1/4 teaspoon pepper
- 1/4 cup cornstarch
- 1/2 cup cold water

- Cut roast in half. Place in a 5-qt. slow cooker. Add the tomatoes, onion, wine, salt, basil, oregano, garlic and pepper. Cover and cook on low for 5-6 hours or until meat is tender.

- Remove meat to a serving platter; keep warm. Skim fat from cooking juices; transfer to a small saucepan. Combine cornstarch and water until smooth. Gradually stir into pan. Bring to a boil; cook and stir for 2 minutes or until thickened. Serve with meat.

I make this hearty pot roast regularly, as it's a favorite of my husband's. It's delicious, so when I serve this dish to guests, I'm always asked for the recipe. After preparing the roast, you'll love how the tender slices of meat seem to melt in your mouth.

—DEBBIE DALY BUCKINGHAM, ILLINOIS

BEEF 'N' CHILI BEANS

I took this dish to the last church meal we had, and it was a hit! Several of the ladies requested the recipe. It's so easy to make—just put the ingredients in the slow cooker, and dinner's ready before you know it.

—**ANITA HUDSON** SAVOY, TEXAS

Beef 'n' Chili Beans

PREP: 15 MIN. ■ **COOK:** 6 HOURS ■ **YIELD:** 6-8 SERVINGS

- 3 pounds beef stew meat, cut into 1-inch cubes
- 2 tablespoons brown sugar
- 1-1/2 teaspoons ground mustard
- 1 teaspoon salt
- 1 teaspoon paprika
- 1/2 teaspoon chili powder
- 1/4 teaspoon pepper
- 1 large onion, chopped
- 2 cans (10 ounces *each*) diced tomatoes and green chilies, undrained
- 1 can (16 ounces) Ranch Style beans (pinto beans in seasoned tomato sauce)
- 1 can (15-1/4 ounces) whole kernel corn, drained

- ■ Place the beef in a 3-qt. slow cooker. Combine the brown sugar, mustard, salt, paprika, chili powder and pepper; sprinkle over beef and toss to coat. Top with onion, tomatoes, beans and corn.

- ■ Cover and cook on low for 6-8 hours or until meat is tender.

Herbed Beef With Noodles

Just a handful of ingredients and a sprinkling of spices go into my hearty dinner. Although it's very simple, it's wonderfully creamy and full of subtle flavors.

—**ROSLYN HURST**
BELMONT, CALIFORNIA

PREP: 25 MIN. ■ **COOK:** 5 HOURS
YIELD: 8 SERVINGS

- 2 pounds beef top round steak
- 1/2 teaspoon salt
- 1/2 teaspoon pepper, *divided*
- 2 teaspoons canola oil
- 1 can (10-3/4 ounces) reduced-fat reduced-sodium condensed cream of celery soup, undiluted
- 1 medium onion, chopped
- 1 tablespoon fat-free milk
- 1 teaspoon dried oregano
- 1/2 teaspoon dried thyme
- 6 cups cooked wide egg noodles

Chopped celery leaves, optional

- ■ Cut steak into serving-size pieces; sprinkle with salt and 1/4 teaspoon pepper. In a large nonstick skillet coated with cooking spray, brown meat in oil on both sides. Transfer to a 3-qt. slow cooker.

- ■ In a small bowl, combine the soup, onion, milk, oregano, thyme and remaining pepper. Pour over meat. Cover and cook on low for 5-6 hours or until meat is tender.

- ■ Serve with noodles. Sprinkle with celery leaves if desired.

- ➡ **NUTRITION FACTS:** 3 ounces cooked beef with 3/4 cup noodles equals 290 calories, 7 g fat (2 g saturated fat), 92 mg cholesterol, 334 mg sodium, 26 g carbohydrate, 2 g fiber, 30 g protein. **DIABETIC EXCHANGES:** 3 lean meat, 1-1/2 starch.

This hearty meal is a great way to start the week. And since most of the work is done by the slow cooker, you'll have very little to do for a satisfying supper.

—TASTE OF HOME TEST KITCHEN

ITALIAN ROAST WITH ALFREDO POTATOES

Italian Roast with Alfredo Potatoes

PREP: 10 MIN. ■ **COOK:** 7 HOURS 20 MIN.
YIELD: 4 SERVINGS PLUS LEFTOVERS

- 1 boneless beef chuck roast (4 pounds), trimmed
- 1 envelope brown gravy mix
- 1 envelope Italian salad dressing mix
- 1/2 cup water
- 1 medium sweet red pepper, cut into 1-inch pieces
- 1 cup chopped green pepper
- 2/3 cup chopped onion
- 8 medium red potatoes, quartered
- 2 tablespoons cornstarch
- 1/4 cup cold water
- 3/4 cup refrigerated Alfredo sauce
- 2 tablespoons butter
- 1/4 teaspoon pepper
- 1 tablespoon minced chives

- Cut roast in half; place in a 5-qt. slow cooker. In a small bowl, combine the gravy mix, dressing mix and water; pour over roast. Top with peppers and onion. Cover and cook on low for 6-8 hours or until meat is tender.

- Place potatoes in a large saucepan; cover with water. Bring to a boil. Reduce heat; cover and simmer for 15-20 minutes or until tender. Meanwhile, remove roast and cut a portion of the meat into cubes, measuring 3 cups; cover and save for another use. Slice the remaining beef and keep warm.

- Skim fat from cooking juices if necessary; pour into a large saucepan. Combine cornstarch and cold water until smooth; stir into cooking juices. Bring to a boil; cook and stir for 2 minutes or until thickened.

- Drain potatoes; mash with Alfredo sauce, butter and pepper. Sprinkle with chives. Serve with sliced beef and gravy.

Thai-Style Beef

This meal gets its Southeast Asian flair from none other than chunky peanut butter, plus tangy lemon juice and cilantro. You can adjust the red pepper flakes to change the heat factor.

—KRIS HAGE
MAPLE GROVE, MINNESOTA

PREP: 20 MIN. ■ **COOK:** 5 HOURS
YIELD: 9 SERVINGS

- 3 pounds beef stew meat
- 1 medium sweet red pepper, sliced
- 3/4 cup chunky peanut butter
- 1/3 cup reduced-sodium soy sauce
- 4 teaspoons canola oil
- 3 garlic cloves, minced
- 1 tablespoon lemon juice
- 1 tablespoon minced fresh cilantro
- 1/2 to 1 teaspoon crushed red pepper flakes
- 1/4 teaspoon pepper

Hot cooked rice, optional

- In a 3- or 4-qt. slow cooker, combine beef and red pepper. In a small bowl, combine the peanut butter, soy sauce, oil, garlic, lemon juice, cilantro, pepper flakes and pepper. Pour over beef; toss to coat.

- Cover and cook on low for 5-6 hours or until beef is tender. Serve with rice if desired.

Poultry

The slow cooker brings out poultry's **naturally delicious flavor** in the comforting recipes featured here. **With hearty chicken stews and saucy main dishes,** finding a new family favorite is a cinch with these classic, satisfying dinners that rely on chicken and turkey.

CORNISH GAME HENS WITH COUSCOUS

- In a large resealable plastic bag, combine the flour, salt, pepper and chili powder. Add hens, one at a time, and shake to coat. In a large skillet, brown hens in oil on all sides. Transfer to a 5- or 6-qt. slow cooker. Add broth to the skillet, stirring to loosen browned bits from pan. Bring to a boil. Reduce heat; simmer, uncovered, for 1-2 minutes. Add to slow cooker.

- Stir in the eggplant, tomatoes, mushrooms, onion, green pepper, garlic and bay leaf. Cover and cook on low for 3-4 hours or until a thermometer reads 180° and vegetables are tender. Discard bay leaf. To serve, split hens in half. Serve with couscous and vegetables.

When I invite people to dinner, they often ask if we're going to have this entree. They think I slave all day in the kitchen, and I don't tell them any different. I suppose my secret's out now!
—**BARBARA LENTO** HOUSTON, PENNSYLVANIA

Cornish Game Hens with Couscous

PREP: 40 MIN. ■ **COOK:** 3 HOURS ■ **YIELD:** 4 SERVINGS

2 tablespoons all-purpose flour

1/2 teaspoon salt

1/2 teaspoon pepper

1/4 teaspoon chili powder

2 Cornish game hens (20 to 24 ounces *each*), thawed

1 tablespoon olive oil

1 can (14-1/2 ounces) reduced-sodium chicken broth

2 cups cubed peeled eggplant

2 large tomatoes, cut into wedges and seeded

2 cups sliced baby portobello mushrooms

1 medium onion, sliced

1 medium green pepper, chopped

1 garlic clove, minced

1 bay leaf

2 cups hot cooked couscous

Baby portobello mushrooms are **similar in appearance to white mushrooms** because they come from the same family. But baby portobellos have **a deeper and earthier flavor** than white mushrooms.

GREEK ORZO CHICKEN

Take your first bite of my flavorful pasta dish and you'll be on a dinner-table tour of the sunny Greek Isles. Sprinkle a touch of lemon zest on top to give it a little extra flair.

—ANGELA BUCHANAN LONGMONT, COLORADO

Greek Orzo Chicken

PREP: 15 MIN. ■ **COOK:** 5-1/2 HOURS ■ **YIELD:** 6 SERVINGS

6	bone-in chicken thighs, (about 2-1/4 pounds), skin removed
1	cup sliced fresh carrots
1	cup chicken broth
1/4	cup lemon juice
1	garlic clove, minced
1	teaspoon dried oregano
1/2	teaspoon salt
1	cup uncooked orzo pasta
1/2	cup sliced pitted green olives
1/4	cup golden raisins
1/2	cup minced fresh parsley
1/2	cup crumbled feta cheese

■ In a 3-qt. slow cooker, combine the chicken, carrots, broth, lemon juice, garlic, oregano and salt. Cover and cook on low for 5-6 hours or until chicken is tender.

■ Stir in the orzo, olives and raisins. Cover and cook 30 minutes longer or until pasta is tender. Sprinkle with parsley and feta cheese.

Tasty Chicken Marsala

A friend shared a company-worthy recipe with me. There's enough of the smooth, creamy sauce to dress both the meat and the noodles, should you choose to serve them, too. It's divine!

—PATRICIA CAMPBELL
VALENCIA, PENNSYLVANIA

PREP: 20 MIN. ■ **COOK:** 5 HOURS
YIELD: 6 SERVINGS

3/4	cup water
1/4	cup butter, melted
1	teaspoon garlic salt
1	teaspoon dried basil
1	teaspoon dried oregano
6	boneless skinless chicken breast halves (5 ounces each)
2	cups sliced fresh mushrooms
2	cans (10-3/4 ounces each) condensed golden mushroom soup, undiluted
1	package (8 ounces) reduced-fat cream cheese, cubed
3/4	cup Marsala wine

Hot cooked noodles, optional

■ In a greased 4- or 5-qt. slow cooker, combine the water, butter, garlic salt, basil and oregano. Add chicken and mushrooms. In a large bowl, combine the soup, cream cheese and wine; pour over chicken. Cover and cook on low for 5-6 hours or until chicken is tender. Serve with noodles if desired.

Looking for a simple way to prepare an elegant dish? The flavors of mushrooms, fresh spinach and herbes de Provence make a delicious backdrop for the succulent pieces of chicken.

—NANCY SWAIN
ST. AUGUSTINE, FLORIDA

Mushroom Chicken Florentine

PREP: 20 MIN. ■ COOK: 4 HOURS ■ YIELD: 4 SERVINGS

1 can (10-3/4 ounces) condensed cream of mushroom soup, undiluted

1/2 cup white wine *or* chicken broth

1/2 cup sour cream

1 teaspoon herbes de Provence

1-1/2 pounds boneless skinless chicken breasts, cut into 2-inch pieces

1-3/4 cups sliced baby portobello mushrooms

6 cups fresh spinach

Hot cooked egg noodles

■ In a 3-qt. slow cooker, combine the soup, wine, sour cream and herbes de Provence. Stir in chicken and mushrooms. Fold in spinach. Cover and cook on low for 4-5 hours or until chicken is no longer pink. Serve with noodles.

EDITOR'S NOTE: Look for herbes de Provence in the spice aisle.

Although **"coq au vin" is French for "rooster with wine,"** it usually calls for a capon or chicken. The traditional French recipe typically requires chicken, **red wine, lardons (or bacon), mushrooms, onion, garlic** and sometimes brandy.

So-Easy Coq Au Vin

Here's my adaptation of the beloved French dish. I substituted boneless skinless chicken breasts for a lighter version that still showcases the traditional and memorable taste.

—SONYA LABBE
WEST HOLLYWOOD, CALIFORNIA

PREP: 20 MIN. ■ COOK: 5 HOURS
YIELD: 4 SERVINGS

4 boneless skinless chicken breast halves (4 ounces *each*)

3 bacon strips, chopped

1/2 pound sliced fresh mushrooms

1 medium onion, chopped

4 garlic cloves, minced

1 bay leaf

1/3 cup all-purpose flour

1/2 cup red wine

1/2 cup chicken broth

1/2 teaspoon dried thyme

1/4 teaspoon pepper

Hot cooked noodles, optional

■ Place chicken in a 3-qt. slow cooker. In a large skillet, cook bacon over medium heat until crisp. Remove to paper towels with a slotted spoon; drain, reserving drippings.

■ In the same skillet, saute the mushrooms, onion and garlic in bacon drippings just until tender. Spoon over chicken. Add bay leaf. In a small bowl, whisk the flour, wine, broth, thyme and pepper until smooth; pour over chicken.

■ Cover and cook on low for 5-7 hours or until a thermometer reads 170°. Discard bay leaf. Serve with noodles if desired.

Apple Chicken Stew

My husband and I enjoy visiting the apple orchards in nearby Nebraska City. We always buy cider to use in this sensational slow-cooked stew.

—**CAROL MATHIAS** LINCOLN, NEBRASKA

PREP: 10 MIN. ■ COOK: 4 HOURS ■ YIELD: 6-8 SERVINGS

4	medium potatoes, cubed
4	medium carrots, cut into 1/4-inch slices
1	medium red onion, halved and sliced
1	celery rib, thinly sliced
1-1/2	teaspoons salt
3/4	teaspoon dried thyme
1/2	teaspoon pepper
1/4	to 1/2 teaspoon caraway seeds

2	pounds boneless skinless chicken breasts, cubed
2	tablespoons olive oil
1	large tart apple, peeled and cubed
1-1/4	cups apple cider or juice
1	tablespoon cider vinegar
1	bay leaf
	Minced fresh parsley

■ In a 5-qt. slow cooker, layer the potatoes, carrots, onion and celery. Combine the salt, thyme, pepper and caraway; sprinkle half over the vegetables.

■ In a large skillet, saute chicken in oil until browned; transfer to slow cooker. Top with apple. In a small bowl, combine apple cider and vinegar; pour over chicken and apple. Sprinkle with remaining salt mixture. Top with bay leaf.

■ Cover and cook on high for 4-5 hours or until chicken is no longer pink and vegetables are tender. Discard bay leaf. Stir before serving. Sprinkle with parsley.

Cider vinegar, which is **made from apples**, has a faint fruity flavor and is used in recipes where a **slightly milder vinegar flavor** is preferred. If you want to add a sharper taste to the dish, simply use white vinegar.

Turkey in Cream Sauce

I've been relying on this recipe for tender turkey since I first moved out on my own years ago.

—**KATHY-JO WINTERBOTTOM** POTTSTOWN, PENNSYLVANIA

PREP: 20 MIN. ■ COOK: 7 HOURS YIELD: 9 SERVINGS

1-1/4	cups white wine or chicken broth
1	medium onion, chopped
2	garlic cloves, minced
2	bay leaves
2	teaspoons dried rosemary, crushed
1/2	teaspoon pepper
3	turkey breast tenderloins (3/4 pound each)
3	tablespoons cornstarch
1/2	cup half-and-half cream or whole milk
1/2	teaspoon salt

■ In a 3-qt. slow cooker, combine the wine, onion, garlic and bay leaves. Combine rosemary and pepper; rub over turkey. Place in slow cooker. Cover and cook on low for 7-8 hours or until a thermometer reads 170°.

■ Remove turkey to a serving platter; keep warm. Strain and skim fat from juices; transfer to a small saucepan. Bring liquid to a boil. Combine cornstarch, cream and salt until smooth; slowly stir into pan. Bring to a boil. Cook; stir for 2 minutes or until thickened. Slice turkey and serve with cream sauce.

➡ **NUTRITION FACTS:** 1 serving (prepared with wine and fat-free milk) equals 179 calories, 1 g fat (0 saturated fat), 82 mg cholesterol, 190 mg sodium, 5 g carbohydrate, 1 g fiber, 30 g protein. **DIABETIC EXCHANGES:** 4 lean meat, 1 vegetable.

SAUCY RASPBERRY CHICKEN

I first had this when I was a teenage babysitter. The children's mom prepared it for us to eat while she was out. The kids loved it, and so did I! Now I make it for my own kids.

—**MELISSA WALES** ELEPHANT BUTTE, NEW MEXICO

Saucy Raspberry Chicken

PREP: 15 MIN. ■ COOK: 5 HOURS ■ YIELD: 5 SERVINGS

5 chicken leg quarters, skin removed	1 teaspoon spicy brown mustard
1/3 cup seedless raspberry spreadable fruit	1/4 teaspoon pepper
3 tablespoons reduced-sodium soy sauce	2 tablespoons cornstarch
	2 tablespoons cold water

■ Place the chicken in a 3-qt. slow cooker. In a small bowl, combine the spreadable fruit, soy sauce, mustard and pepper; pour over chicken. Cover and cook on low for 5-6 hours or until a thermometer reads 180°.

■ Remove chicken to a serving platter; keep warm. Skim fat from cooking juices; transfer to a small saucepan. Bring to a boil. Combine the cornstarch and water until smooth; gradually stir into the pan. Bring to a boil; cook and stir for 2 minutes or until thickened. Serve with chicken.

Satisfying Chicken and Veggies

The best thing about my tasty meal-in-one supper is that I only have one pot to clean.

—**KAT SADI**
SAN LUIS OBISPO, CALIFORNIA

PREP: 20 MIN. ■ COOK: 4 HOURS
YIELD: 6 SERVINGS

- 2 medium potatoes, peeled and cut into 1-inch pieces (about 1-1/2 cups)
- 1 cup thickly sliced onion
- 1/2 cup sliced celery
- 1 medium carrot, cut into 1-inch pieces
- 1 medium sweet yellow pepper, cut into 1-inch pieces
- 1 broiler/fryer chicken (3 to 4 pounds), cut up and skin removed
- 1 jar (24 ounces) meatless spaghetti sauce
- 1 cup water
- 1-1/2 teaspoons minced garlic
- 1/4 teaspoon salt
- 1/4 teaspoon dried oregano
- 1/4 teaspoon dried basil
- 1/4 teaspoon pepper

■ Place the potatoes, onion, celery, carrot and yellow pepper in a 5-qt. slow cooker. Top with chicken. Combine the remaining ingredients; pour over chicken. Cover and cook on low for 4 to 4-1/2 hours or until the chicken juices run clear and vegetables are tender.

HARVEST CHICKEN WITH WALNUT GREMOLATA

This original recipe is based on a classic veal or lamb dish but made more simply in the slow cooker. To lighten it up, I used fat-free chicken broth and removed the skin and excess fat from the chicken legs.

—PATRICIA HARMON BADEN, PENNSYLVANIA

Harvest Chicken with Walnut Gremolata

PREP: 25 MIN. ■ **COOK:** 5-1/4 HOURS ■ **YIELD:** 6 SERVINGS

- 1 medium butternut squash (about 3 pounds), peeled and cubed
- 1 can (14-1/2 ounces) diced tomatoes, drained
- 1 medium onion, chopped
- 1 celery rib, chopped
- 1/2 cup reduced-sodium chicken broth
- 1/4 cup white wine *or* additional reduced-sodium chicken broth
- 1 garlic clove, minced
- 1 teaspoon Italian seasoning
- 1/4 teaspoon coarsely ground pepper, *divided*

- 1/4 cup all-purpose flour
- 1 teaspoon seasoned salt
- 6 chicken drumsticks, skin removed
- 1 cup uncooked orzo pasta

GREMOLATA:
- 2 tablespoons finely chopped walnuts
- 2 tablespoons minced fresh parsley
- 1 garlic clove, minced
- 1 teaspoon grated lemon peel

- In a 5-qt. slow cooker, combine the squash, tomatoes, onion, celery, broth, wine, garlic, Italian seasoning and 1/8 teaspoon pepper.

- In a large resealable plastic bag, combine the flour, seasoned salt and remaining pepper. Add the chicken, a few pieces at a time, and shake to coat. Place the chicken on top of the vegetables. Cover and cook on low for 5 hours or until a thermometer reads 180°. Remove the chicken and keep warm.

- Stir orzo into vegetable mixture; cover and cook 15-20 minutes longer or until orzo is tender. Meanwhile, combine gremolata ingredients.

- Transfer vegetable mixture to a serving platter; top with chicken. Sprinkle with gremolata.

Because of orzo's **similar shape and mild flavor,** it can be substituted for rice in many recipes. Ounce for ounce, **rice and orzo contain similar** amounts of carbohydrates, fat, sugar and even sodium.

My husband and I really like Mexican food, and this is our favorite dish. You can modify it to suit your taste by adding corn, rice or refried beans.

—JENNY MILLER
RALEIGH,
NORTH CAROLINA

HEARTY CHICKEN ENCHILADAS

Hearty Chicken Enchiladas

PREP: 15 MIN. ■ **COOK:** 8 HOURS 25 MIN. ■ **YIELD:** 4 SERVINGS

1 pound boneless skinless chicken breasts	1 can (15 ounces) black beans, rinsed and drained
2 cans (15 ounces *each*) enchilada sauce	8 flour tortillas (6 inches)
1 can (4 ounces) chopped green chilies	1 cup (4 ounces) shredded Mexican cheese blend
	Sour cream, optional

■ In a 3-qt. slow cooker, combine the chicken, enchilada sauce and chilies. Cover and cook on low for 8 hours or until a thermometer reads 170°.

■ Remove chicken and shred with two forks. Reserve 1-2/3 cups cooking juices. Pour the remaining cooking juices into a large bowl; add the beans and shredded chicken. Coat two freezer-safe 8-in. square baking dishes with cooking spray; add 1/2 cup reserved juices to each.

■ Place about 1/3 cup chicken mixture down the center of each tortilla. Roll up and place seam side down in prepared dishes. Pour remaining reserved juices over top; sprinkle with cheese.

■ Cover and freeze one dish for up to 3 months. Cover and bake the second dish at 350° for 20 minutes. Uncover; bake 5 minutes longer or until cheese is lightly browned. Serve with sour cream if desired.

■ **TO USE FROZEN ENCHILADAS:** Thaw in the refrigerator overnight. Remove from the refrigerator 30 minutes before baking. Bake as directed.

Pepper Jack Chicken

Simmer up a low-fat, delicious meal with just a few basic ingredients. Your family is sure to love this colorful medley with tender, juicy chicken and a zippy cheese sauce.

—LINDA FOREMAN
LOCUST GROVE, OKLAHOMA

PREP: 20 MIN. ■ **COOK:** 5 HOURS
YIELD: 6 SERVINGS

6 boneless skinless chicken breast halves (5 ounces *each*), cut into chunks

1 *each* small green, sweet red and orange pepper, cut into thin strips

1 can (10-3/4 ounces) condensed nacho cheese soup, undiluted

1/2 cup chunky salsa

1/8 teaspoon chili powder

4-1/2 cups hot cooked rice

■ In a 3-qt. slow cooker, combine the chicken, peppers, soup, salsa and chili powder. Cover and cook on low for 5-6 hours or until chicken is tender. Serve with rice.

➡ **NUTRITION FACTS:** 1 cup chicken mixture with 3/4 cup rice equals 360 calories, 7 g fat (2 g saturated fat), 84 mg cholesterol, 553 mg sodium, 41 g carbohydrate, 2 g fiber, 34 g protein. **DIABETIC EXCHANGE:** 4 lean meat, 2-1/2 starch, 1/2 fat.

Chicken Chop Suey with a Twist

If you're in for a busy evening, here's a great way to ensure you can still have a healthful supper. It's tasty, traditional, and easy, too!

—MELODY LITTLEWOOD ROYAL CITY, WASHINGTON

PREP: 20 MIN. ■ COOK: 5-1/2 HOURS ■ YIELD: 9 SERVINGS

1-1/2 pounds boneless skinless chicken thighs, cut into 2-inch pieces	1/2 cup frozen shelled edamame
8 ounces sliced fresh mushrooms	1 can (14-1/2 ounces) reduced-sodium chicken broth
2 celery ribs, sliced	1/2 cup reduced-sodium soy sauce
1 medium onion, chopped	1 tablespoon minced fresh gingerroot
1 can (14 ounces) bean sprouts, rinsed and drained	1/4 teaspoon crushed red pepper flakes
1 can (8 ounces) bamboo shoots, drained	2 tablespoons cornstarch
1 can (8 ounces) sliced water chestnuts, drained	2 tablespoons cold water
	Hot cooked rice

■ Place chicken in a 4- or 5-qt. slow cooker. Top with mushrooms, celery, onion, bean sprouts, bamboo shoots, water chestnuts and edamame. In a small bowl, combine the broth, soy sauce, ginger and pepper flakes. Pour over chicken and vegetables. Cover and cook on low for 5-6 hours or until chicken is tender.

■ Combine cornstarch and water until smooth; gradually stir into chop suey. Cover and cook on high 30 minutes longer or until thickened. Serve with rice.

➡➡ **NUTRITION FACTS:** 1 cup (calculated without rice) equals 178 calories, 6 g fat (2 g saturated fat), 50 mg cholesterol, 739 mg sodium, 12 g carbohydrate, 3 g fiber, 19 g protein. **DIABETIC EXCHANGES:** 2 lean meat, 1 vegetable.

Moist & Tender Turkey Breast

This easy dish will be very popular in your home. It's a family-pleasing recipe with great flavor, and you'll love how quickly it comes together.

—HEIDI VAWDREY RIVERTON, UTAH

PREP: 10 MIN. ■ COOK: 4 HOURS ■ YIELD: 12 SERVINGS

1 bone-in turkey breast (6 to 7 pounds)	1 tablespoon brown sugar
4 fresh rosemary sprigs	1/2 teaspoon coarsely ground pepper
4 garlic cloves, peeled	1/4 teaspoon salt

■ Place turkey breast in a 6-qt. slow cooker. Place rosemary and garlic around turkey. Combine brown sugar, pepper and salt; sprinkle over turkey. Cover and cook on low for 4-6 hours or until turkey is tender.

Cajun Chicken Lasagna

PREP: 20 MIN. ■ COOK: 3 HOURS
YIELD: 8 SERVINGS

- 2 pounds ground chicken
- 2 celery ribs with leaves, chopped
- 1 medium green pepper, chopped
- 1 medium onion, chopped
- 1 can (28 ounces) crushed tomatoes, undrained
- 1 cup water
- 1 can (6 ounces) tomato paste
- 3 teaspoons Cajun seasoning
- 1 teaspoon sugar
- 2 cups (8 ounces) shredded part-skim mozzarella cheese
- 1 carton (15 ounces) ricotta cheese
- 9 uncooked lasagna noodles

■ In a large skillet, cook chicken over medium heat until no longer pink. Add the celery, green pepper and onion; cook and stir 5 minutes longer or until tender. Stir in the tomatoes, water, tomato paste, Cajun seasoning and sugar. In a small bowl, combine cheeses.

■ Spread 1 cup meat sauce in a greased oval 5- or 6-qt. slow cooker. Layer with 3 noodles (breaking noodles if necessary to fit), a third of the remaining meat sauce and a third of the cheese mixture. Repeat layers twice. Cover and cook on low for 3-4 hours or until noodles are tender.

Destined to be a new favorite with everyone around the table, this zesty take on traditional Italian lasagna nods to the Gulf Coast. The ground chicken along with the different flavor profile are a nice change. Increase the amount of Cajun seasoning if you like spicier fare.

—**MARY LOU COOK** WELCHES, OREGON

SLOW-COOKED ITALIAN CHICKEN

- Place chicken in a 3-qt. slow cooker. In a bowl, combine the broth, tomatoes, tomato sauce, green pepper, onion, garlic and seasonings; pour over chicken. Cover and cook on low for 4-5 hours or until meat is tender. Remove chicken and keep warm.

- Pour cooking juices into a large saucepan; skim fat. Combine flour and cold water until smooth; stir into juices. Bring to a boil; cook and stir for 2 minutes or until thickened. Serve with chicken and pasta.

➤ **NUTRITION FACTS:** One chicken breast half with 1/2 cup sauce (prepared with reduced-sodium broth, garlic powder and onion powder; calculated without pasta) equals 241 calories, 2 g fat (trace saturated fat), 66 mg cholesterol, 1,003 mg sodium, 25 g carbohydrate, 4 g fiber, 31 g protein. **DIABETIC EXCHANGES:** 2-1/2 lean meat, 1-1/2 starch.

With its nicely seasoned tomato sauce, this enticing chicken entree is especially good over pasta or rice. My father loved it when I made this, and it's a regular entree in my home.

—**DEANNA D'AURIA** BANNING, CALIFORNIA

Slow-Cooked Italian Chicken

PREP: 10 MIN. ■ **COOK:** 4 HOURS 10 MIN. ■ **YIELD:** 4 SERVINGS

4 boneless skinless chicken breast halves (4 ounces each)	3 teaspoons chili powder
1 can (14-1/2 ounces) chicken broth	1 teaspoon ground mustard
1 can (14-1/2 ounces) stewed tomatoes, cut up	1/2 teaspoon garlic salt *or* garlic powder
1 can (8 ounces) tomato sauce	1/2 teaspoon onion salt *or* onion powder
1 medium green pepper, chopped	1/2 teaspoon pepper
1 green onion, chopped	1/3 cup all-purpose flour
1 garlic clove, minced	1/2 cup cold water
	Hot cooked pasta

A medium green pepper, chopped, will yield about 1 cup. A large green pepper, chopped, will yield about 1-1/3 to 1-1/2 cups. Store green peppers in a resealable plastic bag. They can **be frozen for as long as 6 months.**

Pulled Turkey Tenderloin

Not your ordinary pulled turkey sandwich, this one shines thanks to its unique yogurt sauce. Serve the turkey by itself or stack on extra sweet pickle slices and jalapenos to match the dressing.

—**SHANA CONRADT** GREENVILLE, WISCONSIN

PREP: 15 MIN. ■ COOK: 6 HOURS ■ YIELD: 5 SERVINGS

1 package (20 ounces) turkey breast tenderloins	1/2 cup fat-free plain Greek yogurt
2 cups water	1 tablespoon yellow mustard
1/2 cup sweet pickle juice	1/8 teaspoon pepper
1 envelope onion soup mix	5 kaiser rolls, split
2 tablespoons canned diced jalapeno peppers	

■ Place turkey in a 3-qt. slow cooker. In a small bowl, combine the water, pickle juice, soup mix and jalapeno peppers; pour over turkey. Cover and cook on low for 6-8 hours or until a thermometer reads 170°. Remove turkey and shred with two forks. Transfer to a small bowl.

■ Strain cooking juices, reserving 1/2 cup juices. In another small bowl, combine the yogurt, mustard, pepper and reserved cooking juices. Pour over turkey; toss to coat. Serve on rolls.

➡ **NUTRITION FACTS:** 1 sandwich equals 339 calories, 4 g fat (1 g saturated fat), 56 mg cholesterol, 1,074 mg sodium, 40 g carbohydrate, 2 g fiber, 36 g protein. **DIABETIC EXCHANGES:** 4 lean meat, 2 starch.

Moist Italian Turkey Breast

This recipe renders some of the juiciest turkey I have ever eaten. High in lean protein, it's a smart entree for a special occasion.

—**JESSICA KUNZ** SPRINGFIELD, ILLINOIS

PREP: 25 MIN. ■ COOK: 6 HOURS + STANDING ■ YIELD: 12 **SERVINGS**

1 pound medium carrots, cut into 2-inch pieces	1 bone-in turkey breast (6 to 7 pounds), thawed and skin removed
2 medium onions, cut into wedges	2 tablespoons olive oil
3 celery ribs, cut into 2-inch pieces	1-1/2 teaspoons seasoned salt
1 can (14-1/2 ounces) chicken broth	1 teaspoon Italian seasoning
	1/2 teaspoon pepper

■ In a 6- or 7-qt. slow cooker, combine the carrots, onions, celery and broth. Place turkey in slow cooker. Brush with oil. Sprinkle with seasoned salt, Italian seasoning and pepper.

■ Cover and cook on low for 6-8 hours or until a thermometer reads 170°. Let stand for 15 minutes before slicing.

Tangy Tropical Chicken

In this colorful dish, exotic fruits such as mango and pineapple beautifully complement the chicken and lend a pleasant hint of sweetness that's balanced by a bit of soy sauce.

—**CHRISTINA AHO** NAPLES, FLORIDA

PREP: 20 MIN. ■ COOK: 4 HOURS
YIELD: 4 SERVINGS

- 1 pound boneless skinless chicken breasts, cut into 1-inch strips
- 2 cups chopped peeled mangoes
- 1 medium onion, chopped
- 1 medium green pepper, sliced
- 1 garlic clove, minced
- 1 cup unsweetened pineapple juice
- 1 cup orange juice
- 1/4 cup reduced-sodium soy sauce
- 2 tablespoons Thai chili sauce
- 1/4 teaspoon pepper
- 2 tablespoons cornstarch
- 2 tablespoons cold water

Hot cooked rice

■ Place chicken in a 3-qt. slow cooker. Top with mangoes, onion, green pepper and garlic. In a small bowl, combine the pineapple juice, orange juice, soy sauce, chili sauce and pepper; pour over chicken. Cover and cook on low for 4-5 hours or until chicken is tender.

■ Remove chicken mixture to a serving platter; keep warm. Transfer cooking juices to a small saucepan. Bring juices to a boil. Combine cornstarch and water until smooth; gradually stir into the pan. Bring to a boil; cook and stir for 2 minutes or until thickened. Serve with chicken mixture and rice.

During chilly months, I fix this jambalaya at least once a month. It's so easy—just chop the vegetables, dump everything in the slow cooker and forget it! Even my sons, who are picky about spicy things, like this dish.

—CINDI COSS
COPPELL, TEXAS

Forgotten Jambalaya

PREP: 35 MIN. ■ **COOK:** 4-1/4 HOURS ■ **YIELD:** 11 SERVINGS

1	can (14-1/2 ounces) diced tomatoes, undrained
1	can (14-1/2 ounces) beef *or* chicken broth
1	can (6 ounces) tomato paste
2	medium green peppers, chopped
1	medium onion, chopped
3	celery ribs, chopped
5	garlic cloves, minced
3	teaspoons dried parsley flakes
2	teaspoons dried basil
1-1/2	teaspoons dried oregano
1-1/4	teaspoons salt
1/2	teaspoon cayenne pepper
1/2	teaspoon hot pepper sauce
1	pound boneless skinless chicken breasts, cut into 1-inch cubes
1	pound smoked sausage, halved and cut into 1/4-inch slices
1/2	pound uncooked medium shrimp, peeled and deveined
	Hot cooked rice

■ In a 5-qt. slow cooker, combine the tomatoes, broth and tomato paste. Stir in the green peppers, onion, celery, garlic and seasonings. Stir in chicken and sausage.

■ Cover and cook on low for 4-6 hours or until chicken is no longer pink. Stir in shrimp. Cover and cook 15-30 minutes longer or until shrimp turn pink. Serve with rice.

Herbed Chicken And Shrimp

Tender chicken and shrimp make a flavorful combination that's easy to prepare, yet elegant enough to serve at a dinner party. While I clean the house, it practically cooks itself. I serve it over hot cooked rice with crusty bread and a green salad.

—DIANA KNIGHT RENO, NEVADA

PREP: 15 MIN.
COOK: 4 HOURS 20 MIN.
YIELD: 4 SERVINGS

1	teaspoon salt
1	teaspoon pepper
1	broiler/fryer chicken (3 to 4 pounds), cut up and skin removed
1/4	cup butter
1	large onion, chopped
1	can (8 ounces) tomato sauce
1/2	cup white wine *or* chicken broth
1	garlic clove, minced
1	teaspoon dried basil
1	pound uncooked medium shrimp, peeled and deveined

■ Combine salt and pepper; rub over chicken pieces. In a large skillet, brown chicken on all sides in butter. Transfer to an ungreased 5-qt. slow cooker.

■ In a large bowl, combine the onion, tomato sauce, wine, garlic and basil; pour over chicken. Cover and cook on low for 4-5 hours or until chicken is no longer pink.

■ Stir in the shrimp. Cover and cook on high for 20-30 minutes or until the shrimp turn pink.

SUNDAY CHICKEN STEW

I love this recipe because I can prepare the veggies the night before, and in the morning, brown the chicken and assemble everything in the slow cooker before church. Then, I spend time with my family as dinner cooks.

—DIANE HALFERTY CORPUS CHRISTI, TEXAS

Sunday Chicken Stew

PREP: 30 MIN. ■ **COOK:** 6-1/2 HOURS ■ **YIELD:** 6 SERVINGS

1/2 cup all-purpose flour	1 large sweet onion, thinly sliced
1 teaspoon salt	1 teaspoon dried rosemary, crushed
1/2 teaspoon white pepper	1-1/2 cups frozen peas
1 broiler/fryer chicken (3 pounds), cut up and skin removed	**DUMPLINGS:**
2 tablespoons canola oil	1 cup all-purpose flour
3 cups chicken broth	2 teaspoons baking powder
6 large carrots, cut into 1-inch pieces	1/2 teaspoon salt
2 celery ribs, cut into 1/2-inch pieces	1/2 teaspoon dried rosemary, crushed
	1 egg, lightly beaten
	1/2 cup 2% milk

■ In a large resealable plastic bag, combine the flour, salt and pepper; add chicken, a few pieces at a time, and shake to coat. In a large skillet, brown chicken in oil; remove and keep warm. Gradually add broth to skillet; bring to a boil.

■ In a 5-qt. slow cooker, layer the carrots, celery and onion; sprinkle with rosemary. Add the chicken and hot broth. Cover and cook on low for 6-7 hours or until chicken juices run clear, vegetables are tender and stew is bubbling.

■ Remove chicken; when cool enough to handle, remove meat from the bones and discard bones. Cut meat into bite-size pieces and return to the slow cooker. Stir in peas.

■ For dumplings, in a small bowl, combine the flour, baking powder, salt and rosemary. Combine the egg and milk; stir into dry ingredients. Drop by heaping teaspoonfuls onto simmering chicken mixture. Cover and cook on high for 25-30 minutes or until a toothpick inserted in a dumpling comes out clean (do not lift the cover while simmering).

- Place chicken in a greased 4-qt. slow cooker. In a large bowl, combine the corn, beans, tomatoes, jalapeno and seasonings; pour over chicken. Cover and cook on low for 4-5 hours or until the chicken is tender.

- Remove chicken; cool slightly. Shred meat with two forks and return to the slow cooker. Stir in cream cheese. Cover and cook 15 minutes longer or until heated through.

- Spoon 3/4 cup chicken mixture down the center of each tortilla; add toppings of your choice. Fold sides and ends over filling and roll up.

EDITOR'S NOTE: Wear disposable gloves when cutting hot peppers; the oils can burn skin. Avoid touching your face.

FIESTA CHICKEN BURRITOS

Looking for some heat with supper but still want a cool kitchen? Try these slow cooked burritos with a spicy touch the whole family will love! This is a simple recipe to double if you're catering to a crowd.

—**MARGARET LATTA** PADUCAH, KENTUCKY

Fiesta Chicken Burritos

PREP: 30 MIN. ■ COOK: 4-1/4 HOURS ■ YIELD: 8 SERVINGS

1-1/2 pounds boneless skinless chicken breasts

1 can (15-1/4 ounces) whole kernel corn, drained

1 can (15 ounces) black beans, rinsed and drained

1 can (10 ounces) diced tomatoes and green chilies, undrained

1 jalapeno pepper, seeded and finely chopped

3 tablespoons ground cumin

1 teaspoon salt

1 teaspoon paprika

1/2 teaspoon pepper

Dash cayenne pepper

Dash crushed red pepper flakes

1 package (8 ounces) reduced-fat cream cheese

8 flour tortillas (8 inches), warmed

Optional toppings: sour cream, shredded cheddar cheese, shredded lettuce and chopped tomatoes

If you have to cut a large number of hot peppers, try this: **Cut off the tops of the peppers,** then slice them in half lengthwise. **Use the small end of a melon baller** to scrape out seeds and membranes. (Be sure to wear plastic gloves!)

The yummy flavors in this dish make it my favorite slow cooker recipe. The delicious, slightly spicy sauce will win you over, too! It's a great way to enjoy summer flavor any time of the year.

—YVONNE MCKIM
VANCOUVER, WASHINGTON

TROPICAL BBQ CHICKEN

Tropical BBQ Chicken

PREP: 15 MIN. ■ **COOK:** 5 HOURS ■ **YIELD:** 12 **SERVINGS**

6 chicken leg quarters, skin removed	4 teaspoons minced fresh parsley
3/4 cup ketchup	2 teaspoons Worcestershire sauce
1/2 cup orange juice	1 teaspoon garlic salt
1/4 cup packed brown sugar	1/2 teaspoon pepper
1/4 cup red wine vinegar	2 tablespoons plus 2 teaspoons cornstarch
1/4 cup olive oil	1/4 cup water

■ With a sharp knife, cut leg quarters at the joints. Place chicken in a 4-qt. slow cooker.

■ In a small bowl, combine the ketchup, orange juice, brown sugar, vinegar, oil, parsley, Worcestershire sauce, garlic salt and pepper; pour over chicken.

■ Cover and cook on low for 5-6 hours or until a meat thermometer reads 180°.

■ Remove the chicken to a serving platter; keep warm. Skim fat from the cooking juices; transfer 2 cups to a small saucepan. Bring the liquid to a boil.

■ Combine cornstarch and water until smooth. Gradually stir into the pan. Bring to a boil; cook and stir for 2 minutes or until thickened. Serve with chicken.

➡ **NUTRITION FACTS:** 1 serving equals 179 calories, 9 g fat (2 g saturated fat), 45 mg cholesterol, 392 mg sodium, 12 g carbohydrate, trace fiber, 13 g protein. **DIABETIC EXCHANGES:** 2 lean meat, 1 starch, 1 fat.

Chicken in Sour Cream Sauce

Tender chicken is deliciously dressed up in a tasty cream sauce with fresh mushrooms. This is an excellent entree for your family or even guests.

—JANE CARLOVSKY
SEBRING, FLORIDA

PREP: 15 MIN. ■ **COOK:** 6 HOURS
YIELD: 6 SERVINGS

1-1/2 teaspoons salt
1/4 teaspoon pepper
1/4 teaspoon paprika
1/4 teaspoon lemon-pepper seasoning
6 bone-in chicken breast halves, skin removed (7 ounces *each*)
1 can (10-3/4 ounces) condensed cream of mushroom soup, undiluted
1 cup (8 ounces) sour cream
1/2 cup dry white wine *or* chicken broth
1/2 pound fresh mushrooms, sliced

■ In a small bowl, combine the first four ingredients; rub over chicken. Place in a 3-qt. slow cooker. In a large bowl, combine the soup, sour cream, and wine; stir in mushrooms. Pour over chicken.

■ Cover and cook on low for 6-8 hours or until a thermometer reads 170°. Thicken the sauce if desired.

Pork & Other Entrees

49

50

52

Slow cookers aren't just for beef and chicken anymore! These hearty entrees are proof positive. From **pork roasts and ribs to sausage stews and gumbo**, they use ham, ribs, sausage, lamb, shrimp or no meat at all. Try plenty of delectable new ways to make a fun, flavorful—and effortless—meal!

Tropical Triple Pork

With a busy day ahead, I threw this jambalaya-style main dish together using items I had on hand—it was so easy! When I served it at dinner, it earned raves from my guests.

—DEE GUELCHER
ACWORTH, GEORGIA

PREP: 25 MIN. ■ **COOK:** 5 HOURS
YIELD: 8 SERVINGS

1-1/2   pounds boneless pork loin roast
  3/4   pound fully cooked andouille sausage links, sliced
1-1/2   cups cubed fully cooked ham
   1   can (28 ounces) diced tomatoes, undrained
   2   medium mangoes, peeled and chopped
   1   medium onion, chopped
   1   cup roasted sweet red peppers, cut into strips
   1   bay leaf
   1   teaspoon salt
  1/2   teaspoon pepper
Hot cooked rice

■ Place roast in a 5-qt. slow cooker. Add sausage and ham. Stir in the tomatoes, mangoes, onion, red peppers, bay leaf, salt and pepper. Cover and cook on low for 5-6 hours or until meat is tender.

■ Remove roast to a plate. Discard bay leaf. Shred meat with two forks and return to slow cooker; heat through. Serve with rice.

RATATOUILLE WITH A TWIST

Before this variation came along, my family always ate ratatouille as a veggie. My husband's suggestion to incorporate sausage turned out to be a big hit, and now it's an entree we all love!

—SUSAN TREMBLAY BERLIN, NEW HAMPSHIRE

Ratatouille with a Twist

PREP: 25 MIN. ■ **COOK:** 6 HOURS ■ **YIELD:** 6 SERVINGS

4   hot Italian sausage links (4 ounces *each*)
4   cups chopped zucchini
1   can (14-1/2 ounces) stewed tomatoes, cut-up
1   can (10-3/4 ounces) condensed tomato soup, undiluted

1   medium onion, chopped
1   garlic clove, minced
1/2   teaspoon dried basil
1/2   teaspoon dried oregano
Hot cooked pasta

■ In a large skillet, cook sausages until no longer pink. Cut into 1/2-in. slices; transfer to a 3-qt. slow cooker. Add the zucchini, tomatoes, soup, onion, garlic, basil and oregano. Cover and cook on low for 6-8 hours or until flavors are blended. Serve with pasta.

PORK CHOPS & POTATOES IN MUSHROOM SAUCE

This hearty pork dinner is really a keeper! Everyone loves the creamy potatoes, and they always go back for seconds. The fact that the dish is made in a slow cooker makes the recipe even more appealing!

—LINDA FOREMAN LOCUST GROVE, OKLAHOMA

Pork Chops & Potatoes In Mushroom Sauce

PREP: 25 MIN. ■ **COOK:** 3-1/2 HOURS ■ **YIELD:** 6 SERVINGS

1 can (10-3/4 ounces) condensed cream of mushroom soup, undiluted	1/4 teaspoon salt
	1/4 teaspoon pepper
1/4 cup chicken broth	6 medium red potatoes, sliced
1/4 cup country style Dijon mustard	1 medium onion, halved and thinly sliced
1 garlic clove, minced	6 boneless pork loin chops (5 ounces *each*)
1/2 teaspoon dried thyme	

■ In a 5-qt. slow cooker, combine the first seven ingredients. Stir in potatoes and onion. Top with pork chops. Cover and cook on low for 4-6 hours or until potatoes are tender.

Apple-Dijon Pork Roast

This is one of my family favorites for cold-weather comfort. The delicious recipe takes less than five minutes to assemble. I serve the roast with rice and use the tangy sauce as a gravy for both.

—CINDY STEFFEN
CEDARBURG, WISCONSIN

PREP: 15 MIN. ■ **COOK:** 4 HOURS
YIELD: 8 SERVINGS

- 1 boneless whole pork loin roast (2 to 3 pounds)
- 1 can (14-1/2 ounces) chicken broth
- 1 cup unsweetened apple juice
- 1/2 cup Dijon mustard
- 6 tablespoons cornstarch
- 6 tablespoons cold water

■ Place roast in a 5-qt. slow cooker. In a small bowl, combine the broth, apple juice and mustard; pour over roast. Cover and cook on low for 4-5 hours or until tender. Remove roast and keep warm.

■ For gravy, strain cooking juices and skim fat. Pour juices into a small saucepan. Combine cornstarch and water until smooth; gradually stir into juices. Bring to a boil; cook and stir for 2 minutes or until thickened. Serve with the pork.

➡ **NUTRITION FACTS:** 3 ounces cooked pork with about 1/3 cup gravy (prepared with reduced-sodium chicken broth) equals 197 calories, 7 g fat (2 g saturated fat), 56 mg cholesterol, 413 mg sodium, 11 g carbohydrate, trace fiber, 23 g protein. **DIABETIC EXCHANGES:** 3 lean meat, 1/2 starch.

These simple-to-prepare ribs call for everyday ingredients, so I never complain when my family asks me to make them. Everyone enjoys the down-home goodness.

—ALPHA WILSON ROSWELL, NEW MEXICO

SLOW COOKER RIBS

Slow Cooker Ribs

PREP: 15 MIN. ■ **COOK:** 4 HOURS ■ **YIELD:** 4 SERVINGS

3	pounds pork spareribs	
1/2	teaspoon salt	
1/4	teaspoon pepper	

1-3/4 cups sliced onions

1 bottle (18 ounces) barbecue sauce

- Place ribs, meat side up, on a broiling pan. Sprinkle with salt and pepper. Broil 6 in. from the heat for 15-20 minutes or until browned. Cool; cut into serving-size pieces.

- Place onions in a 5-qt. slow cooker; top with ribs. Pour barbecue sauce over all. Cover and cook on high for 1 hour; reduce heat to low and cook 3-4 hours or until ribs are tender.

Spareribs are cut from the side of the hog and are **sometimes called side ribs.** Spareribs cost a bit less than baby backs because spareribs have more bone than meat. But **spareribs also have lots of marbling**, so the ribs have loads of flavor.

Sausage-Veggie Pasta Sauce

With this recipe, I sneak so many vegetables past my young sons—they even ask for seconds! Plus, it smells wonderful simmering all day long. Make it interesting with different pasta shapes.

—TAUSHA KUTIL IRVINE, CALIFORNIA

PREP: 25 MIN. ■ **COOK:** 6 HOURS **YIELD:** 7 SERVINGS

1 pound bulk Italian sausage

1/2 pound sliced fresh mushrooms

1 can (14-1/2 ounces) diced tomatoes, undrained

1 jar (14 ounces) marinara *or* spaghetti sauce

1 cup shredded carrots

1 medium green pepper, chopped

1 medium sweet red pepper, chopped

1 small onion, chopped

1 can (6 ounces) tomato paste

3 garlic cloves, minced

1 tablespoon sugar

1-1/2 teaspoons dried basil

1-1/2 teaspoons dried oregano

Hot cooked spaghetti

- In a large skillet, cook sausage over medium heat until no longer pink; drain. Transfer to a 4-qt. slow cooker. Stir in the mushrooms, tomatoes, marinara sauce, carrots, peppers, onion, tomato paste, garlic, sugar, basil and oregano. Cover and cook on low for 6-8 hours or until vegetables are tender. Serve with spaghetti.

It doesn't get much easier than this quick and hearty all-in-one slow cooker meal. And it doesn't get much tastier, either!

—SANDY MULLEN
GAGE, OKLAHOMA

COUNTRY PORK CHOP SUPPER

Country Pork Chop Supper

PREP: 10 MIN. ■ **COOK:** 5 HOURS ■ **YIELD:** 6 SERVINGS

- 6 boneless pork loin chops (1/2 inch thick and 4 ounces *each*)
- 2 jars (12 ounces *each*) pork gravy
- 1 can (10-3/4 ounces) condensed cream of mushroom soup, undiluted
- 2 tablespoons ketchup
- 1 tablespoon minced chives
- 1 teaspoon pepper
- 1 teaspoon soy sauce
- 1/2 teaspoon seasoned salt
- 3 medium potatoes, peeled and quartered
- 1 package (16 ounces) frozen mixed vegetables

■ Place pork chops in a greased 5-qt. slow cooker. In a large bowl, combine the gravy, soup, ketchup, chives, pepper, soy sauce and seasoned salt; pour over pork.

■ Stir in potatoes; cover and cook on low for 4-5 hours. Stir in the vegetables; cook 1 hour longer or until meat and potatoes are tender.

Unlike beef, **cuts of pork vary little in tenderness.** Use dry-heat cooking methods, such as broiling, grilling and roasting, when firm texture is desired. **Try the moist-heat method of slow cooking** when you want fork-tender pork.

Sweet 'n' Sour Sausage

Carrots, green pepper and pineapple lend color to this slow-cooked sausage supper. Serve this combination stir-fry style over rice or chow mein noodles.

—BARBARA SCHUTZ PANDORA, OHIO

PREP: 15 MIN.
COOK: 4-1/2 HOURS
YIELD: 6 SERVINGS

- 1 pound smoked kielbasa *or* Polish sausage, sliced
- 1 can (20 ounces) unsweetened pineapple chunks, undrained
- 1-1/2 cups fresh baby carrots, quartered lengthwise
- 1 large green pepper, cut into 1-inch pieces
- 1 medium onion, cut into chunks
- 1/3 cup packed brown sugar
- 1 tablespoon soy sauce
- 1/2 teaspoon chicken bouillon granules
- 1/4 teaspoon garlic powder
- 1/4 teaspoon ground ginger
- 2 tablespoons cornstarch
- 1/4 cup cold water

Hot cooked rice *or* chow mein noodles

■ In a 3-qt. slow cooker, combine the first 10 ingredients. Cover and cook on low for 4-5 hours.

■ Mix cornstarch and water until smooth; stir into sausage mixture. Cover; cook on high for 30 minutes or until gravy is thickened. Serve with rice.

➤➤ NUTRITION FACTS: One 1-cup serving (prepared with smoked turkey sausage and reduced-sodium soy sauce; calculated without rice) equals 250 calories, 4 g fat (1 g saturated fat), 34 mg cholesterol, 869 mg sodium, 43 g carbohydrate, 1 g fiber, 10 g protein. DIABETIC EXCHANGES: 2 fruit, 1 lean meat, 1 vegetable, 1/2 starch.

GLAZED LAMB SHANKS

Ideal for a night in for two, these slow-cooked shanks are packed with complex flavors. The Guinness and honey nicely balance the lamb, while garlic imparts a bit of zing.

—ELIZABETH MITCHELL COCHRANVILLE, PENNSYLVANIA

Glazed Lamb Shanks

PREP: 30 MIN. + MARINATING ■ **COOK:** 6 HOURS ■ **YIELD:** 4 SERVINGS

- 4 lamb shanks (about 20 ounces *each*)
- 4 garlic cloves, thinly sliced
- 1 cup lemon juice
- 4 tablespoons olive oil, *divided*
- 1 tablespoon *each* minced fresh thyme, rosemary and parsley
- 1 teaspoon salt
- 1/2 teaspoon pepper

SAUCE:

- 1 cup Guinness (dark beer)
- 1/4 cup honey
- 3 fresh thyme sprigs
- 2 bay leaves
- 1 tablespoon Dijon mustard
- 2 garlic cloves, minced
- 1/2 teaspoon salt
- 1/4 teaspoon pepper
- 1/8 teaspoon crushed red pepper flakes
- 2 pounds Yukon Gold potatoes, peeled and cut into chunks

■ Cut slits into each lamb shank; insert garlic slices. In a large resealable plastic bag, combine juice, 2 tablespoons oil, thyme, rosemary, parsley, salt and pepper. Add lamb; seal bag and turn to coat. Refrigerate overnight.

■ Drain and discard the marinade. In a large skillet, brown the shanks in the remaining oil on all sides in batches. Place the shanks in a 5- or 6-qt. slow cooker.

■ In same skillet, combine beer, honey, thyme sprigs, bay leaves, Dijon, garlic, salt, pepper and pepper flakes. Bring to a boil, stirring constantly. Pour over meat. Cover and cook on low for 6-8 hours or until meat and potatoes are tender, adding the potatoes during the last 2 hours of cooking.

■ Remove lamb and potatoes from slow cooker. Strain sauce and discard bay leaves. If desired, thicken sauce. Serve with lamb and potatoes.

To avoid lamb with a strong flavor, **try grain-fed lamb,** which has a milder flavor than grass-fed lamb. **Domestic lamb is usually grain-fed.**

BAYOU GULF SHRIMP GUMBO

- In a large skillet, cook bacon over medium heat until crisp. Remove to paper towels with a slotted spoon; drain, reserving 2 tablespoons drippings. Saute the celery, onion, green pepper and garlic in drippings until tender.

- Transfer to a 4-qt. slow cooker. Stir in the bacon, clam juice, tomatoes, Worcestershire sauce, salt and marjoram. Cover and cook on low for 4 hours.

- Stir in the shrimp and okra. Cover and cook 1 hour longer or until shrimp turn pink and the okra is heated through. Serve with rice.

This traditional stew from the Louisiana bayou is a natural fit for the slow cooker. The recipe skips the hard-to-find spices that the dish usually calls for but still delivers true seafood flavor.

—WOLFGANG HANAU WEST PALM BEACH, FLORIDA

Bayou Gulf Shrimp Gumbo

PREP: 35 MIN. ■ **COOK:** 5 HOURS ■ **YIELD:** 6 SERVINGS

1/2 pound bacon strips, chopped	2 tablespoons Worcestershire sauce
3 celery ribs, chopped	1 teaspoon kosher salt
1 medium onion, chopped	1 teaspoon dried marjoram
1 medium green pepper, chopped	2 pounds uncooked large shrimp, peeled and deveined
2 garlic cloves, minced	2-1/2 cups frozen sliced okra, thawed
2 bottles (8 ounces *each*) clam juice	Hot cooked rice
1 can (14-1/2 ounces) diced tomatoes, undrained	

Okra originated in **Africa and Southeast Asia** and was later introduced to the southern United States. The elongated green vegetable, which is part of the cotton family, is packed with **vitamin B-6, vitamin C and folate.**

Hawaiian Pork Roast

This is one of my favorite slow-cooker recipes. It's wonderful with rice or potatoes and any vegetable. It also reheats well for lunch the next day.
—**RUTH CHIARENZA** LA VALE, MARYLAND

PREP: 30 MIN. ■ COOK: 4-6 HOURS + STANDING ■ YIELD: 8 SERVINGS

1 boneless whole pork loin roast (3 pounds)	1/2 cup packed brown sugar
1/2 teaspoon salt	1/2 cup sliced celery
1/4 teaspoon pepper	1/2 cup cider vinegar
3 tablespoons canola oil	1/2 cup soy sauce
2 cups unsweetened pineapple juice	1/4 cup cornstarch
1 can (8 ounces) unsweetened crushed pineapple, undrained	1/3 cup cold water

■ Cut pork roast in half. Sprinkle with salt and pepper. In a large skillet, brown roast in oil on all sides; drain. Place in a 5-qt. slow cooker.

■ In a large bowl, combine the pineapple juice, pineapple, brown sugar, celery, vinegar and soy sauce. Pour over the roast. Cover and cook on low for 4-6 hours or until a thermometer reads 160°.

■ Remove roast and keep warm. Let stand for 10 minutes before slicing. Meanwhile, strain cooking juices; transfer to a large saucepan. Combine cornstarch and water until smooth; stir into cooking juices. Bring to a boil; cook and stir for 2 minutes or until thickened. Serve with pork.

Lemon Pork Chops

These chops can simmer all day on low and be super tender by dinnertime. I serve them with a crisp salad and macaroni and cheese as a side dish.
—**BARBARA DE FRANG** HAZEN, NORTH DAKOTA

PREP: 5 MIN. ■ COOK: 6 HOURS ■ YIELD: 4 SERVINGS

4 bone-in pork chops (3/4 inch thick and 7 ounces *each*)	1 medium lemon, cut into 1/4-inch slices
1/2 teaspoon salt	1/4 cup packed brown sugar
1/4 teaspoon pepper	1/4 cup ketchup
1 medium onion, cut into 1/4-inch slices	

■ Place the pork chops in a 3-qt. slow cooker. Sprinkle with salt and pepper. Top with onion and lemon. Sprinkle with brown sugar; drizzle with ketchup. Cover and cook on low for 6 hours or until meat is tender.

Hearty Pork Stew

This spicy slow-cooked stew combines tender chunks of pork with colorful tomatoes and green peppers. I garnish bowls of it with chopped hard-cooked eggs and green onions.
—**REBECCA OVERY** EVANSTON, WYOMING

PREP: 10 MIN.
COOK: 8-1/2 HOURS
YIELD: 8 SERVINGS

1-1/2 to 2 pounds boneless pork, cut into 1-inch cubes

4 cups water

1 can (14-1/2 ounces) stewed tomatoes

1 medium onion, chopped

1 medium green pepper, chopped

1/3 cup soy sauce

1 to 2 tablespoons chili powder

1 tablespoon dried celery flakes

1/2 teaspoon garlic powder

1/2 teaspoon pepper

1/3 cup cornstarch

1/3 cup cold water

Hot cooked noodles

■ In a 3-qt. slow cooker, combine the first 10 ingredients. Cover and cook on low for 8 hours.

■ Combine the cornstarch and water until smooth; gradually stir into slow cooker. Cover and cook on high for 30 minutes or until slightly thickened. Serve in bowls with noodles.

Mint Lamb Stew

The lamb here isn't just tender, it melts in your mouth! This recipe is an adaptation of a stew my mother used to make while I was growing up in England. Now I round it out with local root vegetables.

—MAUREEN EVANS RANCHO CUCAMONGA, CALIFORNIA

PREP: 40 MIN. ■ **COOK:** 7 HOURS ■ **YIELD:** 6 SERVINGS

1/2 cup all-purpose flour	1 large sweet potato, peeled and cubed
1/2 teaspoon salt	
1/4 teaspoon pepper	2 large carrots, cut into 1-inch pieces
1-1/2 pounds lamb stew meat, cubed	
2 shallots, sliced	2 medium parsnips, peeled and cubed
2 tablespoons olive oil	1 garlic clove, minced
1/2 cup red wine	1 tablespoon mint jelly
2 cans (14-1/2 ounces each) beef broth	4 bacon strips, cooked and crumbled
2 medium potatoes, cubed	

■ In a large resealable plastic bag, combine the flour, salt and pepper. Add the meat, a few pieces at a time, and shake to coat. In a large skillet, brown meat and shallots in oil in batches.

■ Transfer to a 5- or 6-qt. slow cooker. Add wine to the skillet, stirring to loosen browned bits from pan. Bring to a boil. Reduce heat; simmer, uncovered, for 1-2 minutes. Add to slow cooker.

■ Stir in the broth, potatoes, sweet potato, carrots, parsnips and garlic. Cover and cook on low for 7-9 hours or until meat is tender. Stir in jelly; sprinkle with bacon.

Ham and Hash Browns

You just can't beat the slow cooker for convenience. I usually use mine two or three times a week all year round. Here's a new way to prepare an old-fashioned favorite.

—MARLENE MUCKENHIRN DELANO, MINNESOTA

PREP: 10 MIN. ■ **COOK:** 7 HOURS ■ **YIELD:** 4 SERVINGS

1 package (28 ounces) frozen O'Brien potatoes	1 can (10-3/4 ounces) condensed cheddar cheese soup, undiluted
2 cups cubed fully cooked ham	3/4 cup milk
1 jar (2 ounces) diced pimientos, drained	1/4 teaspoon pepper

■ In a 3-qt. slow cooker, combine the potatoes, ham and pimientos. In a bowl, combine soup, milk and pepper; pour over potato mixture. Cover and cook on low for 7-8 hours or until potatoes are tender.

Pork Ribs Lo Mein

PREP: 25 MIN.
COOK: 6-1/2 HOURS
YIELD: 6 SERVINGS

1-1/2 pounds boneless country-style pork ribs

3 medium carrots, chopped

1 small onion, sliced

3/4 cup packed brown sugar

1/2 cup reduced-sodium soy sauce

1/2 cup ketchup

1/4 cup honey

2 tablespoons cider vinegar

2 garlic cloves, minced

1/2 teaspoon ground ginger

1/4 to 1/2 teaspoon crushed red pepper flakes

1 cup fresh broccoli florets, chopped

1 can (8 ounces) sliced water chestnuts, drained

1 pound uncooked spaghetti

4 green onions, sliced

■ In a 3-qt. slow cooker, combine the ribs, carrots and onion. In a small bowl, combine the brown sugar, soy sauce, ketchup, honey, vinegar, garlic, ginger and pepper flakes. Pour over ribs. Cover and cook on low for 6-8 hours or until pork is tender. Remove to a plate; shred with two forks and return to slow cooker.

■ Stir in broccoli and water chestnuts. Cover and cook 30 minutes longer or until broccoli is crisp-tender. Meanwhile, cook spaghetti according to package directions; drain. In a large bowl, combine spaghetti and pork mixture. Sprinkle with green onions.

Sweet and savory Asian ingredients, such as soy sauce, garlic and ginger, come together for a mouthwatering and hearty dish that's way better than takeout. Because they're added later in the cooking process, the vegetables still impart fresh flavor and texture.

—**RACHEL RICE** PEA RIDGE, ARKANSAS

No one ever believes how little effort it takes to make these tender, juicy ribs. The flavor of the lightly sweet and tangy sauce penetrates through the meat as the ribs simmer in the slow cooker.

—SANDY ALEXANDER FAYETTEVILLE, NORTH CAROLINA

Sesame Pork Ribs

PREP: 15 MIN. ■ **COOK:** 5 HOURS ■ **YIELD:** 5 SERVINGS

3/4	cup packed brown sugar	1/4	to 1/2 teaspoon crushed red pepper flakes
1/2	cup reduced-sodium soy sauce	5	pounds bone-in country-style pork ribs
1/2	cup ketchup		
1/4	cup honey	1	medium onion, sliced
2	tablespoons white wine vinegar	2	tablespoons sesame seeds, toasted
3	garlic cloves, minced		
1	teaspoon salt	2	tablespoons chopped green onions
1	teaspoon ground ginger		

■ In a large bowl, combine the first nine ingredients. Add ribs and turn to coat. Place the onion in a 5-qt. slow cooker; top with ribs and sauce. Cover and cook on low for 5-6 hours or until meat is tender.

■ Place the ribs on a serving platter; sprinkle with sesame seeds and green onions.

Casserole In the Cooker

For a complete meal-in-one, you'll savor this slow-cooked ham, broccoli and rice dish that has all the goodness of an oven-baked casserole. It's perfect for a Sunday afternoon dinner.

—KRISTA HARRISON BRAZIL, INDIANA

PREP: 10 MIN. ■ **COOK:** 4 HOURS
YIELD: 4 SERVINGS

- 1 package (16 ounces) frozen broccoli cuts, thawed and drained
- 3 cups cubed fully cooked ham
- 1 can (10-3/4 ounces) condensed cream of mushroom soup, undiluted
- 1 jar (8 ounces) process cheese sauce
- 1 cup milk
- 1 cup uncooked instant rice
- 1 celery rib, chopped
- 1 small onion, chopped

■ In a 3-qt. slow cooker, combine the broccoli and ham. Combine the soup, cheese sauce, milk, rice, celery and onion; stir into the broccoli mixture. Cover and cook on low for 4-5 hours or until rice is tender.

Be sure **to use instant rice** in the above recipe. Unlike regular rice, instant rice has been **precooked, dehydrated** and takes just a few minutes to prepare.

Even though a coworker gave me this recipe more than 20 years ago, my family still enjoys it today. The flavorful dish is convenient, hearty and delicious.

—MARTHA NICKERSON
HANCOCK, MAINE

SLOW-COOKED SWEET 'N' SOUR PORK

Slow-Cooked Sweet 'n' Sour Pork

PREP: 20 MIN. ■ COOK: 6-1/2 HOURS ■ YIELD: 6 SERVINGS

2 tablespoons plus 1-1/2 teaspoons paprika

1-1/2 pounds boneless pork loin roast, cut into 1-inch strips

1 tablespoon canola oil

1 can (20 ounces) unsweetened pineapple chunks

1 medium onion, chopped

1 medium green pepper, chopped

1/4 cup cider vinegar

3 tablespoons brown sugar

3 tablespoons reduced-sodium soy sauce

1 tablespoon Worcestershire sauce

1/2 teaspoon salt

2 tablespoons cornstarch

1/4 cup cold water

Hot cooked rice, optional

■ Place paprika in a large resealable plastic bag. Add pork, a few pieces at a time, and shake to coat. In a nonstick skillet, brown pork in oil in batches over medium-high heat. Transfer to a 3-qt. slow cooker.

■ Drain pineapple, reserving juice; refrigerate the pineapple. Add the pineapple juice, onion, green pepper, vinegar, brown sugar, soy sauce, Worcestershire sauce and salt to slow cooker; mix well. Cover and cook on low for 6-8 hours or until meat is tender.

■ Combine cornstarch and water until smooth; stir into pork mixture. Add pineapple. Cover and cook 30 minutes longer or until sauce is thickened. Serve over rice if desired.

➡➡ **NUTRITION FACTS:** 1 cup pork mixture (calculated without rice) equals 312 calories, 10 g fat (3 g saturated fat), 73 mg cholesterol, 592 mg sodium, 28 g carbohydrate, 2 g fiber, 27 g protein. **DIABETIC EXCHANGES:** 3 lean meat, 1 fruit, 1/2 starch, 1/2 fat.

Creole Black Beans 'n' Sausage

I can make this entree any day of the week. I brown the meat, cut up veggies and measure spices the night before, then assemble and begin cooking the next morning. When I get home, I make the rice, and dinner is served!

—CHERYL LANDERS
LATOUR, MISSOURI

PREP: 25 MIN. ■ COOK: 6 HOURS
YIELD: 10 SERVINGS

2 pounds smoked sausage, cut into 1-inch slices

3 cans (15 ounces each) black beans, rinsed and drained

1-1/2 cups each chopped onion, celery and green pepper

1 cup water

1 can (8 ounces) tomato sauce

4 garlic cloves, minced

2 teaspoons dried thyme

1 teaspoon chicken bouillon granules

1 teaspoon white pepper

1/4 teaspoon cayenne pepper

2 bay leaves

Hot cooked rice

■ In a large skillet, brown sausage over medium heat; drain. Transfer to a 5-qt. slow cooker.

■ In a large bowl, combine the beans, onion, celery, green pepper, water, tomato sauce, garlic, thyme, bouillon, white pepper, cayenne and bay leaves; pour over sausage. Cover and cook on low for 6 hours or until vegetables are tender. Discard bay leaves. Serve with rice.

Greek Shrimp Orzo

One of our favorite dishes, Greek Shrimp Orzo is delicious and satisfying and reheats beautifully. My husband would rather have the orzo dish than go out to eat. We like it with crusty bread and salad.

—MOLLY SEIDEL EDGEWOOD, NEW MEXICO

PREP: 45 MIN. ■ COOK: 2 HOURS ■ YIELD: 6 SERVINGS

- 2 cups uncooked orzo pasta
- 2 tablespoons minced fresh basil *or* 2 teaspoons dried basil
- 3 tablespoons olive oil, *divided*
- 1-1/2 tablespoons chopped shallot
- 2 tablespoons butter
- 1 can (14-1/2 ounces) diced tomatoes, drained
- 2 tablespoons minced fresh oregano *or* 2 teaspoons dried oregano
- 3 garlic cloves, minced
- 1 pound uncooked large shrimp, peeled and deveined
- 1 cup oil-packed sun-dried tomatoes, chopped
- 2-1/2 cups (10 ounces) crumbled feta cheese
- 1-1/2 cups pitted Greek olives

■ Cook orzo according to package directions; rinse in cold water and drain. Transfer to a large bowl. Add basil and 1 tablespoon oil; toss to coat and set aside.

■ In a large skillet, saute shallot in butter and remaining oil until tender. Add the diced tomatoes, oregano and garlic; cook and stir for 1-2 minutes. Add shrimp and sun-dried tomatoes; cook and stir for 2-3 minutes or until shrimp turn pink.

■ Transfer to a greased 5-qt. slow cooker. Stir in the orzo mixture, cheese and olives. Cover and cook on low for 2-3 hours or until heated through.

Christmas Carol Ham

Made with healthier-for-you turkey ham, this slow-cooked entree is tender and delicious. Simmered in pineapple juice, the ham slices are so flavorful. My family loves it any time of the year!

—JULIE WILLIQUETTE HARTSELLE, ALABAMA

PREP: 10 MIN. ■ COOK: 2 HOURS ■ YIELD: 8 SERVINGS

- 2 pounds fully cooked boneless ham, cut into eight slices
- 1/2 cup packed brown sugar
- 1/4 cup unsweetened pineapple juice
- 1-1/2 teaspoons white vinegar
- 1/4 teaspoon ground mustard

■ Place ham slices in a 3-qt. slow cooker. In a small bowl, combine the brown sugar, pineapple juice, vinegar and mustard; pour over ham. Cover and cook on low for 2-4 hours or until heated through.

➡ **NUTRITION FACTS:** 1 serving (1 slice) equals 186 calories, 5 g fat (2 g saturated fat), 83 mg cholesterol, 1,237 mg sodium, 15 g carbohydrate, trace fiber, 21 g protein.
DIABETIC EXCHANGES: 3 lean meat, 1 starch.

Blue Cheese and Apple Pork Chops

Tangy apple wedges and smoky, salty bacon create a yummy topping for pork chops. Try this entree alongside mashed potatoes for an especially comforting supper.

—NICOLE EPPERSON SARASOTA, FLORIDA

PREP: 25 MIN. ■ COOK: 5 HOURS YIELD: 4 SERVINGS

- 4 bone-in pork loin chops (8 ounces *each*)
- 1/2 teaspoon salt
- 1/4 teaspoon pepper
- 1 tablespoon olive oil
- 2 large tart apples, peeled and cut into wedges
- 2 medium onions, chopped
- 6 maple-flavored bacon strips, cooked and crumbled
- 2 tablespoons all-purpose flour
- 1 tablespoon sugar
- 1 can (14-1/2 ounces) chicken broth
- 1 cup unsweetened apple juice
- 1 cup (4 ounces) crumbled blue cheese

■ Sprinkle pork with salt and pepper. In a large skillet, brown pork chops in oil in batches.

■ In a 5-qt. slow cooker, combine the apples, onions and bacon. In a large bowl, combine the flour, sugar, broth and apple juice; pour over apple mixture. Top with pork chops. Cover and cook on low for 5-6 hours or until meat is tender.

■ Remove pork from slow cooker. Using a slotted spoon, remove apples; serve with pork. Sprinkle with blue cheese.

- Cut tops off peppers and remove seeds. In a large bowl, combine the beans, corn, broth, rice, onion, orange juice, chili powder and 1 cup cheese; spoon into peppers. Transfer to a greased 5-qt. slow cooker.

- Cover and cook on low for 4-5 hours or until peppers are tender and filling is heated through. Sprinkle with remaining cheese. Cover and cook 10 minutes longer or until cheese is melted.

You can freeze bell peppers for future recipes. Wash the peppers, remove seeds and stems, blanch for 3 minutes, drain well and **freeze on waxed paper-lined cookie sheets.** Then, just store the peppers in resealable plastic bags in your freezer.

BLACK BEAN STUFFED PEPPERS

Mild Southwestern spices pep up this play on the classic meatless main dish. The colorful peppers and cheesy topping invite everyone at the table to dig in!

—MARIE RIZZIO INTERLOCHEN, MICHIGAN

Black Bean Stuffed Peppers

PREP: 20 MIN. ■ **COOK:** 4 HOURS 10 MIN. ■ **YIELD:** 4 SERVINGS

1 *each* large green, sweet red, yellow and orange peppers	1/2 cup uncooked converted rice
1 can (15 ounces) black beans, rinsed and drained	1/2 cup chopped onion
	1/2 cup orange juice
1 can (11 ounces) Mexicorn, drained	2 teaspoons chili powder
1 cup reduced-sodium chicken broth	1-1/4 cups (5 ounces) shredded Monterey Jack cheese, *divided*

Soups, Sides & Sandwiches

65

62

60

The perfect **potluck recipe is waiting for you** in this chapter that features hearty soups, hot sandwiches and yummy side dishes that are family-friendly and easy to make. What a delectable way to **free up stovetop space and kitchen time!**

VEGETABLE BARLEY SOUP

- In a 5-qt. slow cooker, combine the first eight ingredients. Stir in the water, broth, barley, bay leaf and seasonings. Cover and cook on low for 8-10 hours or until the barley and vegetables are tender.

- Stir in tomatoes; cover and cook on high for 10-20 minutes or until heated through. Discard bay leaf.

➡ **NUTRITION FACTS:** 1-1/4 cups equals 128 calories, 1 g fat (trace saturated fat), 0 cholesterol, 812 mg sodium, 28 g carbohydrate, 5 g fiber, 4 g protein. **DIABETIC EXCHANGES:** 1-1/2 starch, 1 vegetable.

Barley, or "groats," is a cereal grain that is used for brewing malt beverages, for making miso and for eating. **Pearl barley is a popular form of barley** because it's processed to make the grain less chewy. **Pearl barley has a mild, nutty flavor.**

My friends and family love this delicious vegetarian soup brimming with veggies and barley. Though it doesn't taste like it, this is low in calories and has only 1 gram of fat!

—**MARY TALLMAN** ARBOR VITAE, WISCONSIN

Vegetable Barley Soup

PREP: 25 MIN. ■ **COOK:** 8-1/4 HOURS
YIELD: 12 SERVINGS (ABOUT 3-1/2 QUARTS)

1	large sweet potato, peeled and cubed	2	cans (14-1/2 ounces *each*) vegetable broth
1-1/2	cups fresh baby carrots, halved	1	cup medium pearl barley
1-1/2	cups frozen cut green beans	1	bay leaf
1-1/2	cups frozen corn	1-3/4	teaspoons salt
3	celery ribs, thinly sliced	1/2	teaspoon fennel seed, crushed
1	small onion, chopped	1/4	teaspoon pepper
1/2	cup chopped green pepper	1	can (14-1/2 ounces) Italian diced tomatoes, undrained
2	garlic cloves, minced		
6	cups water		

FIESTA CORN AND BEANS

- In a large skillet, saute onion and peppers in oil until tender. Add garlic; cook 1 minute longer. Transfer to a 4-qt. slow cooker. Stir in the beans, corn, tomatoes and seasonings.

- Cover and cook on low for 3-4 hours or until heated through. Serve with yogurt and olives if desired.

EDITOR'S NOTE: Wear disposable gloves when cutting hot peppers; the oils can burn skin. Avoid touching your face.

➡ **NUTRITION FACTS:** 3/4 cup (calculated without optional toppings) equals 149 calories, 2 g fat (trace saturated fat), 0 cholesterol, 380 mg sodium, 28 g carbohydrate, 7 g fiber, 8 g protein. **DIABETIC EXCHANGES:** 1 starch, 1 lean meat, 1 vegetable.

Bursting with Southwestern flavors, the zesty veggie medley here can be served as a side dish or a meatless meal-in-one. The dollop of yogurt is a cool, creamy finishing touch.

—**GERALD HETRICK** ERIE, PENNSYLVANIA

Fiesta Corn and Beans

PREP: 25 MIN. ■ **COOK:** 3 HOURS ■ **YIELD:** 10 SERVINGS

- 1 large onion, chopped
- 1 medium green pepper, cut into 1-inch pieces
- 1 to 2 jalapeno peppers, seeded and sliced
- 1 tablespoon olive oil
- 1 garlic clove, minced
- 2 cans (16 ounces *each*) kidney beans, rinsed and drained
- 1 package (16 ounces) frozen corn

- 1 can (14-1/2 ounces) diced tomatoes, undrained
- 1 teaspoon chili powder
- 3/4 teaspoon salt
- 1/2 teaspoon ground cumin
- 1/2 teaspoon pepper

Optional toppings: plain yogurt and sliced ripe olives

An **easy, affordable way to store spices** is in clean, empty jelly jars. **Wrap your favorite recipes** that use the seasoning around the jar and secure with a rubber band. This way you don't waste time searching for the recipes.

Macaroni and cheese: The words alone are enough to make most mouths water. This recipe is a clear example of comfort food at its finest; it's rich, hearty and extra cheesy. And because it's made in the slow cooker, it's extremely easy!

—SHELBY MOLINA
WHITEWATER, WISCONSIN

MAKEOVER SLOW-COOKED MAC 'N' CHEESE

Makeover Slow-Cooked Mac 'n' Cheese

PREP: 25 MIN. ■ **COOK:** 2-3/4 HOURS ■ **YIELD:** 9 SERVINGS

2 cups uncooked elbow macaroni
1 can (12 ounces) reduced-fat evaporated milk
1-1/2 cups fat-free milk
1/3 cup egg substitute
1 tablespoon butter, melted
8 ounces reduced-fat process cheese (Velveeta), cubed
2 cups (8 ounces) shredded sharp cheddar cheese, *divided*

■ Cook macaroni according to package directions; drain and rinse in cold water. In a large bowl, combine the evaporated milk, milk, egg substitute and butter. Stir in the process cheese, 1-1/2 cups sharp cheddar cheese and macaroni.

■ Transfer to a 3-qt. slow cooker coated with cooking spray. Cover and cook on low for 2-3 hours or until center is set, stirring once. Sprinkle with remaining sharp cheddar cheese.

➡ **NUTRITION FACTS:** 3/4 cup equals 300 calories, 12 g fat (9 g saturated fat), 45 mg cholesterol, 647 mg sodium, 29 g carbohydrate, 1 g fiber, 19 g protein. **DIABETIC EXCHANGES:** 2 starch, 2 medium-fat meat.

Southwest Vegetarian Lentil Soup

Even self-avowed carnivores won't miss the meat in this zippy dish. It's chock-full of healthy ingredients that will keep you feeling satisfied.

—LAURIE STOUT-LETZ
BOUNTIFUL, UTAH

PREP: 25 MIN. ■ **COOK:** 7 HOURS
YIELD: 6 SERVINGS (2 QUARTS)

3 cups vegetable broth
1 large onion, chopped
1 can (10 ounces) mild diced tomatoes and green chilies, undrained
1 cup mild salsa
1 cup dried lentils, rinsed
1 cup frozen corn
1 can (8 ounces) tomato sauce
1 can (4 ounces) chopped green chilies
3 garlic cloves, minced
1-1/2 teaspoons chili powder
1 teaspoon ground cumin
1/2 teaspoon celery salt
1/2 teaspoon paprika
1/8 teaspoon cayenne pepper
1 package (16 ounces) firm tofu, drained and cut into 1/4-inch cubes
1 can (4-1/4 ounces) chopped ripe olives
3 green onions, sliced

■ In a 3- or 4-qt. slow cooker, combine the first 14 ingredients. Cover and cook on low for 8-10 hours or until lentils are tender. Sprinkle with tofu, olives and green onions.

BAVARIAN MEATBALLS

Bavarian Meatballs

PREP: 15 MIN. ■ **COOK:** 3-1/2 HOURS ■ **YIELD:** 12 SERVINGS

1 package (32 ounces) frozen fully cooked Italian meatballs	1 can (12 ounces) beer *or* nonalcoholic beer
1/2 cup chopped onion	12 hoagie buns, split
1/4 cup packed brown sugar	3 cups (12 ounces) shredded Swiss cheese
1 envelope onion soup mix	

■ In a 3-qt. slow cooker, combine the meatballs, onion, brown sugar, soup mix and beer. Cover and cook on low for 3 to 4 hours or until heated through.

■ Place six meatballs on each bun bottom. Sprinkle each sandwich with 1/4 cup cheese. Place on baking sheets. Broil 4-6 in. from the heat for 2-3 minutes or until cheese is melted. Replace bun tops.

Dried herbs don't spoil, but they do lose flavor and potency over time. **For maximum flavor in your cooking,** replace herbs that are over a year old. **Store dried herbs in airtight** containers and keep them away from heat and light.

Moist Poultry Dressing

Tasty mushrooms and onions complement the big herb flavor in this stuffing. This dressing stays so moist when cooked this way.

PREP: 20 MIN.
COOK: 4-5 HOURS
YIELD: 12-16 SERVINGS

- 2 jars (4-1/2 ounces *each*) sliced mushrooms, drained
- 4 celery ribs, chopped
- 2 medium onions, chopped
- 1/4 cup minced fresh parsley
- 3/4 cup butter, cubed
- 1-1/2 pounds day-old bread, crusts removed and cubed (about 13 cups)
- 1-1/2 teaspoons salt
- 1-1/2 teaspoons rubbed sage
- 1 teaspoon poultry seasoning
- 1 teaspoon dried thyme
- 1/2 teaspoon pepper
- 2 eggs
- 1 can (14-1/2 ounces) chicken broth *or* 14-1/2 ounces vegetable broth

■ In a large skillet, saute the mushrooms, celery, onions and parsley in butter until the vegetables are tender. In a large bowl, toss the bread cubes with salt, sage, poultry seasoning, thyme and pepper. Add the mushroom mixture. Combine eggs and broth; add to the bread mixture and toss.

■ Transfer to a 5-qt. slow cooker. Cover and cook on low for 4-5 hours or until a thermometer reads 160°.

POSOLE VERDE

With fresh tomatillos, green chilies and hominy, this hearty, healthy soup nods to authentic Mexican fare. Family and friends frequently request it when they're invited for dinner.

—**GAYLE EHRENMAN** WHITE PLAINS, NEW YORK

Posole Verde

PREP: 30 MIN. ■ **COOK:** 7 HOURS ■ **YIELD:** 8 SERVINGS (3 QUARTS)

- 1 pork tenderloin (1 pound), cubed
- 1 package (12 ounces) fully cooked spicy chicken sausage links, sliced
- 8 tomatillos, husks removed and cut into 1-inch pieces
- 2 cans (14 ounces *each*) hominy, rinsed and drained
- 1 can (16 ounces) kidney beans, rinsed and drained
- 1 can (14-1/2 ounces) chicken broth
- 3 cans (4 ounces *each*) chopped green chilies
- 1 large red onion, quartered and sliced
- 2 tablespoons brown sugar
- 3 garlic cloves, minced
- 1 tablespoon ground cumin
- 1 tablespoon chili powder
- 1 teaspoon dried oregano

Minced fresh cilantro, optional

■ In a 6-qt. slow cooker, combine the first 13 ingredients. Cover and cook on low for 8-10 hours or until pork is tender. Sprinkle with cilantro if desired.

Slow-Cooked Chili

This hearty chili can cook for up to 10 hours on low. It's so good to come home to after a long day.

—**SUE CALL** BEECH GROVE, INDIANA

PREP: 15 MIN. ■ **COOK:** 4 HOURS
YIELD: 10 SERVINGS

- 2 pounds lean ground beef (90% lean)
- 2 cans (16 ounces *each*) kidney beans, rinsed and drained
- 2 cans (14-1/2 ounces *each*) diced tomatoes, undrained
- 1 can (8 ounces) tomato sauce
- 2 medium onions, chopped
- 1 green pepper, chopped
- 2 garlic cloves, minced
- 2 tablespoons chili powder
- 2 teaspoons salt, optional
- 1 teaspoon pepper

Shredded cheddar cheese, optional

■ In a large skillet, cook beef over medium heat until no longer pink; drain.

■ Transfer to a 5-qt. slow cooker. Add the next nine ingredients. Cover and cook on low for 8-10 hours or on high for 4 hours. Garnish individual servings with cheese if desired.

➤ **NUTRITION FACTS:** 1 cup (prepared without salt or cheese) equals 330 calories, 13 g fat (0 saturated fat), 60 mg cholesterol, 337 mg sodium, 29 g carbohydrate, 0 fiber, 26 g protein. **DIABETIC EXCHANGES:** 3 meat, 1-1/2 starch, 1 vegetable.

If you're a fan of lamb, don't pass up this aromatic Greek-style soup. Seasoned with classic flavors of rosemary, marjoram and mint, it will transport you straight to the Mediterranean! The optional toppings add just the right touch of salty flavor.

—BRIDGET KLUSMAN OTSEGO, MICHIGAN

Gyro Soup

PREP: 25 MIN. ■ COOK: 6 HOURS ■ YIELD: 6 SERVINGS

2 pounds ground lamb	6 garlic cloves, minced
5 cups water	1 tablespoon dried marjoram
1 can (14-1/2 ounces) diced tomatoes, undrained	1 tablespoon dried rosemary, crushed
1 medium onion, chopped	2 teaspoons salt
1/4 cup red wine	1/2 teaspoon pepper
3 tablespoons minced fresh mint or 1 tablespoon dried mint	Optional toppings: plain Greek yogurt and crumbled feta cheese

■ In a large skillet, cook lamb until no longer pink; drain. Transfer to a 4- or 5-qt. slow cooker. Add the water, tomatoes, onion, wine, mint, garlic, marjoram, rosemary, salt and pepper. Cover and cook on low for 6-8 hours or until flavors are blended.

■ Serve with yogurt and feta cheese if desired.

Trout Chowder

This hearty chowder cooks conveniently in a slow cooker so I can spend more time fishing and less in the kitchen. The broccoli adds fresh taste and lively color to the rich, cheesy broth.

—LINDA KESSELRING CORNING, NEW YORK

PREP: 15 MIN. ■ COOK: 1-1/2 HOURS ■ YIELD: 6 SERVINGS

1 medium onion, chopped	1 cup cubed or shredded cheddar cheese
1 tablespoon butter	
2 cups whole milk	1 cup cubed or shredded Monterey Jack cheese
1 cup ranch salad dressing	
1 pound boneless trout fillets, skin removed	1/4 teaspoon garlic powder
	Paprika, optional
1 package (9 ounces) frozen broccoli cuts, thawed	

■ In a large skillet, saute the onion in butter until tender. Transfer to a 3-qt. slow cooker; add the milk, dressing, fish, broccoli, cheeses and garlic powder.

■ Cover and cook on high for 1-2 hours or until soup is bubbly and fish flakes easily with a fork. Sprinkle with paprika if desired.

Slow-Cooked White Chili

This satisfying slow-simmered chili features chicken, two kinds of beans and crunchy corn. It's quick, easy and delicious. We enjoy the family favorite with corn bread.

—LORI WEBER
WENTZVILLE, MISSOURI

PREP: 25 MIN. ■ COOK: 5 HOURS
YIELD: 8 SERVINGS (2 QUARTS)

- 3/4 pound boneless skinless chicken breasts, cubed
- 1 medium onion, chopped
- 1 tablespoon canola oil
- 1 garlic clove, minced
- 1-1/2 cups water
- 1 can (15 ounces) white kidney or cannellini beans, rinsed and drained
- 1 can (15 ounces) garbanzo beans or chickpeas, rinsed and drained
- 1 can (11 ounces) whole kernel white corn, drained or 1-1/4 cups frozen shoepeg corn
- 1 can (4 ounces) chopped green chilies
- 1 to 2 teaspoons chicken bouillon granules
- 1 teaspoon ground cumin

■ In a large skillet, saute chicken and onion in oil until onion is tender. Add garlic; cook 1 minute longer. Transfer to a 3-qt. slow cooker. Stir in the remaining ingredients. Cover and cook on low for 5-6 hours or until the chicken is no longer pink.

My family loves this recipe. It's such a good all-around dish, either for sandwiches like these, or served with some hot cooked spaghetti.

—ILEAN SCHULTHEISS
COHOCTON, NEW YORK

MELT-IN-YOUR-MOUTH SAUSAGES

Melt-in-Your-Mouth Sausages

PREP: 10 MIN. ■ **COOK:** 4 HOURS ■ **YIELD:** 8 SERVINGS

- 8 Italian sausage links (2 pounds)
- 1 jar (26 ounces) meatless spaghetti sauce
- 1/2 cup water
- 1 can (6 ounces) tomato paste
- 1 large green pepper, thinly sliced
- 1 large onion, thinly sliced
- 1 tablespoon grated Parmesan cheese
- 1 teaspoon dried parsley flakes
- 8 brat buns, split

Additional Parmesan cheese, optional

- Place sausages in a large skillet; cover with water. Bring to a boil. Reduce heat; cover and simmer for 10 minutes or until a thermometer reads 140°; drain well.

- Meanwhile, in a 3-qt. slow cooker, combine the spaghetti sauce, water, tomato paste, green pepper, onion, cheese and parsley. Add sausages. Cover and cook on low for 4-5 hours or until vegetables are tender. Serve in buns. Sprinkle with additional cheese if desired.

When a *Taste of Home* **recipe calls for Italian sausage,** it is referring to **sweet Italian sausage.** Recipes using hot Italian sausage specifically call for that type.

Hearty Split Pea Soup

This slow-cooker soup is one of my favorite meals to make during a busy work week. When I get home, I add the milk and supper is served!

—DEANNA WAGGY
SOUTH BEND, INDIANA

PREP: 5 MIN. ■ **COOK:** 4 HOURS
YIELD: 9 SERVINGS

- 1 package (16 ounces) dried split peas
- 2 cups cubed fully cooked ham
- 1 cup diced carrots
- 1 medium onion, chopped
- 2 garlic cloves, minced
- 2 bay leaves
- 1/2 teaspoon salt
- 1/2 teaspoon pepper
- 5 cups boiling water
- 1 cup hot milk

- In a 5-qt. slow cooker, layer the first nine ingredients in order listed (do not stir). Cover and cook on high for 4-5 hours or until the vegetables are tender. Stir in milk. Discard bay leaves before serving.

➡ **NUTRITION FACTS:** 1 cup equals 214 calories, 3 g fat (1 g saturated fat), 16 mg cholesterol, 542 mg sodium, 31 g carbohydrate, 11 g fiber, 17 g protein. **DIABETIC EXCHANGES:** 2 lean meat, 1-1/2 starch, 1 vegetable.

CHICKEN STEW WITH GNOCCHI

My chicken stew makes the house smell wonderful as it gently simmers in the slow cooker. One whiff of the delectable aroma and my family heads to the kitchen to see if it's ready.

—**MARGE DRAKE** JUNIATA, NEBRASKA

Chicken Stew with Gnocchi

PREP: 25 MIN. ■ **COOK:** 6-1/2 HOURS ■ **YIELD:** 8 SERVINGS (3 QUARTS)

- 3 medium parsnips, peeled and cut into 1/2-inch pieces
- 2 large carrots, cut into 1/2-inch slices
- 2 celery ribs, chopped
- 1 large sweet potato, peeled and cut into 1-inch cubes
- 4 green onions, chopped
- 3 pounds bone-in chicken thighs, skin removed
- 1/2 teaspoon dried sage leaves

- 1/4 teaspoon salt
- 1/4 teaspoon pepper
- 4 cups chicken broth
- 1 cup water
- 3 tablespoons cornstarch
- 1/4 cup cold water
- 1 package (16 ounces) potato gnocchi

Hot pepper sauce, optional

- ■ Place the parsnips, carrots, celery, sweet potato and onions in a 5-qt. slow cooker. Top with chicken; sprinkle with the sage, salt and pepper. Add broth and water. Cover and cook on low for 6-8 hours or until chicken is tender.

- ■ Remove the chicken; when cool enough to handle, remove the meat from bones and discard bones. Cut meat into bite-size pieces and return to the slow cooker.

- ■ Mix cornstarch and cold water until smooth; stir into stew. Add gnocchi. Cover and cook on high for 30 minutes or until thickened. Season with the hot pepper sauce if desired.

Parsnips are a root vegetable similar to carrots. **Don't buy parsnips that are shriveled, limp or spotted.** Store in a plastic bag for up to 2 weeks. **One pound equals 4 medium parsnips** or 2 cups peeled and chopped.

MAPLE-ALMOND BUTTERNUT SQUASH

A heartwarming side dish, especially on chilly days, this tasty take on wonderful butternut squash is a cinch to prepare, making it a good choice for any weeknight. It's sumptuous enough for company, too.

—JUDY LAWSON DEXTER, MICHIGAN

Maple-Almond Butternut Squash

PREP: 30 MIN. ■ **COOK:** 5-1/2 HOURS ■ **YIELD:** 9 SERVINGS

1 medium butternut squash (about 4 pounds), peeled, seeded and cut into 2-inch cubes	1/2 cup butter, melted
	1/2 cup maple syrup
	1/2 cup heavy whipping cream
4 garlic cloves, minced	1/4 cup sliced almonds
1 teaspoon salt	1/4 cup shredded Parmesan cheese
1/2 teaspoon pepper	

■ Place squash in a 4-qt. slow cooker. Sprinkle with garlic, salt and pepper. Add butter and maple syrup; stir to coat. Cover and cook on low for 5-6 hours or until squash is tender.

■ Stir in cream. Cover and cook 30 minutes longer or until heated through. Sprinkle with almonds and cheese.

Creamy Red Potatoes

I put my slow cooker to work to fix these saucy spuds. The side dish features cubed red potatoes that are cooked in a rich combination of ingredients. Be sure to stir the mixture before serving to help the sauce thicken a bit.

—ELAINE RYAN HOLLEY, NEW YORK

PREP: 5 MIN. ■ **COOK:** 5 HOURS
YIELD: 8 SERVINGS

7 cups cubed uncooked red potatoes
1 cup (8 ounces) 4% cottage cheese
1/2 cup sour cream
1/2 cup cubed process cheese (Velveeta)
1 tablespoon dried minced onion
2 garlic cloves, minced
1/2 teaspoon salt
Paprika and minced chives, optional

■ Place the potatoes in a 3-qt. slow cooker. In a blender, puree cottage cheese and sour cream until smooth. Transfer to a large bowl; stir in the process cheese, onion, garlic and salt. Pour over potatoes and mix well.

■ Cover and cook on low for 5-6 hours or until potatoes are tender. Stir well before serving. Garnish with paprika and chives if desired.

Ham Barbecue

We have used this recipe countless times for family gatherings and birthday parties. The sandwiches are so easy to make, and they taste great.

—JENNIFER MIDDLEKAUFF NEW HOLLAND, PENNSYLVANIA

PREP: 10 MIN. ■ **COOK:** 4 HOURS ■ **YIELD:** 12 SERVINGS

2 pounds thinly sliced deli ham	1/4 cup Worcestershire sauce
1 cup water	2 tablespoons white vinegar
1 cup ketchup	2 teaspoons prepared mustard
1/4 cup packed brown sugar	12 hamburger buns, split and toasted

■ Place the ham in a greased 3-qt. slow cooker. In a large bowl, combine the water, ketchup, brown sugar, Worcestershire sauce, vinegar and mustard; pour over ham and stir well. Cover and cook on low for 4-5 hours or until heated through. Serve on buns.

Best Italian Sausage Sandwiches

Need a different type of sandwich for a party? Try this recipe and everyone will be complimenting you on your great-tasting sandwiches.

—TASTE OF HOME TEST KITCHEN

PREP: 10 MIN. ■ **COOK:** 4 HOURS ■ **YIELD:** 10 SERVINGS

2 jars (24 ounces *each*) meatless spaghetti sauce	1/2 teaspoon garlic powder
2 medium green peppers, cut into strips	1/2 teaspoon fennel seed, crushed
2 medium onions, thinly sliced	2 packages (20 ounces *each*) Italian turkey sausage links
	10 sandwich buns, split

■ In a 3-qt. slow cooker, combine the spaghetti sauce, green peppers, onions, garlic powder and fennel seed. Cover and cook on low for 4 hours or until vegetables are tender.

■ Grill the sausages according to package directions. Serve on buns with sauce.

Ranch Beans

This sweet and tangy side dish uses lots of convenient canned goods, so it's a snap to throw together. The recipe was sent to me by a friend. It's nice to serve at a group picnic.

—BARBARA GORDON
ROSWELL, GEORGIA

PREP: 10 MIN. ■ **COOK:** 3 HOURS
YIELD: 8-10 SERVINGS

- 1 can (16 ounces) kidney beans, rinsed and drained
- 1 can (15-3/4 ounces) pork and beans, undrained
- 1 can (15 ounces) lima beans, rinsed and drained
- 1 can (14-1/2 ounces) cut green beans, drained
- 1 bottle (12 ounces) chili sauce
- 3/4 cup packed brown sugar
- 1 small onion, chopped

■ In a 3-qt. slow cooker, combine all the ingredients. Cover and cook on high for 3-4 hours or until mixture is heated through.

The **moisture in brown sugar** tends to trap air between the crystals, so it should be firmly packed when measuring. *Taste of Home* recipes specify packed brown sugar in the ingredient list.

Georgian Bay Baked Beans

My dressed-up baked beans are always a hit at barbecues and potlucks. If you can, prepare them a day ahead, because they get even better with time.
—**CINDY BEDARD** PENETANGUISHENE, ONTARIO

PREP: 30 MIN. + SOAKING ■ COOK: 10 HOURS ■ YIELD: 12 SERVINGS

- 1 pound dried navy beans
- 1 pound thick-sliced bacon strips, chopped
- 6 medium onions, chopped
- 2 medium tomatoes, chopped
- 3 garlic cloves, minced
- 1 cup packed brown sugar
- 1 cup beef stock
- 1 cup strong brewed coffee
- 3/4 cup chili sauce
- 1/2 cup tomato paste
- 1/4 cup molasses
- 1 tablespoon white vinegar
- 1 tablespoon ground mustard
- 3 bay leaves
- 1/2 teaspoon salt
- 1/2 teaspoon ground cinnamon
- 1/2 teaspoon ground cumin
- 1/2 teaspoon pepper
- 1/4 teaspoon ground cloves
- 1/4 teaspoon cayenne pepper
- 1 smoked ham hock

■ Sort beans and rinse in cold water. Place beans in a large bowl; add water to cover by 2 in. Cover and let stand overnight. Drain and rinse beans, discarding liquid. Coat a 5-qt. slow cooker with cooking spray; add beans.

■ In a large skillet, cook bacon over medium heat until crisp. Remove with a slotted spoon to paper towels; drain, reserving 3 tablespoons drippings. Brown onions in drippings. Add tomatoes and garlic; cook 2 minutes longer. Stir into slow cooker with reserved bacon.

■ Combine the brown sugar, stock, coffee, chili sauce, tomato paste, molasses, vinegar, mustard, bay leaves and seasonings. Stir into slow cooker. Add ham hock. Cover and cook on low for 10-12 hours or until beans are tender.

■ Discard bay leaves. Skim fat. Set ham hock aside until cool enough to handle. Remove meat from bone; discard bone. Cut meat into small cubes; return meat to slow cooker. Heat through.

Rinsing dried beans can leave you feeling like you haven't rinsed them enough. **To make this task easier,** submerge the beans in a pitcher with a strainer lid, swirl the beans around to clean them, then **pour the water out through the strainer**.

Cranberry Apple Topping

PREP: 15 MIN.
COOK: 3-1/2 HOURS + COOLING
YIELD: 3-3/4 CUPS

- 4 cups fresh *or* frozen cranberries, thawed
- 2 medium tart apples, peeled and chopped
- 1-1/4 cups sugar
- 1/4 cup orange juice
- 2 teaspoons grated orange peel
- 1/2 teaspoon ground cinnamon
- 2 tablespoons cornstarch
- 2 tablespoons cold water

■ In a 3-qt. slow cooker, combine the first six ingredients. Cover and cook on low for 3-4 hours or until bubbly.

■ In a small bowl, combine cornstarch and water until smooth; stir into cranberry mixture. Cover and cook 30 minutes longer or until thickened. Transfer to a serving bowl; cool.

A generous spoonful of this sweet-tart sauce is a tasty addition to chicken, turkey or pork. The ruby-red color lends a festive look to the meal and is perfect for visitors. The tasty cranberry concoction also tastes great served with vanilla yogurt and chopped nuts.

—LISE ODE DELRAY BEACH, FLORIDA

BROCCOLI-CHEDDAR HASH BROWNS

- In a greased 4- or 5-qt. slow cooker, combine the hash browns, broccoli, onions and 3/4 cup cheese.

- In a small saucepan, melt butter. Stir in flour until smooth; gradually add milk. Bring to a boil; cook and stir for 1 minute or until thickened. Stir in soup, salt and mustard. Pour over potato mixture; stir to combine.

- Cover and cook on low for 4-5 hours or until potatoes are tender. Sprinkle with remaining cheese. Cover and cook 30 minutes longer or until cheese is melted.

Cheddar cheese has its origins in the United Kingdom. **The village of Cheddar** in the English county of Somerset is **how cheddar cheese received its name!**

Need a new go-to comfort food? Hash browns definitely fit the bill! This gooey combo of tender potatoes and broccoli pairs well with a wide variety of entrees.

—**DEBORAH BIGGS** OMAHA, NEBRASKA

Broccoli-Cheddar Hash Browns

PREP: 20 MIN. ■ **COOK:** 4-1/2 HOURS ■ **YIELD:** 8 SERVINGS

- 1 package (30 ounces) frozen shredded hash brown potatoes
- 2 cups frozen broccoli florets
- 2 green onions, chopped
- 1-1/4 cups (5 ounces) shredded sharp cheddar cheese, *divided*
- 2 tablespoons butter
- 2 tablespoons all-purpose flour
- 1/2 cup whole milk
- 1 can (10-3/4 ounces) condensed cream of broccoli soup, undiluted
- 1/2 teaspoon salt
- 1/2 teaspoon Dijon mustard

Hearty Pasta Tomato Soup

I adapted the original recipe for this flavorful soup so I could make it in the slow cooker. It's ideal for staff luncheons at the school where I work, since we don't have easy access to a stove or oven.

—**LYDIA KROESE** PLYMOUTH, MINNESOTA

PREP: 15 MIN. ■ **COOK:** 3-1/2 HOURS
YIELD: 14 SERVINGS (ABOUT 3-1/2 QUARTS)

1 pound bulk Italian sausage	1 medium green pepper, chopped
6 cups beef broth	1/4 cup minced fresh parsley
1 can (28 ounces) stewed tomatoes	2 teaspoons sugar
1 can (15 ounces) tomato sauce	1 teaspoon dried oregano
2 cups sliced zucchini	1 teaspoon dried basil
1 large onion, chopped	1 garlic clove, minced
1 cup sliced carrots	2 cups frozen cheese tortellini
1 cup sliced fresh mushrooms	Grated Parmesan cheese, optional

■ In a skillet, cook the Italian sausage over medium heat until no longer pink; drain. Transfer to a 5-qt. slow cooker; add the next 13 ingredients. Cover and cook on high for 3-4 hours or until the vegetables are tender.

■ Cook tortellini according to package directions; drain. Stir into slow cooker; cover and cook 30 minutes longer. Serve with Parmesan cheese if desired.

Buffalo Chicken Wing Soup

My husband and I love buffalo chicken wings, so we created a soup with the same zippy flavor. It's very popular with guests. Start with a small amount of hot sauce, then add more if needed to suit your family's tastes.

—**PAT FARMER** FALCONER, NEW YORK

PREP: 5 MIN. ■ **COOK:** 4 HOURS ■ **YIELD:** 8 SERVINGS (2 QUARTS)

6 cups 2% milk	1 cup (8 ounces) sour cream
3 cans (10-3/4 ounces each) condensed cream of chicken soup, undiluted	1/4 to 1/2 cup Louisiana-style hot sauce
3 cups shredded cooked chicken (about 1 pound)	

■ Combine all ingredients in a 5-qt. slow cooker. Cover and cook on low for 4-5 hours or until heated through.

Zesty Garbanzo Sausage Soup

Even the busiest home cooks will have time to prepare this Cajun-inspired soup. If your family prefers spicier flavors, use medium salsa instead of mild.

—**PRISCILLA DOYLE** LUTZ, FLORIDA

PREP: 20 MIN.
COOK: 6-1/2 HOURS
YIELD: 7 SERVINGS

- 2 cans (15 ounces each) garbanzo beans or chickpeas, rinsed and drained
- 3 cups water
- 1 jar (16 ounces) mild salsa
- 1 can (14-1/2 ounces) diced tomatoes, undrained
- 2 celery ribs, chopped
- 1 cup sliced fresh or frozen okra
- 1 medium onion, chopped
- 2 teaspoons Cajun seasoning
- 1 pound smoked kielbasa or Polish sausage, cut into 1-inch pieces

■ In a 5-qt. slow cooker, combine the first eight ingredients. Cover and cook on low for 6-8 hours or until the vegetables are tender. Stir in kielbasa. Cover and cook 30 minutes longer or until heated through.

I like to share this dish at potlucks because it can be made ahead, which I especially appreciate during the busy holiday season. The sweet and spicy sauce is always a hit with my guests.

—MARTHA ANNE CARPENTER
MESA, ARIZONA

SLOW COOKER PULLED PORK SANDWICHES

Slow Cooker Pulled Pork Sandwiches

PREP: 20 MIN. ■ **COOK:** 7 HOURS ■ **YIELD:** 10 SERVINGS

- 1 boneless whole pork loin roast (4 pounds)
- 1 can (14-1/2 ounces) beef broth
- 1/3 cup plus 1/2 cup Worcestershire sauce, *divided*
- 1/3 cup plus 1/4 cup Louisiana-style hot sauce, *divided*
- 1 cup ketchup
- 1 cup molasses
- 1/2 cup prepared mustard
- 10 kaiser rolls, split

■ Cut roast in half; place in a 5-qt. slow cooker. In a small bowl, combine the broth, 1/3 cup Worcestershire sauce and 1/3 cup hot sauce; pour over the roast. Cover and cook on low for 8-10 hours or until tender.

■ Remove pork; shred with two forks. Drain and discard cooking liquid. Return shredded pork to the slow cooker. For sauce, combine the ketchup, molasses, mustard and the remaining Worcestershire sauce and hot sauce. Pour over pork. Cover and cook on high for 30 minutes or until heated through. Serve on rolls.

Cheesy Cauliflower Soup

Cheese adds flavor and heartiness to my change-of-pace soup.
—RUTH WORDEN MOSSENA, NEW YORK

PREP: 30 MIN.
COOK: 3-3/4 HOURS
YIELD: 8 SERVINGS (2 QUARTS)

- 1 large head cauliflower, broken into florets
- 2 cups chicken broth
- 2 tablespoons reduced-sodium chicken bouillon granules
- 2 cups half-and-half cream
- 2 cups 2% milk
- 1 medium carrot, shredded
- 2 bay leaves
- 1/4 teaspoon garlic powder
- 1/2 cup mashed potato flakes
- 2 cups (8 ounces) shredded cheddar cheese

Paprika

■ In a large saucepan, combine the cauliflower, broth and bouillon. Bring to a boil. Reduce heat; cover and cook for 20 minutes or until tender. Mash cauliflower.

■ Transfer to a 3-qt. slow cooker. Stir in the cream, milk, carrot, bay leaves and garlic powder. Cover and cook on low for 3 hours. Stir in potato flakes.

■ Cook 30 minutes longer or until thickened. Discard bay leaves. Cool slightly.

■ In a blender, process soup in batches until smooth. Return to the slow cooker; stir in cheese. Cook until soup is heated through and cheese is melted. Garnish with paprika.

SOUTHWESTERN CHICKEN SOUP

This slow cooker recipe brings people back for seconds. Chock-full of chicken, corn, tomatoes, peppers and chilies, the savory soup is sure to put a little zip in mealtime.

—HAROLD TARTAR WEST PALM BEACH, FLORIDA

Southwestern Chicken Soup

PREP: 10 MIN. ■ **COOK:** 7 HOURS ■ **YIELD:** 10 SERVINGS

1-1/4 pounds boneless skinless chicken breasts, cut into thin strips

1 to 2 tablespoons canola oil

2 cans (14-1/2 ounces *each*) chicken broth

1 package (16 ounces) frozen corn, thawed

1 can (14-1/2 ounces) diced tomatoes, undrained

1 medium onion, chopped

1 medium green pepper, chopped

1 medium sweet red pepper, chopped

1 can (4 ounces) chopped green chilies

1-1/2 teaspoons seasoned salt, optional

1 teaspoon ground cumin

1/2 teaspoon garlic powder

■ In a large skillet, saute the chicken in oil until lightly browned. Transfer to a 5-qt. slow cooker with a slotted spoon. Stir in the remaining ingredients. Cover and cook on low for 6-8 hours or until chicken and vegetables are tender. Stir before serving.

▶▶ NUTRITION FACTS: 1 cup (prepared with reduced-sodium broth and without seasoned salt) equals 144 calories, 3 g fat (trace saturated fat), 33 mg cholesterol, 350 mg sodium, 15 g carbohydrate, 3 g fiber, 16 g protein. **DIABETIC EXCHANGES:** 2 lean meat, 1 starch.

Cutting boneless chicken into strips can be tricky if the chicken is cold or at room temperature. **It's easier to slice the chicken** for this recipe if the chicken is slightly frozen.

TURKEY SLOPPY JOES

Letting all the flavors combine in the slow cooker is the key to these mildly sweet sloppy joes. This recipe is sure to be a keeper, and since it calls for turkey, you can feel good about serving it to your family.

—LISA ANN DINUNZIO VINELAND, NEW JERSEY

Turkey Sloppy Joes

PREP: 20 MIN. ■ COOK: 4 HOURS ■ YIELD: 10 SERVINGS

2 pounds lean ground turkey	1 cup water
1 medium onion, finely chopped	2 envelopes sloppy joe mix
1 small green pepper, chopped	1 tablespoon brown sugar
2 cans (8 ounces *each*) no-salt-added tomato sauce	10 hamburger buns, split

■ In a large nonstick skillet coated with cooking spray, cook the turkey, onion and pepper over medium heat until meat is no longer pink; drain. Transfer to a 3-qt. slow cooker.

■ Stir in the tomato sauce, water, sloppy joe mix and brown sugar. Cover and cook on low for 4-5 hours or until flavors are blended. Spoon 1/2 cup onto each bun.

Hamburger Vegetable Soup

I work full time and have a family of four. We sit down to a home-cooked meal just about every night thanks to my slow cooker. This hearty soup is often on the menu.

—THERESA JACKSON
CICERO, NEW YORK

PREP: 15 MIN. ■ COOK: 8 HOURS
YIELD: 10 SERVINGS

1 pound ground beef
1 medium onion, chopped
2 garlic cloves, minced
4 cups V8 juice
1 can (14-1/2 ounces) stewed tomatoes
2 cups coleslaw mix
2 cups frozen green beans
2 cups frozen corn
2 tablespoons Worcestershire sauce
1 teaspoon dried basil
1/2 teaspoon salt
1/4 teaspoon pepper

■ In a large saucepan, cook beef and onion over medium heat until meat is no longer pink. Add garlic; cook 1 minute longer. Drain. In a 5-qt. slow cooker, combine the remaining ingredients. Stir in beef mixture. Cover and cook on low for 8-10 hours or until the vegetables are tender.

➡ NUTRITION FACTS: 1 cup (prepared with lean ground beef) equals 159 calories, 4 g fat (2 g saturated fat), 17 mg cholesterol, 511 mg sodium, 19 g carbohydrate, 3 g fiber, 12 g protein. DIABETIC EXCHANGES: 1 starch, 1 lean meat, 1 vegetable.

I make this zesty salad with potatoes, celery and onion. It's a terrific side dish when served warm with crumbled bacon and fresh parsley sprinkled on top.

—MARLENE MUCKENHIRN DELANO, MINNESOTA

HOT GERMAN POTATO SALAD

Hot German Potato Salad

PREP: 15 MIN. ■ COOK: 4 HOURS ■ YIELD: 8-10 SERVINGS

- 8 medium potatoes, peeled and cut into 1/4-inch slices
- 2 celery ribs, chopped
- 1 large onion, chopped
- 1 cup water
- 2/3 cup cider vinegar
- 1/3 cup sugar
- 2 tablespoons quick-cooking tapioca
- 1 teaspoon salt
- 3/4 teaspoon celery seed
- 1/4 teaspoon pepper
- 6 bacon strips, cooked and crumbled
- 1/4 cup minced fresh parsley

- In a 3-qt. slow cooker, combine the potatoes, celery and onion. In a small bowl, combine water, vinegar, sugar, tapioca, salt, celery seed and pepper. Pour over potatoes; stir gently to coat.

- Cover and cook on high for 4-5 hours or until potatoes are tender. Just before serving, sprinkle with bacon and parsley.

If kept in a cool, dark, well-ventilated place, **most potatoes will keep** for up to 2 weeks. Generally, three medium russett potatoes or **8-10 small new white potatoes equal one pound**.

Italian Beef Hoagies

You'll need just five ingredients to feed a crowd these tender tangy sandwiches. On weekends, I start the roast the night before, so I can shred it in the morning.

—LORI PIATT DANVILLE, ILLINOIS

PREP: 25 MIN. ■ COOK: 8 HOURS
YIELD: 18 SERVINGS

- 1 beef sirloin tip roast (4 pounds), halved
- 2 envelopes Italian salad dressing mix
- 2 cups water
- 1 jar (16 ounces) mild pickled pepper rings, undrained
- 18 hoagie buns, split

- Place roast in a 5-qt. slow cooker. Combine the salad dressing mix and water; pour over roast. Cover and cook on low for 8-10 hours or until meat is tender.

- Remove meat; shred with two forks and return to the slow cooker. Add pepper rings; heat through. Spoon 1/2 cup meat mixture onto each bun.

Slow Cooker Shredded Beef

Our family loves these tasty shredded beef sandwiches with their mild barbecue flavor. The recipe makes a lot, so it's a nice choice for parties.
—**FRAN FRERICHS** GURLEY, NEBRASKA

PREP: 15 MIN. ■ **COOK:** 7 HOURS ■ **YIELD:** 14-16 SERVINGS

3	pounds beef stew meat, cut into 1-inch cubes	1/4	cup cider vinegar
3	medium green peppers, diced	3	tablespoons chili powder
2	large onions, diced	2	teaspoons salt
1	can (6 ounces) tomato paste	2	teaspoons Worcestershire sauce
1/2	cup packed brown sugar	1	teaspoon ground mustard
		14	to 16 sandwich buns, split

- In a 6-qt. slow cooker, combine the beef, green peppers and onions. In a small bowl, combine the tomato paste, brown sugar, vinegar, chili powder, salt, Worcestershire sauce and ground mustard. Stir into the meat mixture. Cover and cook on high for 8-10 hours or until the meat is tender.

- Skim fat from cooking juices. Shred beef, using two forks. With a slotted spoon, place about 1/2 cup beef mixture on each bun.

Sausage Pumpkin Soup

Here, autumn spices complement pumpkin and sausage for a unique and comforting soup. Maple syrup imparts just the right amount of sweetness.
—**LEAH CREMENT** COLLEGE STATION, TEXAS

PREP: 20 MIN. ■ **COOK:** 3 HOURS 10 MIN. ■ **YIELD:** 8 SERVINGS

1	pound bulk pork sausage	1/2	cup maple syrup
1/3	cup chopped onion	1	teaspoon pumpkin pie spice
2	cans (14-1/2 ounces *each*) chicken broth	1/2	teaspoon garlic powder
1	can (15 ounces) solid-pack pumpkin	1/4	teaspoon ground nutmeg
		1	can (12 ounces) evaporated milk

- In a large skillet, cook sausage and onion until sausage is no longer pink; drain.

- Transfer to a 4-qt. slow cooker. Add the broth, pumpkin, syrup, pie spice, garlic powder and nutmeg. Cover and cook on low for 3-4 hours or until flavors are blended. Stir in milk; heat through.

Stewed Zucchini And Tomatoes

PREP: 20 MIN.
COOK: 3-1/2 HOURS
YIELD: 6 SERVINGS

- 3 medium zucchini, cut into 1/4-inch slices
- 1 teaspoon salt, *divided*
- 1/2 teaspoon pepper, *divided*
- 1 medium onion, thinly sliced
- 1 medium green pepper, thinly sliced
- 3 medium tomatoes, sliced
- 2/3 cup condensed tomato soup, undiluted
- 1 teaspoon dried basil
- 1 cup (4 ounces) shredded cheddar cheese

- Place zucchini in a greased 3-qt. slow cooker. Sprinkle with 1/2 teaspoon salt and 1/4 teaspoon pepper. Layer with onion, green pepper and tomatoes. In a small bowl, combine the soup, basil and remaining salt and pepper; spread over tomatoes.

- Cover and cook on low for 3-4 hours or until the vegetables are tender. Sprinkle with cheese. Cover and cook 30 minutes longer or until the cheese is melted.

A fresh take on traditional (and sometimes lackluster) vegetable sides, zucchini, tomatoes and green peppers star in my make-ahead dish. Bubbly cheddar cheese adds a down-home feel. The dish is a wonderful way to use up that end-of-the-summer garden produce!

—BARBARA SMITH SALEM, OREGON

Snacks & Sweets

Celebrating has never been easier with these slow-cooked, scrumptious appetizers, beverages and sweets. There are plenty of menu items to choose from, such as **saucy chicken wings, flavorful coffees, creamy dips, comforting cakes** and more. With the flick of a switch, let the party begin!

LOADED VEGGIE DIP

- In a large skillet, saute the broccoli, cauliflower, carrot, onion, celery and garlic in 2 tablespoons oil until tender. Stir in the artichokes, cream cheese, vegetable recipe mix, garlic powder, white pepper and cayenne; set aside.

- In a 3-qt. slow cooker, combine the broth, cream and remaining oil. Stir in the broccoli mixture, Italian cheese blend and basil. Fold in spinach. Cover and cook on low for 1-2 hours or until cheese is melted and spinach is tender. Serve with crackers.

Packed with veggies and bursting with flavor, this chunky dip is sure to be a hit at your next party. Be sure to serve it with a thick cracker that can be used as a scoop.

—**PATRICE SLAUGHTER** PALM BAY, FLORIDA

Loaded Veggie Dip

PREP: 1 HOUR ■ **COOK:** 1 HOUR ■ **YIELD:** 5 CUPS

3/4 cup finely chopped fresh broccoli

1/2 cup finely chopped cauliflower

1/2 cup finely chopped fresh carrot

1/2 cup finely chopped red onion

1/2 cup finely chopped celery

2 garlic cloves, minced

4 tablespoons olive oil, *divided*

1 can (14 ounces) water-packed artichoke hearts, rinsed, drained and chopped

1 package (6-1/2 ounces) spreadable garlic and herb cream cheese

1 package (1.4 ounces) vegetable recipe mix (Knorr)

1 teaspoon garlic powder

1/2 teaspoon white pepper

1/8 to 1/4 teaspoon cayenne pepper

1/4 cup vegetable broth

1/4 cup half-and-half cream

3 cups (12 ounces) shredded Italian cheese blend

1/2 cup minced fresh basil

1 package (9 ounces) fresh spinach, finely chopped

Assorted crackers *or* baked pita chips

If you use a slow cooker to keep appetizer dips and other foods warm, frequently **check the temperature** of the food with a thermometer. **Hot foods** should be held at 140° or warmer.

I received the recipe for this hearty spread from my daughter. It tastes just like a Reuben sandwich. I keep serving it because it's always popular at get-togethers.

—ROSALIE FUCHS
PAYNESVILLE, MINNESOTA

REUBEN SPREAD

Reuben Spread

PREP: 5 MIN. ■ **COOK:** 2 HOURS ■ **YIELD:** 3-1/2 CUPS

- 1 jar (16 ounces) sauerkraut, rinsed and drained
- 1 package (8 ounces) cream cheese, cubed
- 2 cups (8 ounces) shredded Swiss cheese
- 1 package (3 ounces) deli corned beef, chopped
- 3 tablespoons prepared Thousand Island salad dressing

Snack rye bread *or* crackers

■ In a 1-1/2-qt. slow cooker, combine the first five ingredients. Cover and cook for 2 hours or until cheeses are melted; stir to blend. Serve warm with bread or crackers.

Sweet-and-Sour Smokies

This warm appetizer is so simple to make but so tasty. I use cherry pie filling, chunks of pineapple and a little brown sugar to create a fruity sauce that's just perfect for mini sausage links.
—DEBI HETLAND ROCHELLE, ILLINOIS

PREP: 5 MIN. ■ **COOK:** 4 HOURS ■ **YIELD:** 16-20 SERVINGS

- 2 packages (16 ounces *each*) miniature smoked sausages
- 2 cans (21 ounces *each*) cherry pie filling
- 1 can (20 ounces) pineapple chunks, drained
- 3 tablespoons brown sugar

■ Place sausages in a 3-qt. slow cooker. In a small bowl, combine the pie filling, pineapple and brown sugar; pour over sausages. Cover and cook on low for 4 hours. Keep warm.

Creamy Onion Dip

Here, caramelized onions team up with Gruyere cheese for a rich appetizer fit for a classic cocktail party.
—BECKY WALCH
MANTECA, CALIFORNIA

PREP: 20 MIN. ■ **COOK:** 5 HOURS
YIELD: 5 CUPS.

- 4 cups finely chopped sweet onions
- 1/4 cup butter, cubed
- 1/4 cup white wine *or* chicken broth
- 6 garlic cloves, minced
- 1 bay leaf
- 2 cups (8 ounces) shredded Gruyere *or* Swiss cheese
- 1 package (8 ounces) cream cheese, softened
- 1/4 cup sour cream

Assorted crackers *or* breadsticks

■ In a 3-qt. slow cooker, combine the onions, butter, wine, garlic and bay leaf. Cover and cook on low for 4-5 hours or until onions are tender and golden brown.

■ Discard bay leaf. Stir in the Gruyere cheese, cream cheese and sour cream. Cover and cook 1 hour longer or until cheese is melted. Serve warm with crackers.

- In a small bowl, combine raisins and pineapple; set aside. In a blender, combine the bananas, milk, pina colada mix, pineapple juice, eggs, cream of coconut and rum if desired. Cover and process until smooth.

- Place two-thirds of the bread in a greased 5- or 6-qt. slow cooker. Top with 1 cup raisin mixture. Layer with remaining bread and raisin mixture. Pour banana mixture into slow cooker. Cover and cook on low for 4-5 hours or until a knife inserted near the center comes out clean. Serve warm with whipped cream if desired.

A completely unexpected dessert from the slow cooker, it's moist and sweet with plump, juicy raisins and wonderful tropical flavors of pineapple and coconut.

—ELIZABETH DOSS CALIFORNIA CITY, CALIFORNIA

Caribbean Bread Pudding

PREP: 30 MIN. ■ **COOK:** 4 HOURS ■ **YIELD:** 16 SERVINGS

- 1 cup raisins
- 1 can (8 ounces) crushed pineapple, undrained
- 2 large firm bananas, halved
- 1 can (12 ounces) evaporated milk
- 1 can (10 ounces) frozen non-alcoholic pina colada mix
- 1 can (6 ounces) unsweetened pineapple juice
- 3 eggs
- 1/2 cup cream of coconut
- 1/4 cup light rum, optional
- 1 loaf (1 pound) French bread, cut into 1-inch cubes

Whipped cream, optional

Cream of coconut is a **very thick, smooth and sweet canned liquid** made from fresh coconuts. It's commonly used in mixed drinks and tropical desserts. **Find it in liquor stores.**

MOCHA MINT COFFEE

This doctored-up coffee benefits from hints of mint, cocoa and cinnamon. The marshmallows on top are a playful addition that brings out the youngster in everyone!

—MINDIE HILTON SUSANVILLE, CALIFORNIA

Mocha Mint Coffee

PREP: 10 MIN. ■ COOK: 2 HOURS ■ YIELD: 8 SERVINGS

6 cups hot brewed coffee	4 teaspoons sugar
2 packets instant hot cocoa mix	1 cup miniature marshmallows
1/2 cup dulce de leche	1/2 teaspoon ground cinnamon
1/4 cup peppermint crunch baking chips *or* mint chocolate chips	

■ In a 3-qt. slow cooker, combine the coffee, hot cocoa mix, dulce de leche, baking chips and sugar. Cover and cook on low for 2-3 hours or until hot.

■ Ladle into mugs. Top with marshmallows; sprinkle with cinnamon.

EDITOR'S NOTE: This recipe was tested with Nestle dulce de leche. Look for it in the international foods section.

Winter Fruit Compote

You can make this colorful and easy fruit relish up to a week in advance and refrigerate it. It makes a great accompaniment to turkey, chicken or pork throughout the holiday season.

—ESTHER CHESNEY
CARTHAGE, MISSOURI

PREP: 10 MIN.
COOK: 1-1/4 HOURS + COOLING
YIELD: 2-1/2 CUPS

 1 package (12 ounces) fresh *or* frozen cranberries, thawed
 2/3 cup packed brown sugar
 1/4 cup orange juice concentrate
 2 tablespoons raspberry vinegar
 1/2 cup chopped dried apricots
 1/2 cup golden raisins
 1/2 cup chopped walnuts, toasted

■ In a 1-1/2-qt. slow cooker, combine the cranberries, brown sugar, orange juice concentrate and vinegar. Cover and cook on low for 1-1/4 to 1-3/4 hours or until cranberries pop and mixture is thickened.

■ Turn off the heat; stir in the apricots, raisins and walnuts. Cool to room temperature. Serve or refrigerate.

➡ **NUTRITION FACTS:** 1/4 cup equals 161 calories, 4 g fat (trace saturated fat), 0 cholesterol, 12 mg sodium, 32 g carbohydrate, 3 g fiber, 2 g protein. **DIABETIC EXCHANGES:** 1 starch, 1 fruit, 1/2 fat.

This dessert classic gets a rich twist from butterscotch pudding. We had the warm apple filling bubbling to perfection in a mini slow cooker.

—JOLANTHE ERB
HARRISONBURG, VIRGINIA

BUTTERSCOTCH APPLE CRISP

Butterscotch Apple Crisp

PREP: 10 MIN. ■ **COOK:** 2-1/2 HOURS ■ **YIELD:** 3 SERVINGS

3 cups thinly sliced peeled tart apples (about 3 medium)	1/3 cup cook-and-serve butterscotch pudding mix
1/3 cup packed brown sugar	1/2 teaspoon ground cinnamon
1/4 cup all-purpose flour	1/4 cup cold butter
1/4 cup quick-cooking oats	Vanilla ice cream, optional

■ Place apples in a 1-1/2-qt. slow cooker. In a small bowl, combine the brown sugar, flour, oats, pudding mix and cinnamon. Cut in butter until mixture resembles coarse crumbs. Sprinkle over apples.

■ Cover and cook on low for 2-1/2 to 3-1/2 hours or until apples are tender. Serve with ice cream if desired.

There are plenty of **tart apple varieties to choose from** for baking. Here are a few: Granny Smith, Ida Red, Jonathan, **Lady Apple, McIntosh, Macoun and Winesap.**

Spiced Cranberry Punch

My mom used to serve this festive concoction every Thanksgiving and Christmas. To this day, when I smell it, I can't help but think of the holidays.

—HANNAH SIMPSON
TUPELO, ARKANSAS

PREP: 10 MIN. ■ **COOK:** 2 HOURS
YIELD: 9 SERVINGS

- 1 bottle (32 ounces) cranberry juice
- 3 cups unsweetened pineapple juice
- 1/2 cup sugar
- 1 cinnamon stick (3 inches)
- 12 whole cloves

■ In a 3- or 4-qt. slow cooker, combine the cranberry juice, pineapple juice and sugar. Place cinnamon and cloves on a double thickness of cheesecloth; bring up corners of cloth and tie with string to form a bag. Place in slow cooker.

■ Cover and cook on low for 2-3 hours or until heated through. Discard spice bag. Serve warm in mugs.

Warm Strawberry Fondue

For a delightful dessert, I need only a handful of ingredients to fix this unique fruit fondue. Use grapes, bananas, strawberries and angel food cake cubes as dippers.

—SHARON MENSING GREENFIELD, IOWA

PREP/TOTAL TIME: 15 MIN. ■ YIELD: 1-1/2 CUPS

1 package (10 ounces) frozen sweetened sliced strawberries, thawed	1 teaspoon cornstarch
	1/2 teaspoon lemon juice
1/4 cup half-and-half cream	Angel food cake cubes and fresh fruit

■ In a food processor or blender, combine the strawberries, cream, cornstarch and lemon juice; cover and process until smooth.

■ Pour into saucepan. Bring to a boil; cook and stir for 2 minutes or until slightly thickened. Transfer to a fondue pot or 1-1/2-qt. slow cooker; keep warm. Serve with cake and fruit.

➡ NUTRITION FACTS: 2 tablespoons prepared with fat-free half-and-half; calculated without cake and fruit equals 27 calories, trace fat (0 saturated fat), 0 cholesterol, 6 mg sodium, 7 g carbohydrate, trace fiber, trace protein. DIABETIC EXCHANGES: 1/2 fruit.

Buffet Meatballs

It only takes five ingredients to fix easy appetizers for casual get-togethers. Grape juice and apple jelly are the secrets behind the sweet yet tangy sauce that complements convenient packaged meatballs.

—JANET ANDERSON CARSON CITY, NEVADA

PREP: 10 MIN. ■ COOK: 4 HOURS ■ YIELD: ABOUT 11 DOZEN

1 cup grape juice	1 can (8 ounces) tomato sauce
1 cup apple jelly	1 package (64 ounces) frozen fully cooked Italian meatballs
1 cup ketchup	

■ In a small saucepan, combine the juice, jelly, ketchup and tomato sauce. Cook and stir over medium heat until jelly is melted; remove from the heat.

■ Place meatballs in a 5-qt. slow cooker. Pour sauce over the top and gently stir to coat. Cover and cook on low for 4-5 hours or until heated through.

Chocolate Malt Pudding Cake

PREP: 25 MIN.
COOK: 2 HOURS + STANDING
YIELD: 8 SERVINGS

1/2	cup 2% milk
2	tablespoons canola oil
1/2	teaspoon almond extract
1	cup all-purpose flour
1/2	cup packed brown sugar
2	tablespoons baking cocoa
1-1/2	teaspoons baking powder
1/2	cup coarsely chopped malted milk balls
1/2	cup semisweet chocolate chips
3/4	cup sugar
1/4	cup malted milk powder
1-1/4	cups boiling water
4	ounces cream cheese, softened and cubed
1/4	cup sliced almonds

Vanilla ice cream

■ In a large bowl, combine the milk, oil and extract. Combine the flour, brown sugar, cocoa and baking powder; gradually beat into milk mixture until blended. Stir in milk balls and chocolate chips.

■ Spoon into a greased 3-qt. slow cooker. In a small bowl, combine sugar and milk powder; stir in water and cream cheese. Pour over batter (do not stir).

■ Cover and cook on high for 2 to 2-1/2 hours or until a toothpick inserted near the center of cake comes out clean. Turn off heat. Let stand for 15 minutes. Serve warm with almonds and ice cream.

When I make my warm, comforting cake, I chop the malted milk balls by putting them in a plastic bag and pounding it with a rubber mallet or a pot with a thick bottom. This easy process eliminates the mess of using a cutting board and knife.

—SARAH SKUBINNA CASCADE, MONTANA

HAWAIIAN KIELBASA

Salty, savory sausage teams up with juicy, tangy pineapple for a winning combination that you can prep in a flash. The sweet barbecue-style sauce is a tasty way to tie them together.

—LOUISE KLINE CARROLLTOWN, PENNSYLVANIA

Hawaiian Kielbasa

PREP: 15 MIN. ■ COOK: 3 HOURS ■ YIELD: 12 SERVINGS

2 pounds smoked kielbasa *or* Polish sausage, cut into 1-inch pieces	2 tablespoons yellow mustard
	1 tablespoon cider vinegar
1 can (20 ounces) unsweetened pineapple chunks, undrained	3/4 cup lemon-lime soda
	2 tablespoons cornstarch
1/2 cup ketchup	2 tablespoons cold water
2 tablespoons brown sugar	

■ Place sausage in a 3- or 4-qt. slow cooker. Drain pineapple, reserving 3/4 cup juice; set pineapple aside. In a small bowl, whisk the ketchup, brown sugar, mustard and vinegar. Stir in soda and reserved pineapple juice. Pour over sausage; stir to coat. Cover and cook on low for 2-1/2 to 3 hours or until heated through.

■ Stir in pineapple. In a small bowl, combine cornstarch and water until smooth. Stir into slow cooker. Cover and cook 30 minutes longer or until sauce is thickened. Serve with toothpicks.

Fruit Dessert Topping

You'll quickly warm up to the old-fashioned taste of this fruit topping. Spoon it over vanilla ice cream or slices of pound cake.

—DORIS HEATH
FRANKLIN, NORTH CAROLINA

PREP: 10 MIN.
COOK: 3-1/2 HOURS
YIELD: ABOUT 6 CUPS

- 3 medium tart apples, peeled and sliced
- 3 medium pears, peeled and sliced
- 1 tablespoon lemon juice
- 1/2 cup packed brown sugar
- 1/2 cup maple syrup
- 1/4 cup butter, melted
- 1/2 cup chopped pecans
- 1/4 cup raisins
- 2 cinnamon sticks (3 inches)
- 1 tablespoon cornstarch
- 2 tablespoons cold water

Pound cake *or* ice cream

■ In a 3-qt. slow cooker, toss apples and pears with lemon juice. Combine the brown sugar, maple syrup and butter; pour over fruit. Stir in the pecans, raisins and cinnamon sticks. Cover and cook on low for 3-4 hours.

■ Combine cornstarch and water until smooth; gradually stir into slow cooker. Cover and cook on high for 30-40 minutes or until thickened. Discard cinnamon sticks. Serve topping over pound cake or ice cream.

This spicy fruit mixture is a breeze to make —just open the cans and empty them into the slow cooker. With its pretty color from cherry pie filling, this salad is nice around the holidays or for any special occasion.

—BARB VANDE VOORT
NEW SHARON, IOWA

HOT FRUIT SALAD

Sweet Kahlua Coffee

I have this beverage brewing in my slow cooker at my annual Christmas open house. I set out the whipped cream and grated chocolate in festive dishes so guests can help themselves.

—RUTH GRUCHOW
YORBA LINDA, CALIFORNIA

PREP: 10 MIN. ■ COOK: 4 HOURS
YIELD: 9 SERVINGS
(2-1/4 QUARTS)

- 2 quarts hot water
- 1/2 cup Kahlua (coffee liqueur)
- 1/4 cup creme de cacao
- 3 tablespoons instant coffee granules
- 2 cups heavy whipping cream
- 1/4 cup sugar
- 1 teaspoon vanilla extract
- 2 tablespoons grated chocolate

- In a 4-qt. slow cooker, combine the water, Kahlua, creme de cacao and coffee granules. Cover and cook on low for 3-4 hours or until heated through.

- In a large bowl, beat cream until it begins to thicken. Add sugar and vanilla; beat until stiff peaks form.

- Ladle coffee into mugs. Garnish with whipped cream and grated chocolate.

Hot Fruit Salad

PREP: 5 MIN. ■ COOK: 3 HOURS ■ YIELD: 16 SERVINGS

- 1 jar (25 ounces) chunky applesauce
- 1 can (21 ounces) cherry pie filling
- 1 can (20 ounces) pineapple chunks, undrained
- 1 can (15-1/4 ounces) sliced peaches, undrained
- 1 can (15-1/4 ounces) apricot halves, undrained
- 1 can (15 ounces) mandarin oranges, undrained
- 1/2 cup packed brown sugar
- 1 teaspoon ground cinnamon

- Place the first six ingredients in a 5-qt. slow cooker and stir gently. Combine brown sugar and cinnamon; sprinkle over fruit mixture. Cover and cook on low for 3-4 hours.

➠ **NUTRITION FACTS:** One 3/4-cup serving (prepared with reduced-sugar pie filling, unsweetened applesauce and pineapple, and no-sugar-added peaches and apricots) equals 124 calories, trace fat (0 saturated fat), 0 cholesterol, 12 mg sodium, 32 g carbohydrate, 0 fiber, 1 g protein. **DIABETIC EXCHANGES:** 2 fruit.

Add **an appealing garnish to dessert** by combining several orange peel strips, 1/3 cup fresh cranberries and 1/2 cup sugar. Stir, cover and refrigerate for 1 hour. **Arrange orange peel strips** and cranberries on dessert before serving.

Slow Cooker Mexican Dip

My husband and I love to entertain, and this hearty, seven-ingredient dip is always a hit—as well as a request. It couldn't be much easier to put together, and using our slow cooker leaves us free to share some quality time with our guests. After all, isn't that the purpose of a party?

—**HEATHER COURTNEY** AMES, IOWA

PREP: 15 MIN. ■ **COOK:** 1-1/2 HOURS ■ **YIELD:** 8 CUPS

1-1/2 pounds ground beef	1 can (16 ounces) refried beans
1 pound bulk hot Italian sausage	1 can (10 ounces) enchilada sauce
1 cup chopped onion	1 pound process cheese (Velveeta), cubed
1 package (8.8 ounces) ready-to-serve Spanish rice	1 package tortilla chip scoops

■ In a Dutch oven, cook the beef, sausage and onion over medium heat until meat is no longer pink; drain. Heat rice according to package directions.

■ In a 3-qt. slow cooker, combine the meat mixture, rice, beans, enchilada sauce and cheese. Cover and cook on low for 1-1/2 to 2 hours or until cheese is melted. Serve with tortilla scoops.

Burgundy Pears

These warm spiced pears elevate slow cooking to a new level of elegance, yet they're incredibly easy to make. Your friends won't believe this fancy-looking dessert came from a slow cooker.

—**ELIZABETH HANES** PERALTA, NEW MEXICO

PREP: 10 MIN. ■ **COOK:** 3 HOURS ■ **YIELD:** 6 SERVINGS

6 medium ripe pears	1 tablespoon lemon juice
1/3 cup sugar	1/4 teaspoon ground cinnamon
1/3 cup Burgundy wine or grape juice	1/4 teaspoon ground nutmeg
3 tablespoons orange marmalade	Dash salt
	Whipped cream cheese

■ Peel pears, leaving stems intact. Core from the bottom. Stand pears upright in a 5-qt. slow cooker. In a small bowl, combine the sugar, wine or grape juice, marmalade, lemon juice, cinnamon, nutmeg and salt. Carefully pour over pears.

■ Cover and cook on low for 3-4 hours or until tender. To serve, drizzle pears with sauce and garnish with whipped cream cheese.

Sweet-and-Sour Chicken Wings

PREP: 15 MIN. ■ **COOK:** 3 HOURS
YIELD: 32 APPETIZERS

1 cup sugar
1 cup cider vinegar
1/2 cup ketchup
2 tablespoons reduced-sodium soy sauce
1 teaspoon chicken bouillon granules
16 chicken wings
6 tablespoons cornstarch
1/2 cup cold water

■ In a small saucepan, combine the first five ingredients. Bring to a boil; cook and stir until sugar is dissolved. Cut wings into three sections; discard wing tip sections.

■ Transfer to a 3-qt. slow cooker; add vinegar mixture. Cover and cook on low for 3 to 3-1/2 hours or until chicken juices run clear.

■ Transfer wings to a serving dish and keep warm. Skim fat from cooking juices; transfer to a small saucepan. Bring liquid to a boil.

■ Combine cornstarch and water until smooth. Gradually stir into the pan. Bring to a boil; cook and stir for 2 minutes or until thickened. Spoon over chicken. Serve with a slotted spoon.

EDITOR'S NOTE: Uncooked chicken wing sections (wingettes) may be substituted for whole chicken wings.

Barbecue-style chicken wings are perfect for picnics, potlucks and other fun gatherings. Because this version comes with plenty of sauce, I also like to serve the wings over rice as a main dish. Any way you do it, the sweet and tangy medley will be a hit!

—JUNE EBERHARDT MARYSVILLE, CALIFORNIA

MINI HOT DOGS 'N' MEATBALLS

This recipe is so popular I usually double it and use a larger slow cooker. You can vary the meats to suit your family's tastes, or increase the heat factor by using a zesty barbecue or spaghetti sauce.

—**ANDREA CHAMBERLAIN** MACEDON, NEW YORK

Mini Hot Dogs 'n' Meatballs

PREP: 5 MIN. ■ COOK: 3 HOURS ■ YIELD: 8 CUPS

- 1 package (12 ounces) frozen fully cooked Italian meatballs
- 1 package (16 ounces) miniature hot dogs *or* smoked sausages
- 1 package (3-1/2 ounces) sliced pepperoni
- 1 jar (24 ounces) meatless spaghetti sauce
- 1 bottle (18 ounces) barbecue sauce
- 1 bottle (12 ounces) chili sauce

■ In a 5-qt. slow cooker, combine all ingredients. Cover and cook on low for 3-4 hours or until heated through.

Apple Comfort

Years ago, we were without electricity for nine days during an ice storm. I was able to run the slow cooker from our generator, so I made this dessert. It has been a favorite ever since.

—**AWYNNE THURSTENSON**
SILOAM SPRINGS, ARKANSAS

PREP: 30 MIN. ■ COOK: 4 HOURS
YIELD: 8 SERVINGS

- 8 medium tart apples, peeled and sliced
- 1 cup sugar
- 1/4 cup all-purpose flour
- 2 teaspoons ground cinnamon
- 2 eggs
- 1 cup heavy whipping cream
- 1 teaspoon vanilla extract
- 1 cup graham cracker crumbs
- 1/2 cup chopped pecans
- 1/4 cup butter, melted

Vanilla ice cream, optional

■ In a large bowl, combine the apples, sugar, flour and cinnamon. Spoon into a greased 3-qt. slow cooker. Whisk the eggs, cream and vanilla; pour over apple mixture. Combine the cracker crumbs, pecans and butter; sprinkle over top.

■ Cover and cook on low for 4-5 hours or until apples are tender. Serve warm with ice cream if desired.

Mulled Grape Cider

I came up with this recipe one year when I attempted to make grape jelly and ended up with 30 jars of delicious grape syrup instead. I then simmered the syrup with spices to make a unique beverage.

—SHARON HARMON ORANGE, MASSACHUSETTS

PREP: 20 MIN. ■ **COOK:** 3 HOURS
YIELD: 10-12 SERVINGS (2-3/4 QUARTS)

5 pounds Concord grapes	8 whole cloves
8 cups water, *divided*	4 cinnamon sticks (4 inches)
1-1/2 cups sugar	Dash ground nutmeg

- In a large saucepan or Dutch oven, combine the grapes and 2 cups water; bring to a boil, stirring constantly. Press through a strainer; reserve juice and discard skins and seeds.

- Pour juice through a double layer of cheesecloth into a 5-qt. slow cooker. Add the sugar, cloves, cinnamon sticks, nutmeg and remaining water. Cover and cook on low for 3 hours. Discard cloves and cinnamon sticks.

Spiced Sweet Potato Pudding

One of my favorite fall desserts, this treat's rich flavors are well suited to the chillier months. I like to serve it over a slice of pound cake or a scoop of vanilla ice cream.

—AYSHA SCHURMAN AMMON, IDAHO

PREP: 15 MIN. ■ **COOK:** 3 HOURS ■ **YIELD:** 7 SERVINGS

2 cans (15-3/4 ounces *each*) sweet potatoes, drained and mashed	1/2 cup packed brown sugar
	1/2 cup apple butter
3 eggs	2 tablespoons butter, softened
1 can (12 ounces) evaporated milk	2 teaspoons vanilla extract
	1/3 cup finely chopped pecans
2/3 cup biscuit/baking mix	Pound cake, optional

- In a large bowl, beat the first eight ingredients until well-blended. Pour into a greased 3-qt. slow cooker. Sprinkle with pecans. Cover and cook on low for 3-4 hours or until a thermometer reads 160°. Serve with pound cake if desired.

EDITOR'S NOTE: This recipe was tested with commercially prepared apple butter.

Caramel Hot Chocolate

Perfect on a chilly day in Calgary or anywhere, this recipe makes homemade hot chocolate even more luscious thanks to the addition of a caramel candy bar.

—MAUREEN MITCHELL
CALGARY, ALBERTA

PREP: 5 MIN. ■ **COOK:** 4 HOURS
YIELD: ABOUT 2 QUARTS

- 4 cups nonfat dry milk powder
- 3/4 cup baking cocoa
- 1/2 cup sugar
- 8 cups water
- 1 Caramello candy bar (2.7 ounces), chopped

Whipped cream and grated chocolate, optional

- In a 3-qt. slow cooker, combine the milk powder, cocoa and sugar; gradually whisk in water until smooth. Cover and cook on low for 4 hours or until hot.

- Add candy bar; stir until melted. Garnish with whipped cream and grated chocolate if desired.

"Tender cubes of pork are paired with a flavorful sweet-tart pomegranate pan sauce. For a weekday meal, try using a quick-cooking long grain and wild rice mix."

—**ELIZABETH DUMONT** BOULDER, COLORADO

stovetopsuppers

Beef &
Ground Beef

106

104

101

These speedy single-skillet or one-pot suppers are an easy way to get dinner on the table fast so you can spend more time with your family. The hearty beef and ground beef recipes in this chapter include **quick stir-fries, popular pasta dishes, robust stews, tasty sandwiches** and so much more!

ASPARAGUS BEEF STIR-FRY

I love filet mignon—but not its price! While grocery shopping, I picked up a more affordable beef tenderloin tail, brought it home and came up with this recipe. I cook it once a week and my husband takes leftovers to work.

—**LINDA FLYNN** ELLICOTT CITY, MARYLAND

Asparagus Beef Stir-Fry

PREP/TOTAL TIME: 30 MIN. ■ YIELD: 4 SERVINGS

1 pound beef tenderloin roast, cubed	1 pound fresh asparagus, trimmed and cut into 2-inch pieces
1 green onion, sliced	1/2 pound sliced fresh mushrooms
1/2 teaspoon salt	1/4 cup butter, cubed
1/4 teaspoon pepper	1 tablespoon reduced-sodium soy sauce
1 tablespoon canola oil	1-1/2 teaspoons lemon juice
2 garlic cloves, minced	Hot cooked rice

■ In a wok or large skillet, stir-fry the beef, onion, salt and pepper in oil for 3-5 minutes. Add the garlic; cook 1 minute longer. Remove and keep warm.

■ In the same pan, stir-fry asparagus and mushrooms in butter until asparagus is tender. Return beef mixture to the pan. Stir in soy sauce and lemon juice; heat through. Serve with rice.

Hearty Beef Ravioli

You're only 30 minutes away from a great new pasta dish. Just add a fresh salad and crusty bread, and dinner's done in no time!

—**TASTE OF HOME TEST KITCHEN**

PREP/TOTAL TIME: 30 MIN.
YIELD: 6 SERVINGS

- 1 package (25 ounces) frozen beef ravioli
- 1/2 pound extra-lean ground beef (95% lean)
- 1 medium green pepper, chopped
- 1 can (14-1/2 ounces) no-salt-added diced tomatoes
- 1 can (8 ounces) no-salt-added tomato sauce
- 2 tablespoons reduced-sodium taco seasoning
- 3/4 cup shredded reduced-fat cheddar cheese
- 1 can (2-1/4 ounces) sliced ripe olives, drained

■ Cook ravioli according to package directions.

■ Meanwhile, in a large nonstick skillet, cook beef and green pepper over medium heat until meat is no longer pink. Stir in the tomatoes, tomato sauce and taco seasoning. Bring to a boil. Reduce heat; simmer, uncovered, for 5-7 minutes or until slightly thickened.

■ Drain pasta. Serve with sauce. Sprinkle each serving with 2 tablespoons cheese and about 1 tablespoon olives.

My brother-in-law, Stanley, gave me this recipe more than 30 years ago. He was an officer in the Army, and his fellow officers considered this flavorful steak a high-demand dish. It's simple, straightforward and quick, but tastes better than most restaurant menu fare.

—**DAN MAYER** OLNEY, ILLINOIS

Teriyaki Steak

PREP: 20 MIN. + MARINATING ■ COOK: 15 MIN. ■ YIELD: 6 SERVINGS

1	beef flank steak (1-1/2 to 2 pounds)	2	garlic cloves, minced
1/2	cup plus 1/3 cup reduced-sodium soy sauce, *divided*	2	tablespoons butter, *divided*
1/4	cup balsamic vinegar	3	eggs, beaten
1/4	cup honey	2	cups cold cooked rice
1	teaspoon ground ginger	1	package (9 ounces) frozen peas and pearl onions

■ Place steak in a large resealable plastic bag. In a small bowl, whisk 1/2 cup soy sauce, vinegar, honey, ginger and garlic. Pour half of the marinade over steak. Seal bag and turn to coat; refrigerate overnight. Cover and refrigerate remaining marinade.

■ Drain and discard marinade. Grill steak, covered, over medium heat or broil 3-4 in. from the heat for 7-9 minutes on each side or until meat reaches desired doneness (for medium-rare, a thermometer should read 145°; medium, 160°; well-done, 170°). Let stand for 10 minutes before slicing.

■ Meanwhile, transfer reserved marinade to a small saucepan. Bring to a boil; cook until liquid is reduced by half. Set aside.

■ In a large skillet, heat 1 tablespoon butter over medium-high heat. Pour eggs into skillet. As eggs set, lift edges, letting uncooked portion flow underneath. When eggs are completely cooked, remove to plate. Chop eggs into small pieces; set aside.

■ In the same skillet, stir-fry rice in remaining butter over medium-high heat. Stir in the peas, onions and remaining soy sauce. Add eggs; cook and stir until heated through. Thinly slice steak across the grain; serve over rice. Drizzle with sauce mixture.

When grilling or broiling **flank steak,** you can prevent the edges from curling by scoring the surface with **shallow diagonal cuts,** making simple diamond shapes.

Brown-Bag Burritos

For a change from sandwiches, we like burritos—something many people don't consider in a brown-bag lunch. They're good cold or easy to heat in a microwave.

—**RHONDA CLIETT** BELTON, TEXAS

PREP/TOTAL TIME: 30 MIN. + CHILLING
YIELD: 15-20 SERVINGS

1	pound ground beef
1	can (16 ounces) refried beans
2/3	cup enchilada sauce
1/4	cup water
3	tablespoons finely chopped onion
4-1/2	teaspoons chili powder
1-1/2	teaspoons garlic powder
3/4	teaspoon salt
1/2	teaspoon dried oregano
15	to 20 flour tortillas (8 inches)
1-1/2	to 2-1/2 cups shredded cheddar cheese

■ In a large skillet, cook beef over medium heat until no longer pink; drain. Stir in the next eight ingredients. Bring to a boil. Reduce heat; cover and simmer for 20 minutes.

■ In a microwave, heat tortillas in batches until warm, about 45 seconds. Spoon 3 to 4 tablespoons of beef mixture off center on each tortilla. Sprinkle each with 2 to 3 tablespoons cheese and roll up.

■ Wrap each burrito in paper towel, then in foil. Repeat with remaining tortillas and filling. Refrigerate. Eat burritos cold, or remove foil and microwave paper towel-wrapped burritos on high for 30-60 seconds.

This creamy dish has lots of great earthy flavors; mushrooms and a bit of rosemary make it really special, too. It is sure to become a family favorite!

—TASTE OF HOME TEST KITCHEN

MUSHROOM STEAK 'N' LINGUINE

Mushroom Steak 'n' Linguine

PREP/TOTAL TIME: 30 MIN. ■ **YIELD:** 4 SERVINGS

8	ounces uncooked linguine
1	pound beef top round steak, cut into thin strips
1/4	teaspoon salt
1/4	teaspoon pepper
3	teaspoons olive oil, *divided*
1	cup chopped sweet red pepper
1/2	cup chopped onion
1/2	pound sliced fresh mushrooms
1	cup coarsely chopped fresh spinach
1/2	teaspoon dried rosemary, crushed
3/4	cup spreadable chive and onion cream cheese
1/2	cup sour cream
1	tablespoon whole milk

■ Cook linguine according to package directions. Meanwhile, sprinkle beef with salt and pepper. In a large skillet, saute beef in 2 teaspoons oil until tender. Remove and keep warm.

■ In the same pan, saute the red pepper and onion in remaining oil until tender. Add mushrooms; saute 1-2 minutes longer or until tender. Add spinach and rosemary; cook and stir just until spinach is wilted. Stir in the cream cheese, sour cream and milk; heat through (do not boil).

■ Drain linguine; top with mushroom mixture and beef.

Hamburger Goulash

Goulash over mashed potatoes was my birthday meal of choice while growing up. Now I make the tangy recipe for my family.

—JENNIFER WILLINGHAM
KANSAS CITY, MISSOURI

PREP: 5 MIN. ■ **COOK:** 30 MIN.
YIELD: 6 CUPS

2-1/2	pounds ground beef
1	medium onion, chopped
2	cups water
3/4	cup ketchup
2	tablespoons Worcestershire sauce
2	teaspoons paprika
1	to 2 teaspoons sugar
1	teaspoon salt
1/2	teaspoon ground mustard
1/4	teaspoon garlic powder
2	tablespoons all-purpose flour
1/4	cup cold water

Hot cooked noodles *or* mashed potatoes

■ In a Dutch oven, cook beef and onion over medium heat until meat is no longer pink; drain. Add the water, ketchup, Worcestershire sauce, paprika, sugar, salt, mustard and garlic powder. Bring to a boil. Reduce heat; simmer, uncovered, for 20 minutes.

■ In a small bowl, combine flour and cold water until smooth; stir into meat mixture. Bring to a boil; cook and stir for 2 minutes or until thickened. Serve over noodles or potatoes; or cool and freeze for up to 3 months.

■ **TO USE FROZEN CASSEROLE:** Thaw in refrigerator; place in a saucepan and heat through.

ITALIAN STRIP STEAKS WITH FOCACCIA

- In a large skillet, cook steaks in 2 tablespoons oil over medium heat for 5-6 minutes on each side or until meat reaches desired doneness (for medium-rare, a thermometer should read 145°; medium, 160°; well-done, 170°). Remove and keep warm.

- In the same skillet, saute the mushrooms, shallot and onion in remaining oil. Add garlic and rosemary; saute 1-2 minutes longer. Stir in the red peppers, wine, salt and pepper; heat through.

- Place focaccia on serving plates; top each with a steak and 1/2 cup mushroom mixture. Sprinkle with cheese and olives.

My easy entree lets the host enjoy entertaining. The dish comes together quickly and makes a beautiful presentation. Fans of Italian food are sure to be impressed.

—PATRICIA HARMON BADEN, PENNSYLVANIA

Italian Strip Steaks with Focaccia

PREP: 15 MIN. ■ **COOK:** 25 MIN. ■ **YIELD:** 4 SERVINGS

4 boneless beef top loin steaks (8 ounces *each*)	1/2 cup roasted sweet red peppers, cut into strips
3 tablespoons olive oil, *divided*	1/4 cup dry red wine *or* beef broth
1/2 pound sliced baby portobello mushrooms	1/4 teaspoon salt
1 shallot, finely chopped	1/4 teaspoon coarsely ground pepper
3 tablespoons chopped red onion	1 focaccia bread (12 ounces), cut into quarters
2 garlic cloves, minced	2/3 cup shredded Asiago cheese
2 teaspoons minced fresh rosemary	1/4 cup sliced pimiento-stuffed olives

Top loin steak may be labeled as strip steak, Kansas City steak, New York strip steak, **ambassador steak or boneless club steak** in your region.

HEARTY BEEF AND NOODLES

- In a large skillet, brown beef in oil on all sides; remove and keep warm. In the same skillet, saute onion until tender. Add garlic; cook 1 minute longer. Return beef to the pan; stir in the soup, water, cream, coffee and gravy mix. Bring to a boil. Reduce heat; cover and simmer for 20-25 minutes or until meat is tender, stirring occasionally.

- Meanwhile, cook noodles according to package directions. Add the sour cream, paprika and pepper to skillet; heat through. Drain noodles. Serve with beef.

Here's hefty "man food" at its easy best! It's a longtime family favorite, and my kids always asked to bring home friends on nights we served it. My oldest son in the Army even had his wife call home for the recipe.

—SYLVIA STREU NORMAN, OKLAHOMA

Hearty Beef and Noodles

PREP: 10 MIN. ■ COOK: 25 MIN. ■ YIELD: 6 SERVINGS

1-1/2 pounds beef top sirloin steak, cut into 1/2-inch strips

2 teaspoons olive oil

1/2 cup chopped onion

1-1/2 teaspoons minced garlic

1 can (10-3/4 ounces) condensed cream of mushroom soup, undiluted

1 cup water

1 cup half-and-half cream

1/3 cup brewed coffee

2 envelopes brown gravy mix

5 cups uncooked egg noodles

1 cup (8 ounces) sour cream

1/2 teaspoon paprika

1/4 teaspoon pepper

To cook pasta or noodles evenly, prevent them from sticking together and avoid boil-overs, **always cook in a large pot** or Dutch oven. Unless you have a large pot, don't cook more than 2 pounds of noodles at a time.

I first had this dish during a trip to Argentina a few years ago. It inspired me to recreate it at home. It turned out so well, I wrote "Yum!" on the recipe card!

—KARI CAVEN
POST FALLS, IDAHO

LOADED VEGETABLE BEEF STEW

Loaded Vegetable Beef Stew

PREP: 40 MIN. ■ **COOK:** 8-1/2 HOURS
YIELD: 12 SERVINGS (1-1/3 CUPS EACH)

- 8 bacon strips, diced
- 3 pounds beef stew meat, cut into 1-inch cubes
- 6 medium carrots, cut into 1-inch pieces
- 6 medium tomatoes, peeled and cut into wedges
- 4 medium potatoes, peeled and cubed
- 3 cups cubed peeled butternut squash
- 2 medium green peppers, chopped
- 2 teaspoons dried thyme
- 2 garlic cloves, minced
- 2 cans (14-1/2 ounces *each*) beef broth
- 6 cups chopped cabbage
- 1/2 teaspoon pepper

■ In a large skillet, cook bacon over medium heat until crisp. Using a slotted spoon, remove to paper towels to drain. In the drippings, brown beef in batches. Refrigerate the bacon until serving.

■ In a 5-qt. slow cooker, combine the carrots, tomatoes, potatoes, squash, green peppers, thyme and garlic. Top with beef. Pour broth over the top. Cover and cook on low for 8-10 hours.

■ Stir in cabbage and pepper. Cover and cook on high for 30 minutes or until cabbage is tender. Sprinkle each serving with bacon.

Nacho Mac 'n' Cheese

Creamy and comforting, this family-friendly meal is a great way to ease into the week. And since most of the ingredients are mixed in one dish, cleanup is a breeze!
—TASTE OF HOME TEST KITCHEN

PREP/TOTAL TIME: 25 MIN.
YIELD: 6 SERVINGS

- 3 cups uncooked gemelli *or* spiral pasta
- 1 pound ground beef
- 2 cups chopped sweet red peppers
- 1/4 cup butter, cubed
- 1/4 cup all-purpose flour
- 1 envelope taco seasoning
- 1/4 teaspoon pepper
- 2-1/4 cups 2% milk
- 2 cups (8 ounces) shredded cheddar cheese
- 1 cup frozen corn, thawed
- 1 cup coarsely crushed tortilla chips

■ Cook gemelli according to package directions. Meanwhile, in a Dutch oven, cook beef and red peppers over medium heat until meat is no longer pink; drain.

■ Stir in the butter, flour, taco seasoning and pepper until blended. Gradually stir in milk. Bring to a boil; cook and stir for 2 minutes or until thickened. Remove from the heat. Stir in cheese and corn until cheese is melted.

■ Drain gemelli; add to beef mixture and stir to coat. Sprinkle with tortilla chips.

Mom's Pot Roast

My greatest inspiration to learn how to cook came from my mom. She was always feeding everyone, and that's why I only know how to cook for a crowd. This recipe accommodates groups big or small, because leftovers are great for sandwiches or a hearty barley soup.

—DOROTHY DUDER NORTH HOLLYWOOD, CALIFORNIA

PREP: 45 MIN. ■ COOK: 3 HOURS ■ YIELD: 8 SERVINGS

- 3 tablespoons all-purpose flour, *divided*
- 1 teaspoon salt
- 1/4 teaspoon *each* minced chives, parsley flakes and tarragon
- 1/4 teaspoon pepper
- 1 boneless beef chuck roast (3 to 3-1/2 pounds)
- 2 tablespoons canola oil
- 8 cups water
- 2 tablespoons beef bouillon granules
- 2 tablespoons Worcestershire sauce
- 1 large onion, chopped
- 3 celery ribs, cut into chunks
- 3 garlic cloves, minced
- 2 bay leaves
- 4 medium potatoes, peeled and quartered
- 4 medium carrots, cut into chunks
- 2 tablespoons butter

- ■ Combine 1 tablespoon flour and seasonings; rub over roast. In a Dutch oven, brown roast on all sides in oil over medium-high heat. Add the water, bouillon, Worcestershire sauce, onion, celery, garlic and bay leaves. Bring to a boil. Reduce heat; cover and simmer for 2 hours, turning the roast after 1 hour.

- ■ Turn roast again. Add potatoes and carrots. Cover and simmer 1 hour longer or until meat and vegetables are tender.

- ■ Discard bay leaves. Remove meat and vegetables to a serving platter and keep warm. Pour 2 cups cooking juices and loosened browned bits into a 2-cup measuring cup; skim fat. (Save remaining cooking juices for another use.)

- ■ For gravy, in a small saucepan, melt the butter; stir in the remaining flour until smooth; gradually stir in the cooking juices. Bring to a boil; cook and stir for 2 minutes or until thickened. Serve with the roast and vegetables.

Bohemian Beef Dinner

PREP: 25 MIN. ■ COOK: 2 HOURS
YIELD: 6 SERVINGS

- 3/4 cups all-purpose flour
- 1 teaspoon salt
- 1/4 teaspoon pepper
- 2 pounds beef stew meat, cut into 1-inch cubes
- 2 tablespoons canola oil
- 2 medium onions, chopped
- 1 garlic clove, minced
- 1 teaspoon dill weed
- 1 teaspoon caraway seeds
- 1 teaspoon paprika
- 1/2 cup water
- 1 cup (8 ounces) sour cream
- 2 cans (14 ounces *each*) sauerkraut, rinsed and well drained

Additional paprika

- ■ In a large resealable plastic bag, combine the flour, salt and pepper. Add beef; dredge or shake to coat. In a Dutch oven, brown the beef in oil in batches; drain. Add the onions, garlic, dill, caraway, paprika and water.

- ■ Cover and simmer for 2 hours or until meat is tender, stirring occasionally.

- ■ Stir in sour cream; heat through but do not boil. Heat sauerkraut; drain and spoon onto a serving platter. Top with the beef mixture. Sprinkle with paprika.

One of my favorite things to do when I was growing up was help my mother in the kitchen while she prepared traditional Czech dishes like this one. It's a savory stick-to-your ribs meal with beef and sauerkraut covered in a rich, creamy sauce.

—CARL & ISOBEL WANASEK ROGERS, ARKANSAS

PEPPERONI PIZZA SKILLET

On hectic school nights, no household can have too many hearty, 30-minute meals the whole family asks for. This creamy, flavor-packed skillet supper is sure to be requested again and again.

—ANNA MILLER QUAKER CITY, OHIO

Pepperoni Pizza Skillet

PREP/TOTAL TIME: 30 MIN. ■ **YIELD:** 8 SERVINGS

5	cups uncooked wide egg noodles	1	can (4-1/2 ounces) sliced mushrooms, drained
1-1/2	pounds ground beef	1/2	cup grated Parmesan cheese
1/2	cup chopped onion	1/4	teaspoon garlic powder
1/2	cup chopped green pepper	1/4	teaspoon dried oregano
1-1/2	cups chopped pepperoni	1/2	cup shredded part-skim mozzarella cheese
1	jar (14 ounces) pizza sauce		
1	can (10-3/4 ounces) condensed cream of mushroom soup, undiluted		

- Cook noodles according to package directions. Meanwhile, in a large skillet, cook the beef, onion and pepper over medium heat until meat is no longer pink; drain. Stir in the pepperoni, pizza sauce, soup, mushrooms, Parmesan cheese, garlic powder and oregano.

- Drain the noodles; stir into the skillet and heat through. Sprinkle with mozzarella cheese.

Taco Salad

I came across this recipe while in Arizona. When we return home each spring, our grandchildren ask me to make these tasty salads.

—BETTY JOHNSON
OLYMPIA, WASHINGTON

PREP: 30 MIN. ■ **COOK:** 15 MIN.
YIELD: 8 SERVINGS

- 2 packages (5.6 ounces *each*) refrigerated taco salad shells
- 3 bacon strips, diced
- 1 pound lean ground beef (90% lean)
- 2 large onions, chopped
- 2 garlic cloves, minced
- 3 tablespoons chili powder
- 1 teaspoon salt
- 1 teaspoon ground cumin, optional
- 1 can (14-1/2 ounces) diced tomatoes, undrained
- 1 can (16 ounces) refried beans
- 4 cups shredded lettuce

Toppings: chopped tomatoes, salsa, sour cream, guacamole, olives

- Prepare shells according to package directions; set aside.

- In a large skillet, cook bacon until crisp; drain on paper towels. In the drippings, cook beef, onions, garlic and seasonings over medium heat until meat is no longer pink. Stir in tomatoes. Bring to a boil. Reduce heat; cover and simmer for 10 minutes.

- Stir in beans; heat through, about 5 minutes. Spoon about 1/3 cup meat mixture into each salad shell. Top with 1/2 cup lettuce, another 1/4 cup meat mixture, bacon and toppings of your choice.

If you're tired of the same old boring sloppy joes, here's a tasty twist! These messy, kid-friendly sandwiches have a definite pizza flavor that families will simply love. Be sure to serve them with a fork!

—CONNIE PETTIT
LOGAN, OHIO

Pizza Joes

PREP/TOTAL TIME: 30 MIN. ■ **YIELD:** 6 SERVINGS

- 1 pound lean ground beef (90% lean)
- 1 medium onion, chopped
- 1/4 cup chopped green pepper
- 1 jar (14 ounces) pizza sauce
- 3 ounces sliced turkey pepperoni (about 50 slices), chopped
- 1/2 teaspoon dried basil
- 1/4 teaspoon dried oregano
- 6 hamburger buns, split
- 6 tablespoons shredded part-skim mozzarella cheese

■ In a large nonstick skillet, cook the beef, onion and pepper over medium heat until meat is no longer pink. Drain if necessary. Stir in the pizza sauce, pepperoni and herbs. Bring to a boil. Reduce heat; cover and simmer for 10 minutes.

■ Spoon 2/3 cup beef mixture onto each bun; sprinkle with cheese. Place on a baking sheet. Broil 3-4 in. from the heat for 1 minute or until cheese is melted. Replace tops.

When stacking nonstick skillets on cupboard shelves, place a paper plate or hot pad between each to prevent scratches. **This prolongs the life** of the skillets.

Taco Macaroni

This dish is absolutely loaded with zesty tomato flavor! And it's a hearty way to warm up—and fill up—during the winter!

—MARISSA UNDERCOFLER
HOWARD, PENNSYLVANIA

PREP/TOTAL TIME: 30 MIN.
YIELD: 6 SERVINGS

- 1 package (16 ounces) elbow macaroni
- 1 pound ground beef
- 3/4 cup chopped onion
- 1 can (14-1/2 ounces) diced tomatoes, undrained
- 1 can (10-3/4 ounces) condensed tomato soup, undiluted
- 1 can (8 ounces) tomato sauce
- 1 envelope taco seasoning

Shredded cheddar cheese

■ Cook macaroni according to package directions. Meanwhile, in a Dutch oven, cook beef and onion over medium heat until meat is no longer pink; drain.

■ Stir in the tomatoes, soup, tomato sauce and taco seasoning. Bring to a boil. Reduce heat; simmer, uncovered, for 8-10 minutes or until thickened.

■ Drain macaroni; stir into meat mixture and heat through. Sprinkle with cheddar cheese.

Apricot preserves lend sweetness to this tasty beef stir-fry while red pepper flakes provide a bit of kick. A frozen vegetable medley shaves minutes off prep time—no chopping necessary!

—TASTE OF HOME TEST KITCHEN

APRICOT BEEF STIR-FRY

Apricot Beef Stir-Fry

PREP/TOTAL TIME: 25 MIN. ■ YIELD: 4 SERVINGS

1 teaspoon cornstarch	1 pound beef top sirloin steak, thinly sliced
1/4 cup cold water	
1/2 cup apricot preserves	1 tablespoon canola oil
2 tablespoons soy sauce	1 package (16 ounces) frozen asparagus stir-fry vegetable blend
1/2 teaspoon minced garlic	
1/4 teaspoon salt	Hot cooked rice
1/4 teaspoon crushed red pepper flakes	

■ In a small bowl, whisk cornstarch and cold water until smooth. Stir in the apricot preserves, soy sauce, garlic, salt and pepper flakes; set aside.

■ In a large skillet or wok, stir-fry beef in oil until no longer pink; remove and keep warm. In the same pan, stir fry vegetable blend according to package directions. Return beef to the pan. Stir apricot mixture and add to beef mixture. Cook and stir until slightly thickened. Serve with rice.

Easy Beef Taco Skillet

Busy day? Save time and money with this stovetop supper the whole family will love. It calls for handy convenience products, so it can be on the table in minutes.

—KELLY RODER FAIRFAX, VIRGINIA

PREP/TOTAL TIME: 20 MIN.
YIELD: 6 SERVINGS

1 pound ground beef

1 small red onion, chopped

1 can (15-1/4 ounces) whole kernel corn, drained

10 corn tortillas (6 inches), cut into 1-inch pieces

1 bottle (8 ounces) taco sauce

1-1/4 cups shredded cheddar cheese, *divided*

Hot pepper sauce, optional

■ In a large skillet, cook beef and onion over medium heat until meat is no longer pink; drain. Add the corn, tortillas, taco sauce and 1 cup cheese; heat through. Sprinkle with remaining cheese. Serve with pepper sauce if desired.

To lighten up Mexican dishes, **substitute corn tortillas when flour tortillas** are called for in recipes. Yellow or white **corn tortillas have less fat** and fewer calories than flour varieties.

SPAGHETTI WITH ITALIAN MEATBALLS

The classic, hearty spaghetti dinner is one of my family's favorite recipes. We enjoy servings of the sauce with a variety of pasta shapes and sizes. Leftovers taste great, too!

—**SHARON CRIDER** JUNCTION CITY, KANSAS

Spaghetti with Italian Meatballs

PREP: 20 MIN. ■ COOK: 1-1/4 HOURS ■ YIELD: 10 SERVINGS

3/4	cup chopped onion
1	garlic clove, minced
1	tablespoon olive oil
1	can (28 ounces) Italian crushed tomatoes, undrained
1	can (6 ounces) tomato paste
1	cup water
1-1/2	teaspoons dried oregano
1/2	teaspoon salt
1/2	teaspoon pepper

MEATBALLS:

4	slices white bread, torn
1/2	cup water
2	eggs, lightly beaten
1/2	cup grated Parmesan cheese
1	garlic clove, minced
1	teaspoon dried basil
1	teaspoon dried parsley flakes
1/2	teaspoon salt
1	pound lean ground beef
2	teaspoons olive oil
1	package (16 ounces) spaghetti

■ In a large saucepan, cook onion and garlic in oil until tender. Stir in the tomatoes, tomato paste, water, oregano, salt and pepper. Bring to a boil. Reduce heat; cover and simmer for 30 minutes.

■ Meanwhile, in a small bowl, soak bread in water for 5 minutes. Squeeze out excess liquid. In a large bowl, combine the eggs, Parmesan cheese, garlic, basil, parsley, salt and bread. Crumble beef over mixture and mix well. Shape into 1-in. balls.

■ In a large nonstick skillet coated with cooking spray, brown meatballs in batches in oil over medium heat.

■ Add meatballs to sauce; return to a boil. Reduce heat; simmer, uncovered, for 30 minutes or until meatballs are no longer pink.

■ Cook the spaghetti according to package directions; drain. Serve with the meatballs and sauce.

➡ **NUTRITION FACTS:** 3 meatballs and 1/2 cup sauce with 2/3 cup spaghetti equals 368 calories, 9 g fat (3 g saturated fat), 73 mg cholesterol, 661 mg sodium, 50 g carbohydrate, 3 g fiber, 20 g protein. **DIABETIC EXCHANGES:** 2-1/2 starch, 2 lean meat, 2 vegetable, 1/2 fat.

SKILLET BEEF TAMALES

For a cheesy and delicious skillet supper that doesn't pack in the calories, try these easy beef tamales. The dish doesn't taste light at all and is sure to be a huge hit at the dinner table!

—DEB WILLIAMS PEORIA, ARIZONA

Skillet Beef Tamales

PREP/TOTAL TIME: 30 MIN. ■ YIELD: 5 SERVINGS

1 pound lean ground beef (90% lean)	2 tablespoons water
1/3 cup chopped green pepper	6 corn tortillas (6 inches), halved and cut into 1/2-inch strips
1/3 cup chopped sweet red pepper	3/4 cup shredded reduced-fat cheddar cheese
2 cups salsa	5 tablespoons fat-free sour cream
3/4 cup frozen corn	

- In a large nonstick skillet coated with cooking spray, cook beef and peppers over medium heat until meat is no longer pink; drain. Stir in the salsa, corn and water; bring to a boil.

- Stir in tortilla strips. Reduce heat; cover and simmer for 10-15 minutes or until tortillas are softened. Sprinkle with cheese; cover and cook 2-3 minutes longer or until cheese is melted. Serve with sour cream.

➥ **NUTRITION FACTS:** 1 cup beef mixture with 1 tablespoon sour cream equals 329 calories, 11 g fat (5 g saturated fat), 59 mg cholesterol, 679 mg sodium, 28 g carbohydrate, 6 g fiber, 25 g protein. **DIABETIC EXCHANGES:** 3 lean meat, 1-1/2 starch, 1 vegetable, 1/2 fat.

Onion Loose-Meat Sandwiches

Infused with French onion soup, these sandwiches don't have the typical flavor of most sloppy joes. My sisters and I rely on this recipe from Mom on days when there's little time to cook.

—KATHY PETORSKY
BELLE VERNON, PENNSYLVANIA

PREP/TOTAL TIME: 25 MIN.
YIELD: 6-8 SERVINGS

1-1/2 pounds ground beef
  2 tablespoons all-purpose flour
Salt and pepper to taste
  1 can (10-1/2 ounces) condensed French onion soup, undiluted
  6 to 8 hamburger buns, split
Optional: sliced cheddar cheese and dill pickles

- In a large skillet, cook beef over medium heat until no longer pink; drain. Stir in the flour, salt and pepper until blended. Gradually add soup. Bring to a boil; cook and stir for 2 minutes or until thickened.

- Spoon onto buns; top with cheese and pickles if desired.

When browning ground beef, a pastry blender works great at **breaking up the larger pieces** shortly before the meat is cooked.

Many years ago, the *Farm Journal* published a recipe that became the starting point for my stew. It's as colorful as it is delicious. I often serve it over wide egg noodles or atop steamed rice, but it's also good just as it is.

—SAVILLA ZOOK SEABROOK, MARYLAND

MEATBALL STEW

Bacon Cheeseburger Spaghetti

I run a daycare center and it's always hard to find different foods that the kids will actually eat. I spruced up a variation of this simple and quick recipe to my tastes, and now the kids (and my husband) request it all the time!

—NICHELLE NELL ISLE, MINNESOTA

PREP/TOTAL TIME: 30 MIN.
YIELD: 6 SERVINGS

- 10 ounces uncooked spaghetti
- 1 pound lean ground beef (90% lean)
- 2/3 cup chopped onion
- 6 slices ready-to-serve fully cooked bacon, chopped
- 1-1/2 cups ketchup
- 1 cup chopped dill pickles
- 1 cup barbecue sauce
- 1/2 cup prepared mustard
- 2 cups (8 ounces) shredded cheddar cheese

- ■ Cook spaghetti according to package directions. Meanwhile, in a large skillet, cook beef and onion over medium heat until meat is no longer pink; drain. Stir in the bacon, ketchup, pickles, barbecue sauce and mustard. Bring to a boil. Reduce heat; simmer, uncovered, for 5 minutes. Drain spaghetti; stir into meat mixture.

- ■ Sprinkle with cheese. Remove from the heat; cover and let stand until cheese is melted.

Meatball Stew

PREP: 15 MIN. ■ COOK: 45 MIN. ■ YIELD: 8-10 SERVINGS

- 1 egg, lightly beaten
- 1 cup soft bread crumbs
- 1/4 cup finely chopped onion
- 1 teaspoon salt
- 1/2 teaspoon dried marjoram
- 1/4 teaspoon dried thyme
- 1-1/2 pounds lean ground beef (90% lean)
- 2 tablespoons canola oil

- 2 cans (10-3/4 ounces *each*) condensed tomato soup, undiluted
- 2 cans (10-1/2 ounces *each*) condensed beef broth, undiluted
- 4 medium potatoes, peeled and diced
- 4 medium carrots, diced
- 1 jar (16 ounces) whole onions, drained
- 1/4 cup minced fresh parsley

- ■ In a large bowl, combine the egg, bread crumbs, chopped onion, salt, marjoram and thyme. Crumble beef over the top and mix well. Shape into 24 meatballs. Heat oil in a Dutch oven. Brown meatballs in batches; drain.

- ■ Add the soup, broth, potatoes, carrots and whole onions. Bring to a boil; reduce heat and simmer for 30 minutes or until meat is no longer pink. Garnish with parsley.

Poultry

121

122

116

There's always time for a home-cooked meal with these chicken and turkey skillet dishes. Not only is cleanup a cinch, but **the robust, family-pleasing recipes are easy to prepare** on the stovetop in a flash. Many have combined prep and cooking times of 30 minutes or less!

CREAMY CHICKEN ANGEL HAIR

- Cook pasta according to package directions. Meanwhile, in a large skillet, saute the chicken, salt and pepper in 2 tablespoons oil until no longer pink. Remove and keep warm.

- In the same skillet, saute carrot in butter and remaining oil for 1 minute. Add onion and celery; saute 3-4 minutes longer or until tender. Add the garlic; cook for 1 minute.

- Stir in the cream, bacon, lemon juice and Italian seasoning. Bring to a boil. Reduce heat; simmer, uncovered, for 2-3 minutes or until slightly thickened, stirring constantly. Return chicken to the pan.

- Drain pasta; toss with chicken mixture. Garnish with cheese.

Our pasta-loving family often requests this recipe featuring chicken and vegetables. Lemon juice adds a light citrus touch to the creamy sauce, which is well seasoned with garlic and herbs.

—VANESSA SORENSON ISANTI, MINNESOTA

Creamy Chicken Angel Hair

PREP: 15 MIN. ■ **COOK:** 20 MIN. ■ **YIELD:** 6 SERVINGS

- 1 package (16 ounces) angel hair pasta
- 1-1/4 pounds boneless skinless chicken breasts, cut into 1-inch cubes
- 1/2 teaspoon salt
- 1/4 teaspoon pepper
- 3 tablespoons olive oil, *divided*
- 1 large carrot, diced
- 2 tablespoons butter

- 1 medium onion, chopped
- 1 celery rib, diced
- 3 large garlic cloves, minced
- 2 cups heavy whipping cream
- 5 bacon strips, cooked and crumbled
- 3 tablespoons lemon juice
- 1 teaspoon Italian seasoning
- 1 cup shredded Parmesan cheese

You can **mix your own Italian seasoning** by combining 1/4 teaspoon each of **dried basil, thyme, rosemary and oregano** for each teaspoon of Italian seasoning called for in a recipe.

CHICKEN VERONIQUE

- Sprinkle chicken with salt and nutmeg. In a large nonstick skillet coated with cooking spray, cook chicken in butter over medium heat for 3-5 minutes on each side or until lightly browned.

- In a small bowl, combine the wine, marmalade and tarragon. Add to skillet; bring to a boil. Reduce heat; cover and simmer for 4-6 minutes on each side or until a thermometer reads 170°. Remove chicken and keep warm.

- Combine flour and cream until smooth. Gradually stir into skillet. Bring to a boil; cook 2 minutes longer or until thickened. Stir in grapes; heat through. Serve with chicken.

➡ **NUTRITION FACTS:** 1 chicken breast half with 1/3 cup sauce equals 226 calories, 7 g fat (4 g saturated fat), 79 mg cholesterol, 191 mg sodium, 13 g carbohydrate, 1 g fiber, 24 g protein. **DIABETIC EXCHANGES:** 3 lean meat, 1 fat, 1/2 starch, 1/2 fruit.

I found this classic recipe in one of my gardening books. My family just loves it, and it's super easy to make! We think it's excellent served with rice pilaf on the side.

—ANITA DUDIWKA AKRON, OHIO

Chicken Veronique

PREP: 15 MIN. ■ **COOK:** 20 MIN. ■ **YIELD:** 6 SERVINGS

6 boneless skinless chicken breast halves (4 ounces *each*)	2 tablespoons orange marmalade spreadable fruit
1/4 teaspoon salt	3/4 teaspoon dried tarragon
1/8 teaspoon ground nutmeg	2 teaspoons all-purpose flour
4 teaspoons butter	1/2 cup half-and-half cream
2/3 cup white wine *or* reduced-sodium chicken broth	1-1/2 cups green grapes, halved

The general rule **when cooking with white wine** is to use wine that is high in acidity that you would also drink. This might include **sauvignon blanc, pinot blanc, pinot grigio, pinot gris or semillon.**

Mom's traditional fried chicken always cooked up golden brown and crispy. Drizzled with pan gravy, this dish is real comfort food.

—GINNY WERKMEISTER
TILDEN, NEBRASKA

FRIED CHICKEN WITH PAN GRAVY

Fried Chicken with Pan Gravy

PREP: 15 MIN. ■ **COOK:** 45 MIN. ■ **YIELD:** 6 SERVINGS (1-1/2 CUPS GRAVY)

1 cup all-purpose flour	Oil for frying
3/4 teaspoon salt	**GRAVY:**
1/4 teaspoon dried thyme	2 tablespoons all-purpose flour
1/4 teaspoon rubbed sage	1/8 teaspoon salt
1/4 teaspoon pepper	1-1/3 cups 2% milk
1 broiler/fryer chicken (3-1/2 to 4 pounds), cut up	

■ In a large resealable plastic bag, combine the first five ingredients. Add chicken, a few pieces at a time, and shake to coat.

■ In a large skillet over medium-high heat, heat 1/4 in. of oil; fry chicken until browned on all sides. Reduce heat; cover and cook for 30-35 minutes or until the juices run clear, turning occasionally. Uncover and cook 5 minutes longer. Remove the chicken to paper towels and keep warm.

■ Pour off excess fat from the skillet, reserving the browned bits and 2 tablespoons drippings. Stir in flour and salt until blended; gradually add the milk. Bring to a boil; cook and stir for 1-2 minutes or until thickened. Serve with chicken.

Favorite Skillet Lasagna

Whole wheat noodles, zucchini and ricotta add nutrition to this family-friendly dinner. No one will believe this one's lighter.
—LORIE MINER KAMAS, UTAH

PREP/TOTAL TIME: 30 MIN.
YIELD: 5 SERVINGS

- 1/2 pound Italian turkey sausage links, casings removed
- 1 small onion, chopped
- 1 jar (14 ounces) spaghetti sauce
- 2 cups uncooked whole wheat egg noodles
- 1 cup water
- 1/2 cup chopped zucchini
- 1/2 cup fat-free ricotta cheese
- 2 tablespoons grated Parmesan cheese
- 1 tablespoon minced fresh parsley *or* 1 teaspoon dried parsley flakes
- 1/2 cup shredded part-skim mozzarella cheese

■ In a large nonstick skillet, cook sausage and onion over medium heat until no longer pink; drain. Stir in spaghetti sauce, egg noodles, water and zucchini. Bring to a boil. Reduce heat; cover. Simmer for 8-10 minutes or until pasta is tender, stirring occasionally.

■ Combine ricotta, Parmesan and parsley. Drop by tablespoonfuls over pasta mixture. Sprinkle with mozzarella. Cover and cook 3-5 minutes or until the cheese is melted.

➡ **NUTRITION FACTS:** 1 cup equals 250 calories, 10 g fat (3 g saturated fat), 41 mg cholesterol, 783 mg sodium, 24 g carbohydrate, 3 g fiber, 17 g protein. **DIABETIC EXCHANGES:** 2 lean meat, 1-1/2 starch, 1 fat.

This hearty pasta dinner is packed with flavorful chicken, veggies and cheese. It's also creamy, colorful and quick. Best of all, kids are sure to wolf it down!

—MARTI GUTWEIN
RENSSELAER, INDIANA

MEXICAN CHICKEN PENNE FOR KIDS

Mexican Chicken Penne for Kids

PREP/TOTAL TIME: 25 MIN. ■ YIELD: 6 SERVINGS

1 package (16 ounces) uncooked penne pasta	1-1/4 cups salsa con queso dip
2 cups cubed cooked chicken	1/2 cup milk
	1/4 teaspoon salt

■ Cook pasta according to package directions. Meanwhile, in a large bowl, combine the chicken, dip, milk and salt.

■ Drain pasta; return to pan. Stir in chicken mixture and toss to coat. Heat through.

Different kinds of salt have different sodium contents because they each have varying densities. **Table and iodized salt** each have 2,300 milligrams of sodium per teaspoon. Sea salt has a comparable sodium content, while kosher salt has about 1,180 milligrams of sodium per teaspoon.

Turkey Fried Rice

Generally, fried rice is a dish made with leftover rice from the day before, which serves as a nice base for a catch-all meal.

—TASTE OF HOME TEST KITCHEN

PREP/TOTAL TIME: 30 MIN.
YIELD: 4 SERVINGS

- 1 tablespoon olive oil
- 2 eggs, beaten
- 1/2 pound ground turkey
- 2 green onions, sliced
- 3 cups cold cooked rice
- 1 cup bean sprouts
- 1/4 cup minced fresh cilantro
- 1/4 cup soy sauce
- 2 tablespoons chunky peanut butter
- 1 teaspoon sugar
- 1/2 teaspoon garlic powder
- 1/4 teaspoon crushed red pepper flakes
- 1/4 teaspoon ground ginger

■ In a large skillet, heat oil over medium-high heat. Pour the eggs into skillet. As eggs set, lift the edges, letting uncooked portion flow underneath. When eggs are completely cooked, remove to a plate; set aside.

■ In the same skillet, cook turkey and onions over medium heat until meat is no longer pink. Stir in the rice, bean sprouts and cilantro. In a small bowl, whisk the remaining ingredients until blended; stir into skillet. Chop egg into small pieces; stir into skillet and heat through.

THAI PORTOBELLO CHICKEN STIR-FRY

My husband and I never met a mushroom we didn't like, so this flavorful meal-in-one dish is a favorite. I cook the rice in the morning and reheat it while preparing the mushrooms and chicken.

—**SUSAN BAZAN** SEQUIM, WASHINGTON

Thai Portobello Chicken Stir-Fry

PREP: 25 MIN. ■ COOK: 20 MIN. ■ YIELD: 6 SERVINGS

1/2 cup Thai peanut sauce	2 medium carrots, sliced diagonally
1/2 cup teriyaki sauce	1/2 pound sliced baby portobello mushrooms
1/4 cup chunky peanut butter	
2 teaspoons Worcestershire sauce	4-1/2 teaspoons minced fresh gingerroot
3/4 pound boneless skinless chicken breasts, cut into thin strips	3 garlic cloves, minced
3 tablespoons olive oil, *divided*	1/3 cup thinly sliced green onions
1 tablespoon sesame oil	Hot cooked rice
3 cups chopped sweet onions	
4 celery ribs, sliced diagonally	

- In a small bowl, combine the peanut sauce, teriyaki sauce, peanut butter and Worcestershire sauce; set aside.

- In a large skillet or wok, stir-fry chicken in 1 tablespoon olive oil and sesame oil until no longer pink. Remove and keep warm.

- Stir-fry the sweet onions, celery and carrots in remaining oil for 4 minutes. Add the mushrooms, ginger and garlic; stir-fry 4-6 minutes longer or until vegetables are crisp-tender.

- Stir sauce mixture and add to the pan. Bring to a boil; cook and stir for 2 minutes or until thickened. Add chicken; heat through. Sprinkle with green onions. Serve with rice.

For easy stir-frying, prepare all the ingredients before you begin to stir-fry.

Select a wok or skillet large enough to hold the food you'll be stir-frying. If the food is too crowded in the pan, it will steam. If necessary, cook the food in batches.

I have four boys and have to trick them into eating healthy. It's not an easy task, but this is a favorite! With whole wheat pasta, plenty of vegetables, healthier turkey sausage and reduced-fat ingredients, a hearty pasta dish is made good for you.

—TOMISSA HUART UNION, ILLINOIS

Pronto Penne Pasta

PREP/TOTAL TIME: 30 MIN. ■ YIELD: 6 SERVINGS

2-1/4 cups uncooked whole wheat
     penne pasta

1 pound Italian turkey sausage
  links, casings removed

1 medium red onion, chopped

1 medium green pepper, chopped

1 can (14-1/2 ounces) no-salt-
  added diced tomatoes,
  undrained

1 can (14-1/2 ounces) reduced-
  sodium chicken broth

2 garlic cloves, minced

2 teaspoons dried tarragon

2 teaspoons dried basil

1/4 teaspoon cayenne pepper

1/4 cup all-purpose flour

1/2 cup fat-free milk

1/2 cup shredded reduced-fat
  cheddar cheese

1/4 cup grated Parmesan cheese

■ Cook pasta according to package directions. Meanwhile, crumble sausage into a large nonstick skillet coated with cooking spray. Add onion and green pepper; cook and stir over medium heat until meat is no longer pink. Drain. Stir in the tomatoes, broth, garlic, tarragon, basil and cayenne.

■ In a small bowl, combine the flour and milk until smooth; stir into sausage mixture. Bring to a boil; cook and stir for 2 minutes or until thickened.

■ Remove from the heat. Stir in cheddar cheese until melted. Drain pasta; toss with sausage mixture. Sprinkle each serving with 2 teaspoons Parmesan cheese.

➥ **NUTRITION FACTS:** 1 cup equals 373 calories, 11 g fat (3 g saturated fat), 55 mg cholesterol, 800 mg sodium, 45 g carbohydrate, 4 g fiber, 24 g protein. **DIABETIC EXCHANGES:** 2-1/2 starch, 2 medium-fat meat, 1 vegetable.

To mince or chop, hold the handle of a chef's knife with one hand, and rest the fingers of your other hand on the top of the blade near the tip. **Using the handle as a guide,** move your knife in an arc across the food with a rocking motion.

Buffalo Chicken Wraps

This fuss-free meal is a favorite in our house, with its tender chicken, tortillas, crunchy vegetables and spicy buffalo wing sauce. Feel free to change the veggies to suit your family's tastes.

—**SARAH GOTTSCHALK**
RICHMOND, INDIANA

PREP/TOTAL TIME: 30 MIN.
YIELD: 8 SERVINGS

1-1/2 pounds chicken tenderloins

1 cup buffalo wing sauce, *divided*

8 lettuce leaves

8 flour tortillas (10 inches),
  warmed

16 bacon strips, cooked

1 small green pepper, cut into
  strips

1/2 cup ranch salad dressing

■ In a large skillet, bring chicken and 1/2 cup buffalo wing sauce to a boil. Reduce heat; cover and simmer for 10-12 minutes or until meat is no longer pink. Remove from the heat; cool slightly. Shred chicken with two forks.

■ Place a lettuce leaf on each tortilla; spoon about 1/2 cup chicken mixture down the center. Top with bacon and green pepper. Drizzle with ranch dressing and remaining buffalo wing sauce; roll up.

This chicken is so fast and tasty. The light and sweet sauce perfectly offsets the bold jerk seasoning in the one-dish meal.

—**LAURA MCALLISTER**
MORGANTON, NORTH CAROLINA

CARIBBEAN CHICKEN TENDERLOINS

Caribbean Chicken Tenderloins

PREP/TOTAL TIME: 20 MIN. ■ YIELD: 4 SERVINGS

1 pound chicken tenderloins	4 green onions, chopped
2 teaspoons Caribbean jerk seasoning	2 teaspoons cornstarch
3 teaspoons olive oil, *divided*	1 cup unsweetened pineapple juice
2-1/2 cups cut fresh asparagus (2-inch pieces)	1 tablespoon spicy brown mustard
1 cup pineapple tidbits, drained	2 cups hot cooked rice

■ Rub chicken with jerk seasoning. In a large skillet coated with cooking spray, cook chicken in 1 teaspoon oil over medium heat for 3-4 minutes on each side or until the juices run clear. Remove and keep warm.

■ In the same skillet, saute the asparagus, pineapple and onions in remaining oil for 2-3 minutes or until tender.

■ Combine the cornstarch, pineapple juice and mustard until smooth; gradually stir into the pan. Bring to a boil; cook and stir for 2 minutes or until thickened. Serve with chicken and rice.

➡➡ **NUTRITION FACTS:** 3 ounces cooked chicken with 1/2 cup asparagus mixture and 1/2 cup rice equals 314 calories, 4 g fat (1 g saturated fat), 67 mg cholesterol, 247 mg sodium, 40 g carbohydrate, 2 g fiber, 29 g protein. **DIABETIC EXCHANGES:** 3 lean meat, 2 starch, 1/2 fruit, 1/2 fat.

Roasted Pepper Chicken Penne

My husband calls me an aerobic cook because I can make this Italian dish in just 30 minutes.

—**REGINA COWLES**
BOULDER, COLORADO

PREP/TOTAL TIME: 30 MIN.
YIELD: 8 SERVINGS

- 1 pound boneless skinless chicken breasts, cut into 1-inch strips
- 1/4 cup balsamic vinegar
- 1 package (16 ounces) penne pasta
- 1 medium onion, sliced
- 3 garlic cloves, sliced
- 1/4 cup olive oil
- 1 can (28 ounces) crushed tomatoes
- 1 cup julienned roasted sweet red peppers
- 1 cup chicken broth
- 3 teaspoons Italian seasoning
- 1/4 teaspoon salt
- 1 cup shredded Parmesan cheese

■ Place chicken in a large resealable plastic bag; add vinegar. Seal bag and turn to coat; refrigerate for 15 minutes.

■ Cook pasta according to package directions. Meanwhile, in a large skillet, saute onion and garlic in oil for 1 minute. Drain and discard vinegar. Add chicken to skillet; cook for 4-5 minutes or until meat is no longer pink.

■ Stir in tomatoes, red peppers, broth, seasoning and salt. Bring to a boil over medium heat. Cook; stir for 4-5 minutes or until heated through. Drain pasta; toss with chicken mixture. Sprinkle with cheese.

ITALIAN CHICKEN

- In a shallow bowl, beat egg and 1 tablespoon water. Place the bread crumbs in another shallow bowl. Dip chicken in egg mixture, then coat with crumbs. Let stand for 5 minutes.

- In a large skillet, fry chicken in oil until golden brown on all sides. Reduce heat to medium; cook until a thermometer reads 180°, about 15 minutes.

- Meanwhile, in a small saucepan, combine the soup, onion, garlic powder, basil, oregano and remaining water. Bring to a gentle boil over medium heat. Reduce heat; cover and cook for 3-5 minutes or until onion is tender. Serve chicken with sauce; sprinkle with cheeses.

After coating chicken in bread crumbs and frying it, I simmer the breaded chicken in a tomatoey sauce seasoned with garlic, oregano and basil. A sprinkling of cheeses gives it a fast final touch.

—**BOBBY TAYLOR** LAPORTE, INDIANA

Italian Chicken

PREP: 10 MIN. ■ COOK: 30 MIN. ■ YIELD: 4 SERVINGS

- 1 egg
- 1 tablespoon plus 1/4 cup water, *divided*
- 1/2 cup seasoned bread crumbs
- 1 broiler/fryer chicken (2 to 3 pounds), cut up
- 2 tablespoons canola oil
- 1 can (10-3/4 ounces) condensed tomato soup, undiluted

- 1/4 cup chopped onion
- 1/2 teaspoon garlic powder
- 1/2 teaspoon dried basil
- 1/2 teaspoon dried oregano
- 1 cup (4 ounces) shredded part-skim mozzarella cheese

Shredded Parmesan cheese

To make seasoned bread crumbs, **break slices of dried bread** into pieces and process until fine. **Then season the crumbs** with dried spices, grated cheese, salt and paprika. Start with small amounts of seasonings and add more as needed.

OPEN-FACED CHICKEN AVOCADO BURGERS

A creamy avocado spread and thick slices of fresh mozzarella and tomato dress up these chicken patties. They're wonderful with buttered boiled potatoes or a salad.

—LISA HUNDLEY ABERDEEN, NORTH CAROLINA

Open-Faced Chicken Avocado Burgers

PREP: 30 MIN. ■ **COOK:** 15 MIN.
YIELD: 4 SERVINGS PLUS 1/4 CUP LEFTOVER SPREAD.

1 tablespoon lemon juice	1/4 teaspoon salt
1/4 teaspoon Worcestershire sauce	1 pound ground chicken
1/2 medium ripe avocado, peeled	4 tablespoons olive oil, *divided*
1/2 cup mayonnaise	1/2 pound fresh mozzarella cheese, cut into 4 slices
1/4 cup sour cream	4 slices Italian bread (3/4 inch thick)
4 green onions, coarsely chopped	2 cups fresh arugula *or* baby spinach
1/2 teaspoon salt	
1/2 teaspoon cayenne pepper	8 slices tomato
BURGERS:	1/4 teaspoon dried basil
1/4 cup shredded Parmesan cheese	1/4 teaspoon pepper
2 tablespoons prepared pesto	
3 garlic cloves, minced	

■ In a blender, combine the first eight ingredients; cover and process until smooth. Chill until serving. For burgers, in a small bowl, combine the Parmesan cheese, pesto, garlic and salt. Crumble chicken over mixture and mix well. Shape into four patties.

■ In a large skillet over medium heat, cook burgers in 2 tablespoons oil for 5-7 minutes on each side or until a thermometer reads 165° and juices run clear. Top with cheese; cover and cook 1 minute longer.

■ Meanwhile, brush bread with remaining oil; place on a baking sheet. Broil 3-4 in. from the heat for 1-2 minutes on each side or until toasted.

■ Spread each slice of toast with 2 tablespoons avocado spread (refrigerate remaining spread for another use). Top with arugula, a burger and sliced tomato. Sprinkle with basil and pepper.

This is one of my favorite meals my mom used to make. Traditionally, it's made with veal, but I created my own version with chicken since it's a little easier to find.

—KRISTIN KOSSAK
BOZEMAN, MONTANA

CHICKEN SALTIMBOCCA

Chicken Saltimbocca

PREP: 25 MIN. ■ COOK: 20 MIN. ■ YIELD: 8 SERVINGS

2 medium onions, chopped	1/2 teaspoon salt
2 tablespoons butter	1/4 teaspoon pepper
2 cups uncooked long grain rice	2 tablespoons olive oil
4 cups chicken broth	1/2 cup white wine
8 boneless skinless chicken breast halves (4 ounces *each*)	1/4 cup sour cream
4 thin slices prosciutto *or* deli ham, halved	1/2 teaspoon sugar
16 fresh sage leaves	1 teaspoon minced fresh sage

■ In a large saucepan, saute onions in butter until tender. Add rice and stir to coat. Stir in broth and bring to a boil. Reduce heat; cover and simmer for 15-20 minutes or until tender. Fluff with a fork.

■ Meanwhile, cut a slit lengthwise through the thickest part of each chicken breast; fill with prosciutto and two sage leaves. Sprinkle with salt and pepper.

■ In a large skillet over medium heat, brown chicken in oil in batches for 1-2 minutes on each side; return all to the pan. Reduce heat to low. Cover and cook for 8-10 minutes or until a thermometer reads 170°. Remove and keep warm.

■ Add the white wine to the pan. Bring to a boil. Reduce heat; simmer, uncovered, for 2-3 minutes or until slightly reduced. Stir in the sour cream, sugar and minced sage; heat through (do not boil). Serve with chicken and rice.

Penne Gorgonzola With Chicken

The winner of America's-Best-Loved-Recipe Contest, my rich pasta dish is a snap to throw together for a weeknight meal.

—GEORGE SCHROEDER
PORT MURRAY, NEW JERSEY

PREP/TOTAL TIME: 30 MIN.
YIELD: 8 SERVINGS

1 package (16 ounces) penne pasta
1 pound boneless skinless chicken breasts, cut into 1/2-inch pieces
1 tablespoon olive oil
1 large garlic clove, minced
1/4 cup white wine
1 cup heavy whipping cream
1/4 cup chicken broth
2 cups (8 ounces) crumbled Gorgonzola cheese
6 to 8 fresh sage leaves, thinly sliced
Salt and pepper to taste
Grated Parmigiano-Reggiano cheese and minced fresh parsley

■ Cook pasta according to package directions. Meanwhile, in a large skillet over medium heat, brown chicken in oil on all sides. Add garlic; cook 1 minute longer. Add wine, stirring to loosen browned bits from pan.

■ Add cream and broth; cook until sauce is slightly thickened and chicken is no longer pink. Stir in the Gorgonzola cheese, sage, salt and pepper; cook just until cheese is melted.

■ Drain pasta; toss with sauce. Sprinkle with Parmigiano-Reggiano cheese and parsley.

Last year, I decided to grow basil, sage and thyme. The scent of sage is very enticing to me, so I included it in this recipe. The rest just happened.

—LORRAINE CALAND
SHUNIAH, ONTARIO

PROSCIUTTO CHICKEN IN WINE SAUCE

Prosciutto Chicken in Wine Sauce

PREP: 25 MIN. ■ **COOK:** 30 MIN. ■ **YIELD:** 6 SERVINGS

1 broiler/fryer chicken (3 pounds), cut up and skin removed

1/2 teaspoon salt

1/4 teaspoon pepper

1 tablespoon olive oil

1 tablespoon butter

1 cup white wine *or* reduced-sodium chicken broth

4 thin slices prosciutto *or* deli ham, chopped

1 shallot, chopped

1 tablespoon fresh sage *or* 1 teaspoon dried sage leaves

1 garlic clove, minced

■ Sprinkle the chicken with salt and pepper. In a large nonstick skillet coated with cooking spray, brown the chicken on all sides in the olive oil and butter.

■ Add the remaining ingredients, stirring to loosen browned bits. Bring to a boil. Reduce heat; cover and simmer for 20-25 minutes or until chicken juices run clear. Remove chicken and keep warm. Bring sauce to a boil; cook for 10-12 minutes or until liquid is reduced to 3/4 cup. Serve with chicken.

➤➤ **NUTRITION FACTS:** 3 ounces cooked chicken with 2 tablespoons sauce equals 231 calories, 11 g fat (4 g saturated fat), 87 mg cholesterol, 456 mg sodium, 2 g carbohydrate, trace fiber, 27 g protein. **DIABETIC EXCHANGES:** 4 lean meat, 1 fat.

Spicy Chicken Lettuce Wraps

PREP/TOTAL TIME: 30 MIN.
YIELD: 4 SERVINGS

1 pound chicken tenderloins, cut into 1/2-inch pieces

1/8 teaspoon pepper

2 tablespoons canola oil, *divided*

1 medium onion, finely chopped

1 small green pepper, finely chopped

1 small sweet red pepper, finely chopped

1 can (8 ounces) sliced water chestnuts, drained and finely chopped

1 can (4 ounces) mushroom stems and pieces, drained and finely chopped

2 garlic cloves, minced

1/3 cup stir-fry sauce

1 teaspoon reduced-sodium soy sauce

8 Bibb *or* Boston lettuce leaves

1/4 cup salted peanuts

2 teaspoons minced fresh cilantro

■ Sprinkle chicken with pepper. In a large skillet or wok, stir-fry chicken in 1 tablespoon oil until no longer pink. Remove and set aside.

■ Stir-fry onion and peppers in remaining oil for 5 minutes. Add the water chestnuts, mushrooms and garlic; stir-fry 2-3 minutes longer or until vegetables are crisp-tender. Add stir-fry sauce and soy sauce. Stir in chicken; heat through.

■ Place 1/2 cup chicken mixture on each lettuce leaf; sprinkle each with 1-1/2 teaspoons peanuts and 1/4 teaspoon cilantro. Fold the lettuce over the filling.

This is one of my go-to meals when I want a fun and colorful dinner. I love the spicy Asian flavors against the cool lettuce and the added crunch of peanuts and water chestnuts. On weekends I make a little extra so I can take the leftovers to work during the week.

—BRITTANY ALLYN NASHVILLE, TENNESSEE

CITRUS CHICKEN WITH PEPPERS

- Prepare rice according to package directions. Meanwhile, in a large skillet over medium heat, cook chicken in oil for 4-5 minutes on each side or until a thermometer reads 170°. Remove and keep warm.

- In the same skillet, saute peppers until tender. In a small bowl, combine the cornstarch, orange juice, water and lime juice until smooth; stir in the honey, salt, paprika and pepper. Stir into the pan. Bring to a boil; cook and stir for 2 minutes or until thickened.

- Return chicken to the pan; heat through. Serve with rice. Sprinkle with basil if desired.

➡ **NUTRITION FACTS:** 1 chicken breast half with peppers and 1/2 cup rice equals 330 calories, 7 g fat (1 g saturated fat), 63 mg cholesterol, 206 mg sodium, 41 g carbohydrate, 2 g fiber, 26 g protein. **DIABETIC EXCHANGES:** 3 starch, 3 lean meat, 1/2 fat.

This dish is so bright, attractive and healthy. I tried a similar recipe, but the addition of citrus and honey makes the chicken taste so much better. The big flavor makes me feel as if I'm eating something higher in calories.

—**MARY WILHELM** SPARTA, WISCONSIN

Citrus Chicken with Peppers

PREP/TOTAL TIME: 30 MIN. ■ **YIELD:** 4 SERVINGS

1 cup uncooked instant brown rice

4 boneless skinless chicken breast halves (4 ounces *each*)

1 tablespoon canola oil

1 medium sweet orange pepper, sliced

1 medium sweet red pepper, sliced

1 tablespoon cornstarch

1/3 cup orange juice

2 tablespoons water

2 tablespoons lime juice

2 tablespoons honey

1/4 teaspoon salt

1/4 teaspoon paprika

Dash pepper

Minced fresh basil, optional

To liquefy crystallized honey, **place the jar in warm water** and stir until the crystals dissolve. Or try to **microwave honey** on high in a microwave-safe container, stirring every 30 seconds until the crystals dissolve.

With their creamy filling and delightfully crispy crust, these elegant entrees are easy enough for weeknights, yet special enough for company, too.

—TASTE OF HOME TEST KITCHEN

SPINACH-STUFFED CHICKEN POCKETS

Spinach-Stuffed Chicken Pockets

PREP/TOTAL TIME: 30 MIN. ■ YIELD: 4 SERVINGS

4	cups fresh baby spinach
1	garlic clove, minced
2	teaspoons plus 1/4 cup olive oil, *divided*
1/2	cup garlic-herb cheese spread
2/3	cup plus 1/4 cup seasoned bread crumbs, *divided*

1/2	teaspoon salt, *divided*
4	boneless skinless chicken breast halves (5 ounces *each*)
1	egg, beaten
1/4	teaspoon pepper

■ In a large skillet, saute spinach and garlic in 2 teaspoons oil until spinach is wilted. Remove from the heat. Stir in the cheese spread, 2/3 cup bread crumbs and 1/4 teaspoon salt. Cut a pocket in the thickest part of each chicken breast; fill with spinach mixture. Secure with toothpicks.

■ Place egg in a shallow bowl. In another shallow bowl, combine the pepper and remaining bread crumbs and salt. Dip chicken in egg, then coat with bread crumb mixture.

■ In a large skillet over medium heat, cook chicken in remaining oil for 6-8 minutes on each side or until a thermometer reads 170°. Discard toothpicks before serving.

Cran-Apple Turkey Skillet

This quick and easy meal has such wide appeal that it will become one of your favorite recipes.

—LISA RENSHAW
KANSAS CITY, MISSOURI

PREP/TOTAL TIME: 20 MIN.
YIELD: 6 SERVINGS

2	medium apples, peeled and thinly sliced
3/4	cup apple cider *or* unsweetened apple juice
3/4	cup reduced-sodium chicken broth
1/3	cup dried cranberries
1/8	teaspoon ground nutmeg
3	cups cubed cooked turkey breast
1	package (6 ounces) corn bread stuffing mix

■ In a large skillet, combine the apples, apple cider, broth, cranberries and nutmeg. Bring to a boil. Reduce heat; cover and simmer for 4-5 minutes or until apples are tender, stirring occasionally.

■ Stir in turkey and stuffing mix. Cover and cook for 2-3 minutes or until heated through.

➤➤ **NUTRITION FACTS:** 1 cup equals 267 calories, 2 g fat (trace saturated fat), 60 mg cholesterol, 630 mg sodium, 36 g carbohydrate, 2 g fiber, 25 g protein. **DIABETIC EXCHANGES:** 3 lean meat, 1 starch, 1 fruit.

Pork

141

134

136

Pork chops, tenderloin, stir-fries and pasta dishes are just a sampling of the tasty recipes in this chapter that feature the succulent flavor of pork, ham or sausage. Shared by other family cooks, **these stovetop suppers are ready fast** to make mealtime easy on hurried weeknights!

CHERRY-STUFFED PORK CHOPS

Have a stand-out meal in about an hour with this delicious recipe. Filled with a flavorful stuffing made with dried cherries and aromatics, these hearty pork chops are sure to impress!

—TASTE of HOME TEST KITCHEN

Cherry-Stuffed Pork Chops

PREP: 35 MIN. ■ **COOK:** 20 MIN. ■ **YIELD:** 4 SERVINGS

1/4   cup dried cherries

2   tablespoons water

3   tablespoons chopped onion

2   tablespoons chopped celery

1   tablespoon shredded carrot

2   teaspoons dried parsley flakes

1   tablespoon butter

3/4   cup sage stuffing mix

1/3   cup reduced-sodium chicken broth

4   boneless pork loin chops (1 inch thick and 6 ounces *each*)

1/4   teaspoon pepper

2   tablespoons vegetable oil

GRAVY:

2   tablespoons all-purpose flour

1/4   teaspoon dried rosemary, crushed

1/8   teaspoon salt

3/4   cup plus 2 tablespoons reduced-sodium chicken broth

1/4   cup heavy whipping cream

- In a small saucepan, bring cherries and water to a boil. Remove from the heat; set aside (do not drain).

- In a small skillet, saute the onion, celery, carrot and parsley in butter until tender. Stir in the stuffing mix, broth and cherries. Remove from the heat; cover and let stand for 5 minutes or until moisture is absorbed.

- Cut a deep slit in each pork chop, forming a pocket. Stuff about 1/4 cup cherry mixture into each chop; secure with toothpicks. Sprinkle with pepper. In a large skillet, cook chops in oil for 8-10 minutes on each side until pork is no longer pink and a meat thermometer reads 160°. Remove and keep warm.

- Add flour, rosemary and salt to the pan juices; stir until blended. Gradually stir in broth and cream. Bring to a boil; cook and stir for 2 minutes or until thickened. Serve with pork chops.

PORK CHOPS CREOLE

This recipe is one of my family's favorites, and it usually becomes a favorite of whoever tries it. It's so easy to make. You can't beat a one-skillet dish!

—AMY GROSS SWANTON, OHIO

Pork Chops Creole

PREP: 25 MIN. ■ COOK: 15 MIN. ■ YIELD: 8 SERVINGS

- 8   boneless pork loin chops (3/4 inch thick and 6 ounces *each*)
- 4   teaspoons canola oil
- 2   large onions, sliced
- 1   medium green pepper, cut into strips
- 1   medium sweet yellow pepper, cut into strips
- 1   can (10-3/4 ounces) condensed tomato soup, undiluted
- 2/3   cup water
- 1   teaspoon Creole seasoning
- 1/2   teaspoon pepper
- 1/4   teaspoon salt
  Hot cooked rice, optional

- ■ In a large skillet, brown the pork chops in oil on both sides in batches. Set aside and keep warm. In the same skillet, saute the onions, green pepper and yellow pepper until tender.

- ■ Return pork chops to the skillet. Combine the soup, water, Creole seasoning, pepper and salt; pour over chops. Bring to a boil. Reduce heat; cover and simmer for 12-14 minutes or until the meat is tender.

- ■ Serve immediately with rice if desired, or cool before placing in a freezer container. Cover and freeze for up to 3 months.

- ■ **TO USE FROZEN PORK CHOPS:** Thaw in the refrigerator overnight. Place in a skillet; bring to a boil. Reduce heat; cover and simmer for 8-12 minutes or until a thermometer reads 165°.

EDITOR'S NOTE: The following spices may be substituted for 1 teaspoon Creole seasoning: 1/4 teaspoon *each* salt, garlic powder and paprika; and a pinch *each* of dried thyme, ground cumin and cayenne pepper.

➡ NUTRITION FACTS: 1 pork chop with 1/2 cup sauce mixture (calculated without rice) equals 221 calories, 9 g fat (3 g saturated fat), 54 mg cholesterol, 412 mg sodium, 11 g carbohydrate, 1 g fiber, 23 g protein. DIABETIC EXCHANGES: 3 lean meat, 1 vegetable, 1 fat, 1/2 starch.

I absolutely love this creamy and cheesy recipe. I serve it with a side salad and rolls to make a complete meal without much fuss.

—CINDI BAUER
MARSHFIELD, WISCONSIN

PASTA CARBONARA

Pasta Carbonara

PREP/TOTAL TIME: 30 MIN. ■ **YIELD:** 4 SERVINGS

2-1/2 cups uncooked mostaccioli
8 bacon strips, diced
1 jar (4-1/2 ounces) whole mushrooms, drained
3/4 cup half-and-half cream
1/3 cup butter, cubed
1 teaspoon dried parsley flakes
1 teaspoon minced garlic
6 to 8 drops hot pepper sauce
1/2 teaspoon salt, optional
1/3 cup grated Parmesan cheese
1/4 cup sliced green onions

■ Cook mostaccioli according to package directions.

■ Meanwhile, in a large skillet, cook bacon over medium heat until crisp. Using a slotted spoon, remove to paper towels to drain. Brown mushrooms in drippings; remove to paper towels. Drain drippings from pan.

■ Add the cream, butter, parsley, garlic, pepper sauce and salt if desired to the skillet; cook and stir over medium heat until butter is melted. Drain mostaccioli; add to cream mixture. Stir in the bacon, mushrooms and cheese; heat through. Remove from the heat. Sprinkle with green onions.

Ham Fried Rice

My husband and I lived in Japan for a few years and came to love the country's traditional dishes. This one captures Asian flavor better than any other recipes I've tried.
—GRACE CLARK HARLINGEN, TEXAS

PREP/TOTAL TIME: 25 MIN.
YIELD: 5 SERVINGS

4-1/2 teaspoons olive oil
2 eggs, lightly beaten
1/4 cup chopped onion
1/2 cup chopped celery
2 cups cooked long grain rice
1-1/2 cups cubed fully cooked ham (3/4-inch cubes)
3/4 cup frozen peas
3/4 cup frozen corn
1 tablespoon soy sauce

■ In a large skillet over medium-high heat, heat 2-1/4 teaspoons of oil. Pour eggs into skillet. As eggs set, lift edges, letting uncooked portion flow underneath. Remove eggs to a plate; set aside.

■ In the same skillet, saute onion and celery in remaining oil until crisp-tender. Reduce heat. Add rice and ham; heat through. Stir in peas and corn; heat through.

■ Meanwhile, chop egg into small pieces; gently fold into the rice mixture. Drizzle with soy sauce.

In this meal, milk and cheese make a creamy sauce for macaroni, Italian sausage and broccoli. A dish your family is sure to love!

—MARGIE HAEN
MENOMONEE FALLS, WISCONSIN

SAUSAGE MACARONI SUPPER

Sausage Macaroni Supper

PREP/TOTAL TIME: 25 MIN. ■ YIELD: 6 SERVINGS

2 cups uncooked elbow macaroni

1 pound bulk Italian sausage

1 cup chopped onion

2 teaspoons canola oil

1 can (11 ounces) condensed cream of tomato bisque soup, undiluted

1/2 cup 2% milk

1/2 cup shredded Parmesan cheese

2 teaspoons Italian seasoning

4 cups frozen broccoli florets, thawed

■ Cook macaroni according to package directions. Meanwhile, in a Dutch oven, cook sausage and onion over medium heat in oil until meat is no longer pink; drain.

■ Stir in the soup, milk, cheese and Italian seasoning. Bring to a boil; reduce heat. Drain macaroni; add to sausage mixture. Stir in broccoli; heat through.

Pork and Apple Supper

Our part of upstate New York was settled by the Dutch, and this recipe originated there. This is also apple country, with at least 10 major orchards within a 15-mile radius of our home.

—SHARON ROOT
WYNANTSKILL, NEW YORK

PREP: 10 MIN. ■ COOK: 2 HOURS
YIELD: 6-8 SERVINGS

1-1/2 pounds boneless pork, cubed

1 tablespoon canola oil

4 cups water

1 tablespoon chicken bouillon granules

1 teaspoon dried thyme

1/4 teaspoon pepper

1 bay leaf

10 to 12 small red potatoes (about 2 pounds), quartered

4 medium tart apples, peeled and cut into wedges

2 tablespoons cornstarch

2 tablespoons cold water

■ In a Dutch oven, brown pork in oil. Add water, bouillon, thyme, pepper and bay leaf; bring to a boil. Reduce heat; cover and simmer for 1-1/2 to 2 hours or until pork is tender.

■ Add potatoes; cover and cook for 15 minutes. Add apples; cover and cook for 10-12 minutes or until crisp-tender. Discard bay leaf.

■ Combine cornstarch and cold water until smooth; stir into pork mixture. Bring to a boil; cook and stir for 2 minutes or until thickened.

ITALIAN PORK SKILLET

Here's a recipe that uses ground pork and Italian-style ingredients for a pleasing, family-friendly meal. This is one unbelievable dish that will really satisfy on chilly evenings.

—TASTE OF HOME TEST KITCHEN

- Cook noodles according to package directions. Meanwhile, in a large skillet, cook the pork and onion over medium heat until meat is no longer pink. Add garlic; cook 1 minute longer. Drain.

- Add the marinara sauce, peppers, 1/2 cup broth, parsley, Worcestershire sauce, salt, sage, thyme and pepper. Bring to a boil. Reduce heat; simmer, uncovered, for 5 minutes.

- Combine cornstarch and remaining broth until smooth. Gradually stir into the skillet. Bring to a boil; cook and stir for 2 minutes or until thickened. Drain noodles; stir into the pork mixture. Remove from the heat; dollop with cheese.

Italian Pork Skillet

PREP/TOTAL TIME: 30 MIN. ■ YIELD: 4 SERVINGS

1-1/2 cups frozen home-style egg noodles

1 pound ground pork

1/2 cup chopped onion

1 teaspoon minced garlic

1 jar (15 ounces) marinara *or* spaghetti sauce

1 cup frozen pepper strips, thawed and chopped

3/4 cup beef broth, *divided*

1-1/2 teaspoons dried parsley flakes

1/2 teaspoon Worcestershire sauce

1/4 teaspoon salt

1/4 teaspoon rubbed sage

1/4 teaspoon dried thyme

1/4 teaspoon pepper

2 teaspoons cornstarch

1/2 cup ricotta cheese

Use **cornstarch to thicken foods** by dissolving it in a small amount of cold liquid before adding it to a hot mixture. To produce **a nicely thickened sauce,** cook and stir for a full 2 minutes after adding the cornstarch.

PORK IN ORANGE SAUCE

- Cook rice according to package directions.

- In a small bowl, combine the cornstarch, sugar, ginger and orange peel. Stir in orange juice and soy sauce until smooth; set aside.

- In a large skillet or wok, stir-fry the celery, carrots and cashews in oil until vegetables are crisp-tender.

- Stir cornstarch mixture and add to the pan. Bring to a boil; cook and stir for 1 minute or until thickened.

- Add pork; heat through. Serve with rice; top with noodles and onion.

Here's an Asian-inspired stir-fry with huge flavor from a winning combination of ginger, fresh orange juice and soy sauce. The dish pairs nicely with a cucumber salad in vinaigrette dressing.

—**MARLENE KROLL** CHICAGO, ILLINOIS

Pork in Orange Sauce

PREP/TOTAL TIME: 30 MIN. ■ YIELD: 4 SERVINGS

1	cup uncooked long grain rice	2	celery ribs, chopped
2	teaspoons cornstarch	2	medium carrots, thinly sliced
1	teaspoon sugar	1/4	cup lightly salted cashews
1	teaspoon ground ginger	1	tablespoon canola oil
1	teaspoon grated orange peel	2	cups cubed cooked pork
1	cup orange juice	1/2	cup chow mein noodles
1	teaspoon soy sauce	1	green onion, julienned

The French term **"julienne" means to cut foods into long, thin matchstick** shapes that are about **2 inches long and 1/8 inch thick.**

A friend gave me this recipe when she learned that I love muffuletta sandwiches. Very rich and filling, this easy skillet supper goes together quickly on a busy weeknight. Serve with some cheesy garlic bread.

—JAN HOLLINGSWORTH
HOUSTON, MISSISSIPPI

MUFFULETTA PASTA

Muffuletta Pasta

PREP/TOTAL TIME: 25 MIN. ■ **YIELD:** 8 SERVINGS

1 package (16 ounces) bow tie pasta

1 bunch green onions, chopped

2 teaspoons plus 1/4 cup butter, *divided*

1 tablespoon minced garlic

1 package (16 ounces) cubed fully cooked ham

1 jar (12.36 ounces) tapenade *or* ripe olive bruschetta topping, drained

1 package (3-1/2 ounces) sliced pepperoni

1 cup heavy whipping cream

2 cups (8 ounces) shredded Italian cheese blend

■ Cook pasta according to package directions. Meanwhile, in a large skillet, saute onions in 2 teaspoons butter until tender. Add garlic; cook 1 minute longer. Add the ham, tapenade and pepperoni; saute 2 minutes longer.

■ Cube the remaining butter; stir the butter and cream into skillet. Bring to a boil over medium heat. Reduce heat; simmer, uncovered, for 3 minutes.

■ Drain pasta; toss with ham mixture. Sprinkle with cheese.

His Favorite Ravioli

Turn refrigerated ravioli into a gourmet meal in no time! The rich flavors and interesting textures give this dish its character.

—CHRISTA RISPOLI
NEWFOUNDLAND, NEW JERSEY

PREP/TOTAL TIME: 30 MIN.
YIELD: 4 SERVINGS

2 packages (8.8 ounces *each*) refrigerated pumpkin ravioli *or* ravioli of your choice

1-2/3 cups sliced baby portobello mushrooms

1 small onion, finely chopped

4 thin slices prosciutto *or* deli ham, chopped

1 teaspoon olive oil

1/2 teaspoon minced fresh sage

2 cups half-and-half cream

1/2 cup frozen peas, thawed

2 tablespoons grated Parmigiano-Reggiano cheese

1/4 teaspoon salt

1/4 teaspoon pepper

■ Cook ravioli according to package directions. Meanwhile, in a large skillet, saute the mushrooms, onion and prosciutto in oil until vegetables are tender. Add sage; cook 1 minute longer. Stir in cream. Bring to a boil over medium heat. Reduce heat; simmer, uncovered, for 8-10 minutes or until slightly thickened.

■ Stir in the peas, cheese, salt and pepper; heat through. Drain ravioli; toss with sauce.

After dating my husband for a month, I wanted to impress him with my cooking. When I fixed this recipe, it convinced him I was "the one!" We've been married for several years.

—LINDY BONNELL
LOVELAND, COLORADO

PORK WITH ARTICHOKES AND CAPERS

Pork with Artichokes and Capers

PREP: 20 MIN. ■ COOK: 20 MIN. ■ YIELD: 4 SERVINGS

2 pork tenderloins (3/4 pound *each*)

1 tablespoon butter

1 green onion, finely chopped

1 can (14 ounces) water-packed artichoke hearts, rinsed, drained and chopped

1/4 cup reduced-sodium chicken broth

1 tablespoon capers, drained

1 teaspoon Dijon mustard

1 tablespoon minced fresh parsley

Lemon slices

■ Cut pork into 1-in. slices; flatten to 1/4-in. thickness. In a large nonstick skillet over medium heat, cook pork in butter in batches until juices run clear. Transfer to a serving platter and keep warm.

■ In the same skillet, cook and stir onion until tender. Stir in the artichokes, broth, capers and mustard; heat through. Serve over pork; sprinkle with parsley. Garnish with lemon.

➡ **NUTRITION FACTS:** 5 ounces cooked pork with 1/4 cup artichoke mixture equals 263 calories, 9 g fat (4 g saturated fat), 102 mg cholesterol, 479 mg sodium, 7 g carbohydrate, trace fiber, 37 g protein. **DIABETIC EXCHANGES:** 5 lean meat, 1 vegetable.

Capers are actually pickled flower buds. Look for them near the pickles and olives in the grocery store. **They're very salty and should always be rinsed** before using.

Potato Kielbasa Skillet

PREP/TOTAL TIME: 30 MIN.
YIELD: 4 SERVINGS

1 pound red potatoes, cubed

3 tablespoons water

3/4 pound smoked kielbasa *or* Polish sausage, cut into 1/4-inch slices

1/2 cup chopped onion

1 tablespoon olive oil

2 tablespoons brown sugar

2 tablespoons cider vinegar

1 tablespoon Dijon mustard

1/2 teaspoon dried thyme

1/4 teaspoon pepper

4 cups fresh baby spinach

5 bacon strips, cooked and crumbled

■ Place potatoes and water in a microwave-safe dish. Cover and microwave on high for 4 minutes or until tender; drain.

■ In a large skillet, saute kielbasa and onion in oil until onion is tender. Add potatoes; saute 3-5 minutes longer or until kielbasa and potatoes are lightly browned.

■ Combine the brown sugar, vinegar, mustard, thyme and pepper; stir into skillet. Bring to a boil. Reduce heat; simmer, uncovered, for 2-3 minutes or until heated through. Add spinach and bacon; cook and stir until spinach is wilted.

Smoky kielbasa steals the show in this hearty, home-style all-in-one meal. This is perfect on those cold, late fall and early winter nights when you crave something filling. If you have a larger family or want leftovers, it's easy to double the recipe, too.

—TASTE OF HOME TEST KITCHEN

SPICED PORK LOIN WITH PLUMS

- In a small bowl, combine the first six ingredients; rub over roast. In a Dutch oven, brown the roast in 1 tablespoon oil on all sides. Remove roast and set aside.

- In the same pan, cook onion in remaining oil over medium heat until tender. Add sugar; cook, stirring occasionally, 3-4 minutes longer. Add cranberry juice; bring to a boil. Cook until liquid is reduced by half.

- Return roast to the pan; add broth. Bring to a boil. Reduce heat; cover and simmer for 1-1/4 hours.

- Add plums; cover and simmer 30-45 minutes longer or until a thermometer reads 160°. Thicken pan juices if desired.

When plums are in season, I make this every other week. I originally used chicken, but I discovered it was better with pork. I fixed it for 70 people for my granddaughter's christening, and everyone wanted the recipe.

—**RUTH KOLARITSCH** TOWACO, NEW JERSEY

Spiced Pork Loin with Plums

PREP: 25 MIN. ■ **COOK:** 1-1/2 HOURS ■ **YIELD:** 8-10 SERVINGS

1 tablespoon ground cumin	2 tablespoons olive oil, *divided*
1 teaspoon ground cinnamon	1 large onion, chopped
1/2 teaspoon salt	2 tablespoons sugar
1/2 teaspoon ground allspice	1/2 cup cranberry juice
1/4 teaspoon pepper	1 cup chicken broth
1/4 teaspoon ground cloves	4 medium fresh plums, pitted and sliced
1 boneless whole pork loin roast (3 to 4 pounds)	

Plums are stone fruit (fruit that contains a pit) with smooth skin that are a little larger than apricots. Plums come in **a variety of colors** that range from green and yellow to purple, red and black.

Sauteed onions top this smoky ham steak flavored with apple juice and apple butter. If you have some on hand, use homemade apple butter for a personalized touch.

—TASTE OF HOME TEST KITCHEN

HARVEST HAM STEAK

Harvest Ham Steak

PREP/TOTAL TIME: 20 MIN. ■ **YIELD:** 4 SERVINGS

- 1 medium onion, halved and thinly sliced
- 1/4 teaspoon pepper
- 2 tablespoons butter
- 1 boneless fully cooked ham steak (1 pound)
- 1 teaspoon cornstarch
- 1/2 cup unsweetened apple juice
- 1/2 cup apple butter

■ In a large skillet, saute onion and pepper in butter until crisp-tender. Remove from pan and set aside. Cut ham steak into four pieces. In the same skillet, brown ham on both sides.

■ Meanwhile, combine cornstarch and apple juice until smooth; pour over ham. Bring to a boil; cook and stir 1-2 minutes or until slightly thickened. Reduce heat; spread apple butter over ham. Top with onion. Cover and simmer for 5-7 minutes or until heated through.

EDITOR'S NOTE: This recipe was tested with commercially prepared apple butter.

Pork Medallions With Asian Flair

When I became serious about losing weight and getting healthy, my kids missed the Chinese delivery that I used to order so often. I combined a few recipes to come up with this tasty winner.

—DIANNE LUEHRING
EDMOND, OKLAHOMA

PREP/TOTAL TIME: 25 MIN.
YIELD: 4 SERVINGS

- 1 pork tenderloin (1 pound), halved and thinly sliced
- 1 tablespoon sesame oil
- 1/4 cup sherry *or* reduced-sodium chicken broth
- 3 tablespoons reduced-sodium soy sauce
- 1 tablespoon brown sugar
- 1 tablespoon hoisin sauce
- 1 garlic clove, minced
- 1/8 teaspoon cayenne pepper

Hot cooked brown rice, optional

■ In a large nonstick skillet, saute pork in oil in batches until no longer pink. Remove and keep warm. Add the remaining ingredients (except rice) to the pan; cook and stir over medium heat for 3-4 minutes or until thickened. Return the pork to the pan; heat through. Serve with rice if desired.

➡➡ **NUTRITION FACTS:** 3 ounces cooked pork (calculated without rice) equals 202 calories, 7 g fat (2 g saturated fat), 63 mg cholesterol, 566 mg sodium, 6 g carbohydrate, trace fiber, 23 g protein. **DIABETIC EXCHANGES:** 3 lean meat, 1/2 starch, 1/2 fat.

I stir up a homemade sweet-and-sour sauce for this colorful combo of tender pork, crunchy vegetables and a little oh-so-tangy pineapple.

—ELEANOR DUNBAR
PEORIA, ILLINOIS

SWEET-AND-SOUR PORK

Sweet-and-Sour Pork

PREP: 15 MIN. + MARINATING ■ COOK: 20 MIN. ■ YIELD: 4 SERVINGS

2/3 cup packed brown sugar

2/3 cup cider vinegar

2/3 cup ketchup

2 teaspoons soy sauce

1 pound boneless pork loin, cut into 1-inch cubes

1 tablespoon canola oil

1 medium onion, cut into chunks

2 medium carrots, sliced

1 medium green pepper, cut into 1-inch pieces

1/2 teaspoon minced garlic

1/4 teaspoon ground ginger

1 can (8 ounces) pineapple chunks, drained

Hot cooked rice, optional

■ Combine the brown sugar, vinegar, ketchup and soy sauce. Pour half into a large resealable plastic bag; add pork. Seal bag and turn to coat; refrigerate for 30 minutes. Set remaining marinade aside.

■ Drain and discard marinade from pork. In a large skillet, cook pork in oil for 3 minutes. Add the onion, carrots, green pepper, garlic and ginger; saute until pork is no longer pink. Add reserved marinade. Bring to a boil; cook for 1 minute. Stir in the pineapple. Serve with rice if desired.

Hash Brown Pork Skillet

Here, we added potatoes and veggies to leftover pork tenderloin for an easy, creamy weeknight supper in minutes!
—TASTE OF HOME TEST KITCHEN

PREP/TOTAL TIME: 25 MIN.
YIELD: 6 SERVINGS

4 cups frozen O'Brien potatoes, thawed

1 cup chopped onion

1 cup chopped green pepper

2 tablespoons butter

2 cups cubed cooked pork

2 teaspoons chicken bouillon granules

1/4 teaspoon pepper

2 teaspoons all-purpose flour

1/2 cup milk

3/4 cup shredded cheddar cheese

■ In a large skillet, cook the potatoes, onion and green pepper in butter over medium heat until almost tender. Stir in the pork, bouillon and pepper; heat through.

■ In a small bowl, combine flour and milk until smooth; add to skillet. Cook on medium-low heat for 4-5 minutes or until mixture is thickened, stirring frequently.

■ Sprinkle with cheese. Remove from the heat; cover and let stand until cheese is melted.

POMEGRANATE PORK TENDERLOIN

Tender cubes of pork are paired with a flavorful sweet-tart pomegranate-juice pan sauce. For a weekday meal, try using a quick-cooking long grain and wild rice mix.

—ELIZABETH DUMONT BOULDER, COLORADO

Pomegranate Pork Tenderloin

PREP: 20 MIN. ■ **COOK:** 20 MIN. ■ **YIELD:** 4 SERVINGS

1/4	cup all-purpose flour	1	cup pomegranate juice
1/4	cup cornmeal	2	tablespoons sugar
2	teaspoons grated lemon peel	1	to 2 garlic cloves, minced
1-1/2	teaspoons salt, *divided*	1/4	teaspoon ground ginger
1/2	teaspoon pepper	1/8	teaspoon cayenne pepper
1	to 1-1/4 pounds pork tenderloin, cut into 2-inch pieces	2	tablespoons cornstarch
2	tablespoons olive oil	3	tablespoons cold water
1	cup reduced-sodium chicken broth	2	cups hot cooked wild rice

- In a large resealable plastic bag, combine the flour, cornmeal, lemon peel, 1 teaspoon salt and pepper. Add pork, a few pieces at a time, and shake to coat.

- In a large skillet, cook pork in oil for 5-7 minutes on each side or until a thermometer reads 160°. Remove and keep warm.

- In the same skillet, combine the broth, juice, sugar, garlic, ginger, cayenne and remaining salt. Bring to a boil. Reduce heat; simmer, uncovered, for 5 minutes.

- Combine cornstarch and water until smooth; gradually stir into the pan. Bring to a boil; cook and stir for 2 minutes or until thickened. Return pork to the pan and heat through. Serve with rice.

➡ **NUTRITION FACTS:** 4 ounces cooked pork with 1/2 cup sauce and 1/2 cup rice equals 374 calories, 11 g fat (2 g saturated fat), 63 mg cholesterol, 694 mg sodium, 41 g carbohydrate, 2 g fiber, 27 g protein. **DIABETIC EXCHANGES:** 3 lean meat, 2 starch, 1 fat, 1/2 fruit.

Keep pork tenderloin in the freezer for last-minute meals since it thaws and cooks quickly. **Thaw using the defrost cycle** of your microwave.

- Cook fettuccine according to package directions. Meanwhile, in a large skillet, saute onion in butter until tender. Add garlic; cook 1 minute longer. Add the ham, mushrooms if desired, oregano, basil, parsley and pepper flakes. Cook and stir for 4-5 minutes or until mushrooms are tender.

- Stir in spaghetti sauce. Bring to a boil; cook for 2 minutes. Remove from the heat; stir in cream. Drain fettuccine; toss with ham mixture.

Heavy whipping cream is a rich cream that **ranges from 36-40% butterfat** and doubles in volume when whipped. It's often labeled as either **heavy cream or whipping cream.**

HAM FETTUCCINE

Once you make this easy-to-fix recipe, you'll crave it all the time. The standout meal will win rave reviews from your family and friends. Be sure to give it a try!

—PATRICIA MOORE TOLEDO, OHIO

Ham Fettuccine

PREP/TOTAL TIME: 25 MIN. ■ **YIELD:** 6 SERVINGS

12	ounces uncooked fettuccine	1-1/4	teaspoons dried oregano
1/4	cup chopped onion	1-1/4	teaspoons dried basil
3	tablespoons butter	1-1/4	teaspoons dried parsley flakes
1	teaspoon minced garlic	1/2	teaspoon crushed red pepper flakes
3	cups cubed fully cooked ham	1	cup meatless spaghetti sauce
1/2	pound sliced fresh mushrooms, optional	3/4	cup heavy whipping cream

Peppy Parmesan Pasta

When my husband and I needed dinner in a hurry, we came up with this dish that gets spicy flavor from pepperoni. We like to use angel hair pasta because it cooks faster than other noodles.

—**DEBBIE HORST** PHOENIX, ARIZONA

PREP/TOTAL TIME: 10 MIN. ■ YIELD: 4 SERVINGS

8	ounces angel hair pasta	1/4	cup grated Parmesan cheese
1	large tomato, chopped	3	tablespoons olive oil
1	package (3 ounces) sliced pepperoni	1/2	teaspoon salt *or* salt-free seasoning blend, optional
1	can (2-1/4 ounces) sliced ripe olives, drained	1/4	teaspoon garlic powder

■ Cook pasta according to package directions. Meanwhile, in a serving bowl, combine the tomato, pepperoni, olives, cheese, oil, salt if desired and garlic powder. Drain pasta; add to the tomato mixture and toss to coat.

Skillet Franks

Kids will have as much fun helping make this all-in-one supper as they will have eating it! The noodles cook right in the skillet and it's been a super-easy standby at my home for decades.

—**RUTH NOLAND** SAN JOSE, CALIFORNIA

PREP/TOTAL TIME: 30 MIN. ■ YIELD: 6 SERVINGS

1	medium green pepper, julienned	1	cup tomato juice
1/2	cup chopped onion	1	teaspoon salt
2	tablespoons butter	1/2	teaspoon dried marjoram
1	pound hot dogs, halved lengthwise and cut into bite-size pieces	1/2	teaspoon minced garlic
		1/4	teaspoon dried basil
1	can (14-1/2 ounces) diced tomatoes, undrained	1/8	teaspoon pepper
		3	cups uncooked egg noodles

■ In a large skillet, saute green pepper and onion in butter until tender. Add the hot dogs, tomatoes, tomato juice, salt, marjoram, garlic, basil and pepper. Bring to a boil; add the noodles. Reduce heat; cover and simmer for 10-12 minutes or until noodles are tender.

Harvest Stew

This special stew is packed with pork and all of the fabulous flavors of an autumn harvest. Your family will surely ask for seconds!

—**TASTE OF HOME TEST KITCHEN**

PREP: 20 MIN. ■ COOK: 40 MIN.
YIELD: 6 SERVINGS

1-1/2	pounds boneless pork loin roast, cut into 1-inch cubes
1	medium onion, chopped
2	tablespoons butter
2	garlic cloves, minced
3	cups chicken broth
3/4	teaspoon salt
1/4	teaspoon dried rosemary, crushed
1/4	teaspoon rubbed sage
1	bay leaf
1	medium butternut squash, peeled and cubed (3 cups)
2	medium apples, peeled and cubed

■ In a large saucepan, cook pork and onion in butter until meat is no longer pink. Add garlic; cook 1 minute longer. Drain. Add the broth, salt, rosemary, sage and bay leaf. Cover and simmer for 20 minutes.

■ Stir in squash and apples; simmer, uncovered, for 20 minutes or until the squash and apples are tender. Discard the bay leaf.

Fish & Seafood

154 153 150

Reel in shrimp, scallops and fish for these tasty stovetop entrees that are a welcome break from heavier meat-and-potatoes fare. These **light meals are quick and easy to prepare,** and many come with Nutrition Facts to help those who are closely watching what they eat.

TILAPIA WITH SAUTEED SPINACH

- Place egg in a shallow bowl. In another shallow bowl, combine the bread crumbs, Italian seasoning, 1/2 teaspoon salt, garlic powder and paprika. Dip fillets in egg, then bread crumb mixture.

- In a large skillet, cook fillets in 3 tablespoons oil over medium heat for 4-5 minutes on each side or until golden brown and the fish flakes easily with a fork. Remove and keep warm.

- In the same skillet, saute onion in remaining oil until tender. Add garlic; cook 1 minute longer. Stir in the spinach, pepper flakes, pepper and remaining salt. Cook and stir for 3-4 minutes or until spinach is wilted. Serve with fillets; sprinkle with walnuts.

You'll love this delicious restaurant-quality meal fit for guests that's also a healthy choice for those watching calories. Plus, since it's all cooked in the same skillet, cleanup won't be a chore at all.

—TASTE of HOME TEST KITCHEN

Tilapia with Sauteed Spinach

PREP: 20 MIN. ■ COOK: 15 MIN. ■ YIELD: 4 SERVINGS

1	egg, lightly beaten	1	small onion, chopped
1/2	cup dry bread crumbs	1	garlic clove, minced
1	teaspoon Italian seasoning	5	cups fresh baby spinach
3/4	teaspoon salt, *divided*	1/8	teaspoon crushed red pepper flakes
1/4	teaspoon garlic powder	1/8	teaspoon pepper
1/4	teaspoon paprika	1/4	cup chopped walnuts, toasted
4	tilapia fillets (6 ounces *each*)		
4	tablespoons olive oil, *divided*		

To check the doneness of fish fillets, **insert a fork at an angle** into the thickest part of the fish and gently part the meat. **When it is opaque and flakes** into sections, it is cooked completely.

PAELLA

A big pan of paella full of tasty chorizo and other flavorful ingredients is the perfect choice when cooking for a crowd. All you need to round out the meal is fresh bread and a green salad.

—**JANE MONTGOMERY** HILLIARD, OHIO

Paella

PREP: 55 MIN. ■ **COOK:** 35 MIN. ■ **YIELD:** 24 SERVINGS (1 CUP EACH)

3	pounds uncooked skinless turkey breast, cubed
4	pounds uncooked chorizo, cut into 1-1/2-inch pieces *or* bulk spicy pork sausage
3	tablespoons olive oil
2	medium onions, chopped
1	medium sweet red pepper, chopped
4	garlic cloves, minced
1/2	teaspoon cayenne pepper
2	cups tomato puree
1	cup white wine *or* chicken broth

5	cups water
4	cups uncooked long grain rice
3-1/2	cups chicken broth
2	teaspoons salt
1	teaspoon dried thyme
3/4	teaspoon saffron threads *or* 2 teaspoons ground turmeric
1	bay leaf
2	pounds uncooked medium shrimp, peeled and deveined
3/4	cup pitted Greek olives
1/2	cup minced fresh parsley

■ In a large skillet, cook turkey and chorizo in oil in batches until browned. Remove with a slotted spoon and keep warm.

■ In the same skillet, saute onions and red pepper until tender. Add garlic and cayenne; cook 1 minute longer. Stir in tomato puree and wine. Bring to a boil; cook and stir for 2 minutes or until thickened.

■ Transfer to a stockpot. Stir in the water, rice, broth, salt, thyme, saffron, bay leaf, turkey and chorizo. Bring to a boil. Reduce heat; cover and simmer for 20 minutes or until rice is tender.

■ Add shrimp; cook for 2-3 minutes or until shrimp turn pink. Remove from the heat; discard bay leaf. Stir in olives and parsley.

Saffron is a rare and expensive herb with a pungent flavor made from the **stigma of the saffron flower.** It is hand-harvested, and **it takes at least 4,000 stigmas** to produce only 1 ounce of saffron.

This savory recipe takes just minutes. If it's cheaper, I'll sometimes thaw out frozen tilapia fillets in the fridge overnight instead of using fresh fillets.

—MICHELLE WILLIAMS
FORT WORTH, TEXAS

TILAPIA WRAPS

Tilapia Wraps

PREP/TOTAL TIME: 15 MIN. ■ YIELD: 6 SERVINGS

- 3/4 cup salsa
- 1 can (4 ounces) chopped green chilies
- 6 tilapia fillets (6 ounces *each*)
- 2 tablespoons olive oil
- 2 tablespoons steak seasoning
- 12 flour tortillas (6 inches), warmed
- 3/4 cup shredded cheddar cheese

- In a small bowl, combine salsa and chilies; set aside. Drizzle fillets with oil; sprinkle both sides with steak seasoning. Transfer to a large skillet. Cook, uncovered, over medium heat for 5-8 minutes or until the fish flakes easily with a fork. Add the reserved salsa mixture, stirring gently.

- Spoon a heaping 1/3 cupful onto each tortilla; top with cheese. Roll up; serve immediately.

EDITOR'S NOTE: This recipe was tested with McCormick's Montreal Steak Seasoning. Look for it in the spice aisle.

Easy Crab Lo Mein

I came up with this one night when I had some leftover spaghetti that I needed to use.

—LAURA MRYYAN TOPEKA, KANSAS

PREP/TOTAL TIME: 25 MIN.
YIELD: 6 SERVINGS

- 4 ounces uncooked angel hair pasta *or* thin spaghetti
- 1 medium onion, thinly sliced
- 1 medium green pepper, cut into 1-inch strips
- 1 package (9 ounces) frozen broccoli cuts, thawed
- 1/4 cup sliced fresh mushrooms
- 2 tablespoons canola oil
- 1 tablespoon cornstarch
- 1-1/4 cups chicken broth
- 1/4 cup water
- 1/4 cup soy sauce
- 12 ounces imitation crabmeat, cut into 1-inch pieces

- Cook pasta according to package directions. Meanwhile, in a large skillet or wok, stir-fry the onion, green pepper, broccoli and mushrooms in oil for 3-4 minutes or until crisp-tender.

- In a small bowl, combine the cornstarch, broth, water and soy sauce until smooth. Gradually stir into skillet. Bring to a boil; cook and stir for 2 minutes or until thickened. Stir in crab; cook 2-3 minutes longer or until heated through. Drain pasta; toss with crab mixture.

Marinated in lime juice, these mouthwatering fish fillets are truly special, thanks to their delicate flavor and zippy Vera Cruz sauce.

—MIKE BASS
ALVIN, TEXAS

RED SNAPPER VERA CRUZ

Red Snapper Vera Cruz

PREP: 25 MIN. + CHILLING ■ **COOK:** 20 MIN. ■ **YIELD:** 4 **SERVINGS**

VERA CRUZ SAUCE:
- 1 medium onion, thinly sliced
- 2 tablespoons olive oil
- 3 garlic cloves, minced
- 3 large tomatoes, seeded and chopped
- 12 pitted green olives, cut in half
- 2 jalapeno peppers, seeded and cut into thin strips
- 2 tablespoons capers, drained
- 1 bay leaf
- 1/2 teaspoon salt
- 1/2 teaspoon dried oregano
- 1/4 teaspoon pepper

FISH:
- 4 red snapper fillets (8 ounces *each*)
- 2 tablespoons lime juice
- Salt and pepper to taste
- 1/2 cup all-purpose flour
- 2 eggs
- 1/4 cup milk
- 3 tablespoons butter
- 3 tablespoons olive oil

■ In a large skillet, saute onion in oil until onion is tender. Add garlic; cook 1 minute longer. Add the tomatoes, olives, jalapenos, capers, bay leaf, salt, oregano and pepper. Cook for 10 minutes or until sauce is reduced by half. Remove from the heat; discard bay leaf. Keep warm.

■ Sprinkle fillets with lime juice, salt and pepper. Cover and refrigerate for 15 minutes. Place flour in a shallow bowl. In another shallow bowl, whisk eggs and milk. Drain and discard lime juice. Coat fillets with flour, then dip in egg mixture.

■ In a large skillet, fry fillets in butter and oil for 8-10 minutes on each side or until fish flakes easily with a fork. Serve with sauce.

EDITOR'S NOTE: Wear disposable gloves when cutting hot peppers; the oils can burn skin. Avoid touching your face.

Favorite Jiffy Jambalaya

PREP/TOTAL TIME: 30 MIN.
YIELD: 4 SERVINGS

- 1 package (8 ounces) red beans and rice mix
- 1/2 pound smoked sausage, sliced
- 1/2 cup chopped onion
- 1 tablespoon olive oil
- 1/2 pound cooked medium shrimp, peeled and deveined
- 1 can (14-1/2 ounces) diced tomatoes, drained
- 1 teaspoon brown sugar
- 1/4 teaspoon Louisiana-style hot sauce, optional

■ Cook red beans and rice mix according to package directions.

■ Meanwhile, in a large skillet, saute sausage and onion in oil until onion is tender. Add the shrimp, tomatoes, brown sugar and hot sauce if desired. Cook for 3-4 minutes or until heated through. Stir in rice mixture.

Shrimp in the shell
are available in various sizes and can range in color from gray or brown to pink or red. Fresh shrimp should have a **firm texture with a mild odor**.

Your family will love this hearty dish that comes together in a snap. This speedier version of the traditional Louisiana stew gets its heat and flavor from smoked sausage and hot sauce. A basic rice mix gets a quick makeover for a deliciously filling meal.

—TASTE OF HOME TEST KITCHEN

SHRIMP GUMBO

- In a Dutch oven over medium heat, cook and stir the flour and oil until caramel-colored, about 12 minutes (do not burn). Add the celery, green pepper and onion; cook and stir for 5-6 minutes or until tender. Stir in the broth, garlic, salt, pepper and cayenne; bring to a boil. Reduce the heat; cover and simmer for 30 minutes.

- Stir in the shrimp, okra, green onions and tomato. Return to a boil. Reduce heat; cover and simmer for 10 minutes or until shrimp turn pink. Stir in file powder. Serve with rice.

➤ **NUTRITION FACTS:** 1 cup gumbo (calculated without rice) equals 159 calories, 7 g fat (1 g saturated fat), 102 mg cholesterol, 681 mg sodium, 9 g carbohydrate, 2 g fiber, 15 g protein. **DIABETIC EXCHANGES:** 2 lean meat, 1 vegetable, 1 fat.

Mardi Gras just isn't the same if you don't have gumbo! Enjoy this authentic stew, well-seasoned with onion, peppers, garlic and cayenne, even if you're not from the bayou.

—JO ANN GRAHAM OVILLA, TEXAS

Shrimp Gumbo

PREP: 30 MIN. ■ **COOK:** 1 HOUR ■ **YIELD:** 11 SERVINGS

1/4 cup all-purpose flour	1/2 teaspoon cayenne pepper
1/4 cup canola oil	2 pounds uncooked large shrimp, peeled and deveined
3 celery ribs, chopped	
1 medium green pepper, chopped	1 package (16 ounces) frozen sliced okra
1 medium onion, chopped	
1 carton (32 ounces) chicken broth	4 green onions, sliced
	1 medium tomato, chopped
3 garlic cloves, minced	1-1/2 teaspoons gumbo file powder
1 teaspoon salt	Hot cooked rice
1 teaspoon pepper	

Gumbo file powder is used to thicken and flavor Creole recipes. Instead, you can **mix 2 tablespoons each cornstarch and cold water** until smooth. Slowly stir into the gumbo, bring to a boil, cook and stir 2 minutes until thickened.

My daughter loves this simple recipe. It's the only way she'll eat fish. To top it off, it's good for her!

—JEANNETTE BAYE
AGASSIZ,
BRITISH COLUMBIA

PEPPERED SOLE

Peppered Sole

PREP/TOTAL TIME: 25 MIN. ■ YIELD: 4 SERVINGS

2 cups sliced fresh mushrooms	1/4 teaspoon paprika
2 tablespoons butter	1/8 teaspoon cayenne pepper
2 garlic cloves, minced	1 medium tomato, chopped
4 sole fillets (4 ounces *each*)	2 green onions, thinly sliced
1/4 teaspoon lemon-pepper seasoning	

■ In a large skillet, saute mushrooms in butter until tender. Add garlic; saute 1 minute longer. Place fillets over mushrooms. Sprinkle with lemon pepper, paprika and cayenne.

■ Cover and cook over medium heat for 5-10 minutes or until fish flakes easily with a fork. Sprinkle with tomato and onions.

➤➤ **NUTRITION FACTS:** 1 serving equals 174 calories, 7 g fat (4 g saturated fat), 69 mg cholesterol, 166 mg sodium, 4 g carbohydrate, 1 g fiber, 23 g protein. **DIABETIC EXCHANGES:** 3 lean meat, 1-1/2 fat.

Salmon With Broccoli And Pasta

This dinner is meant to help you eat healthy while saving time cooking and cleaning. The recipe takes roughly 20 minutes from start to finish and is a breeze to clean up.

—LINDA HALONE
ROCHESTER, MINNESOTA

PREP/TOTAL TIME: 30 MIN.
YIELD: 6 SERVINGS

8 ounces uncooked whole wheat spaghetti

3-1/2 cups chopped fresh broccoli

6 salmon fillets (4 ounces *each*)

3/4 teaspoon seafood seasoning

2-1/2 cups chopped fresh tomatoes

1 package (7 ounces) mozzarella and Asiago cheese with roasted garlic

1/4 cup olive oil

1/2 teaspoon salt

1/4 teaspoon pepper

■ In a large saucepan, cook spaghetti according to package directions, adding broccoli during the last 5 minutes of cooking.

■ Meanwhile, sprinkle salmon with seafood seasoning. Cook in batches on an indoor grill for 5 minutes or until fish flakes easily with a fork.

■ Drain spaghetti and broccoli; transfer to a large bowl. Add the tomatoes, cheese, oil, salt and pepper; toss to coat. Serve with salmon.

Sesame Shrimp & Rice

A handful of convenience items and a flash in the skillet allow you to put a delightful, high-quality meal on the table in minutes.

—TASTE OF HOME TEST KITCHEN

PREP/TOTAL TIME: 10 MIN. ■ YIELD: 4 SERVINGS

1 package (8.8 ounces) ready-to-serve long grain rice

1 cup fresh *or* frozen snow peas, thawed

2 green onions, sliced

1 teaspoon canola oil

1 pound cooked medium shrimp, peeled and deveined

1 can (20 ounces) pineapple tidbits, drained

1 can (11 ounces) mandarin oranges, drained

1/4 cup sesame ginger salad dressing

2 tablespoons slivered almonds, toasted

■ Microwave rice according to package directions. Meanwhile, in a large skillet or wok, stir-fry snow peas and onions in oil for 1 minute. Add the shrimp, pineapple, oranges and salad dressing; cook until heated through and vegetables are crisp-tender.

■ Sprinkle with almonds. Serve with rice.

Healthy Shrimp Piccata Pasta

Want a quick, easy and tasty way to serve shrimp? A light and tangy sauce spiked with capers makes this pasta an instant classic.

—CAROLE BESS WHITE PORTLAND, OREGON

PREP/TOTAL TIME: 20 MIN. ■ YIELD: 4 SERVINGS

6 ounces uncooked spaghetti

2 shallots, chopped

1 tablespoon olive oil

1 pound uncooked medium shrimp, peeled and deveined

1 jar (3 ounces) capers, drained

3 tablespoons lemon juice

1/2 teaspoon garlic powder

■ Cook spaghetti according to package directions. Meanwhile, in a large nonstick skillet, saute shallots in oil until tender. Add the shrimp, capers, lemon juice and garlic powder; cook and stir for 5-6 minutes or until shrimp turn pink.

■ Drain spaghetti; toss with shrimp mixture.

➤➤ **NUTRITION FACTS:** 1-1/4 cups equals 293 calories, 5 g fat (1 g saturated fat), 168 mg cholesterol, 453 mg sodium, 37 g carbohydrate, 2 g fiber, 24 g protein. **DIABETIC EXCHANGES:** 3 lean meat, 2 starch, 1/2 fat.

Pasta Primavera With Shrimp

I added shrimp to a simple, easy primavera, and the result was a timely and fabulous dinner bursting with flavor in every bite.

—KIMBERLY WAGNER
CASTLE ROCK, COLORADO

PREP/TOTAL TIME: 30 MIN.
YIELD: 6 SERVINGS

1 package (16 ounces) linguine

1 pound uncooked medium shrimp, peeled and deveined

2 cups chopped fresh broccoli

1 cup sliced fresh carrots

1 cup fresh green beans, cut into 2-inch pieces

1 medium zucchini, cut into 1/4-inch slices

1 medium sweet red pepper, julienned

2 tablespoons all-purpose flour

1-1/4 cups heavy whipping cream

3/4 cup chicken broth

1/4 cup grated Parmesan cheese

3/4 teaspoon salt

1/2 teaspoon pepper

■ In a Dutch oven, cook linguine according to package directions, adding shrimp and vegetables during the last 4 minutes.

■ Meanwhile, in a small saucepan, combine the flour, cream and broth until smooth. Add the cheese, salt and pepper. Bring to a boil over medium heat; cook and stir for 2 minutes or until thickened.

■ Drain linguine mixture and return to the pan. Add cream sauce; toss to coat.

VEGGIE TUNA BURGERS

- In a large nonstick skillet coated with cooking spray, saute onion and garlic for 1 minute. Add the zucchini, yellow squash and carrots; saute until tender. Drain and cool to room temperature.

- In a large bowl, combine the egg, bread crumbs, tuna, salt and pepper. Add vegetable mixture. Shape into six 3-1/2-in. patties.

- Coat the same skillet again with cooking spray; cook the patties in butter for 3-5 minutes on each side or until lightly browned. Serve on buns with cheese, lettuce and tomato.

➡ **NUTRITION FACTS:** 1 burger equals 275 calories, 8 g fat (4 g saturated fat), 58 mg cholesterol, 643 mg sodium, 32 g carbohydrate, 3 g fiber, 20 g protein. **DIABETIC EXCHANGES:** 2 starch, 2 lean meat, 1 vegetable.

You don't have to be a health nut to enjoy the flavor of these moist and nutritious burgers. They're a delicious and easy way to get my children to eat their vegetables.

—**LAURA DAVIS** RUSTON, LOUISIANA

Veggie Tuna Burgers

PREP/TOTAL TIME: 30 MIN. ■ **YIELD:** 6 SERVINGS

1/4 cup finely chopped onion	1/4 teaspoon salt
1 garlic clove, minced	1/4 teaspoon pepper
1 cup *each* shredded zucchini, yellow summer squash and carrots	1 teaspoon butter
	6 hamburger buns, split
1 egg, lightly beaten	6 slices reduced-fat cheddar cheese
2 cups soft whole wheat bread crumbs	6 lettuce leaves
1 can (6 ounces) light water-packed tuna, drained and flaked	6 slices tomato

To freeze zucchini, steam shredded zucchini for 1 to 2 minutes or until translucent, then drain well. **Pack in measured amounts** into freezer containers. Cool, seal and freeze.

ASPARAGUS SCALLOP STIR-FRY

With the mild flavors of fresh asparagus, mushrooms, scallops and water chestnuts, this meal truly captures the essence of spring. To lighten the multidimensional flavor even more, use low sodium soy sauce.

—MARY ANN GRIFFIN BOWLING GREEN, KENTUCKY

Asparagus Scallop Stir-Fry

PREP/TOTAL TIME: 25 MIN. ■ YIELD: 4 SERVINGS

1 pound bay scallops	1/2 cup chopped celery
3 tablespoons cornstarch	2 tablespoons canola oil, *divided*
2 cups chicken broth	1 cup sliced fresh mushrooms
2 tablespoons soy sauce	1 can (8 ounces) sliced water chestnuts, drained
2 cups cut fresh asparagus (2-inch pieces)	1/4 cup slivered almonds
1/2 cup chopped onion	Hot cooked rice, optional

■ If scallops are large, cut in half and set aside. In a small bowl, combine the cornstarch, chicken broth and soy sauce until smooth; set aside.

■ In a large skillet, saute the asparagus, onion and celery in 1 tablespoon oil for 3 minutes. Add mushrooms and water chestnuts; stir-fry for 2-3 minutes or until crisp-tender. Remove vegetable mixture and set aside.

■ In the same skillet, stir-fry scallops in remaining oil for 2-3 minutes or until scallops are firm and opaque. Stir chicken broth mixture; add to pan. Bring to a boil; cook and stir for 2 minutes or until thickened. Add vegetables; heat through. Sprinkle with almonds. Serve with rice if desired.

A member of the bivalve mollusk family, **scallops are often found in two groups:** the sea scallop and the much smaller bay scallop. They come shucked, are **sold fresh or frozen** and range in color from pale beige to creamy pink.

I didn't want to hide the ocean freshness of the scallops I bought on the dock from a local fisherman, so I used simple but perfect ingredients to showcase them.

—JOAN CHURCHILL
DOVER,
NEW HAMPSHIRE

SCALLOPS IN SAGE CREAM

Scallops in Sage Cream

PREP/TOTAL TIME: 20 MIN. ■ YIELD: 4 SERVINGS

1-1/2 pounds sea scallops	1/2 cup chopped shallots
1/4 teaspoon salt	3/4 cup heavy whipping cream
1/8 teaspoon pepper	6 fresh sage leaves, thinly sliced
3 tablespoons olive oil, *divided*	Hot cooked pasta, optional

■ Sprinkle scallops with salt and pepper. In a large skillet, cook scallops in 2 tablespoons oil for 1-1/2 to 2 minutes on each side or until firm and opaque. Remove and keep warm.

■ In the same skillet, saute shallots in the remaining oil until tender. Add cream; bring to a boil. Cook and stir for 30 seconds or until slightly thickened.

■ Return scallops to the pan; heat through. Stir in sage. Serve with pasta if desired.

Cod & Vegetable Skillet

This one-dish meal combines lean protein with a colorful vegetable medley. A well-flavored sauce pulls it all together, creating a lovely weeknight dinner.

—TASTE OF HOME TEST KITCHEN

PREP/TOTAL TIME: 30 MIN.
YIELD: 4 SERVINGS

1/2 pound fresh green beans, trimmed

1 cup fresh baby carrots, cut in half lengthwise

1 medium onion, halved and sliced

3 tablespoons butter

1 tablespoon all-purpose flour

1/2 teaspoon dried thyme

1/2 teaspoon salt

1/4 teaspoon pepper

1 cup reduced-sodium chicken broth

1/4 cup white wine *or* reduced-sodium chicken broth

4 cod *or* haddock fillets (4 ounces *each*)

■ In a large skillet, saute the beans, carrots and onion in butter for 2 minutes. Stir in flour and seasonings until blended; gradually add broth and wine. Bring to a boil; cook and stir for 2 minutes or until thickened.

■ Add fillets to the pan. Reduce heat; cover and simmer for 10-12 minutes or until fish flakes easily with a fork.

➥ **NUTRITION FACTS:** 1 fillet with 3/4 cup vegetable mixture equals 229 calories, 9 g fat (6 g saturated fat), 88 mg cholesterol, 621 mg sodium, 12 g carbohydrate, 3 g fiber, 24 g protein. **DIABETIC EXCHANGES:** 3 lean meat, 2 vegetable, 1-1/2 fat.

"My husband requests this hearty ground beef dish for dinner at least once a month. I keep the simple ingredients on hand for last-minute preparation."

—**TRANN FOLEY** COLUMBIA, MISSOURI

ovenentrees

Beef & Ground Beef

162   169   175

Comforting beef dishes fresh from the oven are a surefire way to satisfy hunger. This chapter is full of beefy mainstays, such as **casseroles, meat loaves, pizzas, roasts, baked pastas** and other filling recipes that always make wonderful additions to any busy cook's repertoire.

LOADED SPAGHETTI BAKE

- Cook spaghetti according to package directions. Meanwhile, in a large skillet, cook the beef, onion and pepper over medium heat until meat is no longer pink; drain. Add the spaghetti sauce, mushrooms and olives. Drain spaghetti; add to skillet.

- Transfer to a greased 13-in. x 9-in. baking dish. Sprinkle with 1 cup cheddar cheese. Combine the soup, Alfredo sauce and Parmesan cheese; spread over cheddar cheese. In another bowl, combine cornflake crumbs and remaining cheddar cheese; sprinkle over the top.

- Bake, uncovered, at 350° for 30 minutes or until bubbly and cheese is melted. Let stand for 5 minutes before serving.

This versatile recipe is also great made with leftover chicken from the previous night's dinner. You might prefer another hard cheese for the Parmesan, or just go with the cheddar and cornflake crumbs.

—**MARIAN PAPPAS** LAKE STEVENS, WASHINGTON

Loaded Spaghetti Bake

PREP: 25 MIN. ■ BAKE: 30 MIN. ■ YIELD: 8 SERVINGS

12 ounces uncooked spaghetti

1 pound lean ground beef (90% lean)

1 cup chopped onion

1 cup chopped green pepper

1 jar (26 ounces) spaghetti sauce

1 can (4 ounces) mushroom stems and pieces, drained

1 can (2-1/4 ounces) sliced ripe olives, drained

2 cups (8 ounces) shredded cheddar cheese, *divided*

1 can (10-3/4 ounces) condensed cream of chicken soup, undiluted

1 carton (10 ounces) refrigerated Alfredo sauce

1/4 cup grated Parmesan cheese

1/2 cup cornflake crumbs

After browning ground beef, push the meat to one side of the pan and tilt the pan so the grease runs to the opposite side. Then **easily draw it out** using a turkey baster.

TACO PIE

I combine flavorful taco fixings with biscuit mix to create this zippy main dish pie. You can make it as mild or as hot as you'd like. It pairs extremely well with a tossed salad.

—**SHELLY WINKLEBLACK** INTERLAKEN, NEW YORK

Taco Pie

PREP: 20 MIN. ■ BAKE: 25 MIN. ■ YIELD: 6 SERVINGS

1 pound ground beef	1 cup (4 ounces) shredded cheddar cheese
1 large onion, chopped	2 eggs
1/2 cup salsa	1 cup milk
2 tablespoons taco seasoning	1/2 cup biscuit/baking mix
1/4 teaspoon pepper	

■ In a large skillet, cook beef and onion over medium heat until meat is no longer pink; drain. Stir in the salsa, taco seasoning and pepper. Transfer to a greased 9-in. pie plate; sprinkle with cheese.

■ In a large bowl, combine the eggs, milk and biscuit mix just until combined; pour over cheese. Bake at 400° for 25-30 minutes or until a knife inserted near the center comes out clean.

Steak over Potatoes

I enjoy preparing this dish since it is one of the easiest hearty meals I serve—so tasty, too. The chicken gumbo soup adds a unique flavor to the rest of the ingredients.

—**DENNIS ROBINSON**
LAUREL, MONTANA

PREP: 5 MIN. ■ BAKE: 2 HOURS
YIELD: 8 SERVINGS

2-1/2 pounds beef top round steak
   1 can (10-3/4 ounces) condensed cream of onion soup, undiluted
   1 can (10-1/2 ounces) condensed chicken gumbo soup, undiluted
 1/4 teaspoon pepper
   8 baking potatoes

■ Cut steak into 3-in. x 1/4-in. strips; place in a bowl. Stir in soups and pepper.

■ Transfer to a greased 2-1/2-qt. baking dish. Cover and bake at 350° for 30 minutes.

■ Place potatoes on a baking pan. Bake potatoes and steak mixture for 1-1/2 hours or until meat and potatoes are tender. Serve steak over the potatoes.

Round steak is a less-tender cut of beef and is **best cooked with liquid** in a covered pan over low heat. Round steak can also be tenderized before cooking.

This may not be a true Reuben, but the taste is still fantastic and it's a lot easier to make than individual sandwiches. I like to pair servings of this hot dish with bowls of homemade soup.

—KATHY KITTELL
LENEXA, KANSAS

REUBEN CRESCENT BAKE

Reuben Crescent Bake

PREP: 20 MIN. ■ **BAKE:** 15 MIN. ■ **YIELD:** 8 SERVINGS

- 2 tubes (8 ounces *each*) refrigerated crescent rolls
- 1 pound sliced Swiss cheese, *divided*
- 1-1/4 pounds sliced deli corned beef
- 1 can (14 ounces) sauerkraut, rinsed and well drained
- 2/3 cup Thousand Island salad dressing
- 1 egg white, lightly beaten
- 3 teaspoons caraway seeds

■ Unroll one tube of crescent dough into one long rectangle; seal seams and perforations. Press onto the bottom of a greased 13-in. x 9-in. baking dish. Bake at 375° for 8-10 minutes or until golden brown.

■ Layer with half of the cheese and all of the corned beef. Combine the sauerkraut and salad dressing; spread over the beef. Top with the remaining cheese.

■ On a lightly floured surface, press or roll second tube of crescent dough into a 13-in. x 9-in. rectangle, sealing seams and perforations. Place over the cheese. Brush with beaten egg white; sprinkle with caraway seeds.

■ Bake for 12-16 minutes or until heated through and crust is golden brown. Let stand for 5 minutes before cutting.

Meaty Noodle Casserole

This recipe is fast and easy to make and many of the ingredients are already in my pantry.

—LANA BACKUS
VONORE, TENNESSEE

PREP: 20 MIN. ■ **BAKE:** 30 MIN.
YIELD: 8 SERVINGS

- 1 package (12 ounces) wide egg noodles
- 1 pound ground beef
- 1/2 pound bulk pork sausage
- 3 tablespoons chopped onion
- 1/4 teaspoon garlic powder
- 1 can (14-3/4 ounces) cream-style corn
- 1 can (14-1/2 ounces) stewed tomatoes, cut up
- 1 can (10-3/4 ounces) condensed cream of chicken soup, undiluted
- 1 cup chopped pimiento-stuffed olives
- 2 tablespoons minced fresh parsley
- 1-1/2 cups (6 ounces) shredded cheddar cheese

■ Cook pasta according to package directions. Meanwhile, in a Dutch oven, cook the beef, pork sausage, onion and garlic powder over medium heat until meat is no longer pink; drain. Add the corn, tomatoes, soup, olives and parsley; heat through.

■ Drain pasta; stir into meat mixture. Transfer to a greased 13-in. x 9-in. baking dish. Sprinkle with cheese. Cover and bake at 350° for 25 minutes. Uncover; bake 5-10 minutes longer or until cheese is melted.

Here in beef country, we find all sorts of different ways to serve beef. A former boss gave me this recipe. It was an immediate hit with my family! The soy sauce, ketchup, brown sugar and other seasonings make a great barbecue sauce for the ribs.

—CONNIE MCDOWELL
LINCOLN, NEBRASKA

ASIAN BARBECUED SHORT RIBS

Asian Barbecued Short Ribs

PREP: 25 MIN. ■ **BAKE:** 1-3/4 HOURS ■ **YIELD:** 8 SERVINGS

4 pounds bone-in beef short ribs	1 tablespoon brown sugar
1 tablespoon canola oil	1 teaspoon ground mustard
1 medium onion, sliced	1/2 teaspoon ground ginger
3/4 cup ketchup	1/4 teaspoon salt
3/4 cup water, *divided*	1/8 teaspoon pepper
1/4 cup reduced-sodium soy sauce	1 bay leaf
2 tablespoons lemon juice	2 tablespoons all-purpose flour

■ In a Dutch oven, brown ribs in oil on all sides in batches. Remove ribs; discard pan drippings. In the same pan, saute onion for 2 minutes or until tender. Return ribs to the pan.

■ Combine the ketchup, 1/2 cup water, soy sauce, lemon juice, brown sugar, mustard, ginger, salt, pepper and bay leaf; pour over ribs.

■ Cover and bake at 325° for 1-3/4 to 2 hours or until meat is tender.

■ Remove ribs and keep warm. Discard bay leaf. Skim fat from pan drippings. In a small bowl, combine flour and remaining water until smooth; gradually stir into drippings. Bring to a boil; cook and stir for 2 minutes or until thickened. Serve with ribs.

Beef Spinach Hot Dish

My family, which includes my parents and six brothers and sisters, all love this dinner. Sometimes I use ground turkey in place of the ground beef.

—RACHEL JONES
ROLAND, ARKANSAS

PREP: 30 MIN. ■ **BAKE:** 20 MIN.
YIELD: 6-8 SERVINGS

1 pound ground beef

1 medium onion, chopped

2 garlic cloves, minced

1 can (4 ounces) mushroom stems and pieces, drained

1 teaspoon salt

1 teaspoon dried oregano

1/4 teaspoon pepper

2 packages (10 ounces *each*) frozen chopped spinach, thawed and squeezed dry

1 can (10-3/4 ounces) condensed cream of celery soup, undiluted

1 cup (8 ounces) sour cream

2 cups (8 ounces) shredded part-skim mozzarella cheese, *divided*

■ In a large skillet, cook beef and onion over medium heat until the meat is no longer pink. Add garlic; cook 1 minute longer. Drain. Stir in the mushrooms, salt, oregano and pepper. Add the spinach, soup and sour cream. Stir in half of the cheese.

■ Transfer to a greased 2-qt. baking dish. Bake, uncovered, at 350° for 15 minutes. Sprinkle with the remaining cheese; bake 5 minutes longer or until cheese is melted.

CRESCENT-TOPPED CASSEROLE

- In a large skillet, cook beef and onion over medium heat until meat is no longer pink; drain. Stir in tomato sauce and spaghetti sauce mix. Reduce heat; simmer, uncovered, for 5 minutes. Remove from the heat; stir in sour cream. Spoon into a greased 13-in. x 9-in. baking dish. Sprinkle with mozzarella cheese.

- Unroll crescent dough into one rectangle; seal seams and perforations. Place over mozzarella cheese. Brush with butter and sprinkle with Parmesan cheese.

- Bake, uncovered, at 375° for 25-30 minutes or until casserole is golden brown.

My husband requests this hearty ground beef dish for dinner at least once a month. I always try to keep the simple ingredients on hand for last-minute preparation.

—**TRANN FOLEY** COLUMBIA, MISSOURI

Crescent-Topped Casserole

PREP: 15 MIN. ■ **BAKE:** 25 MIN. ■ **YIELD:** 6-8 SERVINGS

2   pounds ground beef
1/4 cup chopped onion
2   cans (8 ounces *each*) tomato sauce
1   envelope spaghetti sauce mix
3/4 cup sour cream

2   cups (8 ounces) shredded part-skim mozzarella cheese
1   tube (8 ounces) refrigerated crescent rolls
2   tablespoons butter, melted
1/3 cup grated Parmesan cheese

As a general rule, do not use utensils that were used to prepare uncooked meats to later stir or serve cooked foods. To avoid cross-contamination, **wash utensils in hot, soapy water** before reusing—or use different utensils.

A coffee-enhanced rub lends robust flavor to juicy beef tenderloin. This recipe is special enough that I often prepare it for my family around the holidays instead of the traditional turkey or ham. The rich mashed potato stuffing adds an extra-special touch.

—REBECCA ANDERSON AUSTIN, TEXAS

Pepper-Crusted Beef Tenderloin

PREP: 30 MIN. + MARINATING ■ BAKE: 40 MIN. + STANDING
YIELD: 8 SERVINGS

- 1 cup plus 2 tablespoons dry red wine *or* beef broth, *divided*
- 1 beef tenderloin roast (2 pounds)
- 1 large potato, quartered
- 1/2 cup grated Parmesan cheese
- 3 tablespoons milk
- 4 tablespoons butter, *divided*
- 2 bacon strips, cooked and crumbled
- 1 tablespoon horseradish sauce
- 5 garlic cloves, minced, *divided*
- 1/2 teaspoon garlic salt
- 1 tablespoon minced chives, optional
- 3 tablespoons ground coffee
- 1 tablespoon brown sugar
- 1 tablespoon coarsely ground pepper
- 1-1/4 teaspoons salt, *divided*
- 1 medium onion, halved and sliced
- 1 tablespoon olive oil
- 1 teaspoon lemon juice

■ Pour 1 cup wine into a large resealable plastic bag; add the beef. Seal bag and turn to coat; refrigerate at least 1 hour.

■ Place potato in a small saucepan and cover with water. Bring to a boil. Reduce heat; cover and cook for 15-20 minutes or until tender. Drain; mash with cheese, milk, 2 tablespoons butter, bacon, horseradish sauce, 2 garlic cloves, garlic salt and chives if desired; set aside.

■ Drain and discard marinade. In a small bowl, combine the coffee, brown sugar, pepper and 1 teaspoon salt; rub over beef. Cut a lengthwise slit down the center of the tenderloin to within 3/4 in. of bottom. Open tenderloin so it lies flat; cover with plastic wrap. Flatten to 3/4 in. thickness. Remove plastic wrap; mound potato mixture over the center. Close tenderloin; tie at 2-in. intervals with kitchen string. Place on a rack in a shallow roasting pan.

■ Bake, uncovered, at 425° for 40-45 minutes or until meat reaches desired doneness (for medium-rare, a thermometer should read 145°; medium, 160°; well-done, 170°). Remove meat to a serving platter. Cover and let stand for 10 minutes.

■ Meanwhile, in a small skillet, cook onion and remaining garlic in oil and remaining butter over medium heat for 15-20 minutes or until onion is golden brown, stirring frequently. Stir in the lemon juice, remaining wine and salt. Slice tenderloin; serve with sauce.

Traditional Meat Loaf

Topped with a sweet sauce, this meat loaf tastes so good that you might want to double the recipe so everyone can have seconds. It also freezes well for last-minute meals.

—GAIL GRAHAM
MAPLE RIDGE, BRITISH COLUMBIA

PREP: 15 MIN.
BAKE: 1 HOUR + STANDING
YIELD: 6 SERVINGS

- 1 egg, lightly beaten
- 2/3 cup 2% milk
- 3 slices bread, crumbled
- 1 cup (4 ounces) shredded cheddar cheese
- 1 medium onion, chopped
- 1/2 cup finely shredded carrot
- 1 teaspoon salt
- 1/4 teaspoon pepper
- 1-1/2 pounds ground beef
- 1/4 cup packed brown sugar
- 1/4 cup ketchup
- 1 tablespoon prepared mustard

■ In a large bowl, combine the first eight ingredients. Crumble beef over mixture and mix well. Shape into a loaf. Place in a greased 9-in. x 5-in. loaf pan.

■ In a small bowl, combine the brown sugar, ketchup and mustard; spread over loaf. Bake at 350° for 60-75 minutes or until no pink remains and a thermometer reads 160°. Drain. Let stand for 10 minutes before slicing.

I had so many requests for this recipe that I made up cards to hand out every time I serve it at a get-together. My husband and son think it's world-class eating!

—CAROLYN WELLS
NORTH SYRACUSE, NEW YORK

HOMEMADE ITALIAN POT ROAST

Homemade Italian Pot Roast

PREP: 20 MIN. ■ BAKE: 2 HOURS ■ YIELD: 8-10 SERVINGS (3 CUPS GRAVY)

1 tablespoon all-purpose flour
1 large oven roasting bag
1 boneless beef chuck roast (3 pounds)
1-2/3 cups water
1 can (10-3/4 ounces) condensed tomato soup, undiluted
1 envelope onion soup mix
1-1/2 teaspoons Italian seasoning
1 garlic clove, minced
1/4 cup cornstarch
1/4 cup cold water

■ Sprinkle flour into oven bag; shake to coat. Place in a 13-in. x 9-in. baking pan; add roast. In a small bowl, combine the water, tomato soup, soup mix, Italian seasoning and garlic; pour into oven bag.

■ Cut six 1/2-in. slits in top of bag; close with tie provided. Bake at 325° for 2 to 2-1/2 hours or until meat is tender.

■ Remove roast to a serving platter and keep warm. Transfer cooking juices to a small saucepan; skim fat. Bring to a boil. Combine cornstarch and cold water until smooth; stir into cooking juices. Return to a boil; cook and stir for 2 minutes or until thickened. Slice roast; serve with gravy.

Chinese Beef Casserole

Crispy chow mein noodles top this twist on chop suey that's sure to be a family favorite.

—WILLIE DEWAARD
CORALVILLE, IOWA

PREP: 15 MIN. ■ BAKE: 45 MIN.
YIELD: 8 SERVINGS

2 pounds ground beef
1 cup chopped onion
1 cup chopped celery
2 cans (10-3/4 ounces *each*) condensed cream of mushroom soup, undiluted
1 can (14 ounces) bean sprouts, undrained
1/4 cup reduced-sodium soy sauce
1/2 teaspoon pepper
1 cup uncooked long grain rice
1 can (8 ounces) sliced water chestnuts, drained
2 cups frozen peas, thawed
1 can (5 ounces) chow mein noodles

■ In a large skillet, cook the beef, onion and celery over medium heat until meat is no longer pink; drain. Return to skillet. Stir in the soup, bean sprouts, soy sauce and pepper. Bring to a boil. Pour into a greased 3-qt. baking dish. Stir in rice and water chestnuts.

■ Cover and bake at 350° for 30 minutes. Uncover; stir in peas and sprinkle with noodles. Bake 15-20 minutes longer or until heated through.

ENCHILADAS VERDES

These enchiladas are easy to make ahead and refrigerate until you're ready to bake. After quickly cooking the tortillas in hot oil, I layer them between paper napkins to soak up excess oil.

—**JOAN HALLFORD** NORTH RICHLAND HILLS, TEXAS

Enchiladas Verdes

PREP: 45 MIN. ■ **BAKE:** 25 MIN. ■ **YIELD:** 6 SERVINGS

- 1 pound lean ground beef (90% lean)
- 1 large onion, chopped
- 1/4 teaspoon salt
- 1 small garlic clove, minced
- 2 cups (8 ounces) shredded cheddar cheese
- 1 can (10-3/4 ounces) condensed cream of chicken soup, undiluted
- 1 package (8 ounces) process cheese (Velveeta), cubed
- 3/4 cup evaporated milk
- 1 can (4 ounces) chopped green chilies, drained
- 1 jar (2 ounces) diced pimientos, drained
- 12 corn tortillas (6 inches)
- 1/4 cup canola oil

- In a large skillet, cook the beef, onion and salt over medium heat until meat is no longer pink. Add garlic; cook 1 minute longer. Drain. Stir in cheddar cheese; set aside.

- Meanwhile, in a large saucepan, cook and stir the soup, process cheese and milk over medium heat until cheese is melted. Stir in chilies and pimientos.

- In a large skillet, fry the tortillas, one at a time, in oil for 5 seconds on each side or until golden brown. Drain on paper towels.

- Place a scant 1/4 cup of reserved meat mixture down the center of each tortilla. Roll up and place seam side down in greased 13-in. x 9-in. baking dish. Pour cheese sauce over the top.

- Cover and bake at 350° for 25-30 minutes or until heated through.

If your **cheese slicer sticks** when cutting through soft cheese like Velveeta, **spritz the roller bar** with a little bit of nonstick cooking spray.

SOUTHWEST PASTA BAKE

Fat-free cream cheese and reduced-fat cheddar make this creamy casserole lower in fat and calories. Disguising the spinach is a good way to get our kids to eat it!

—CAROL LEPAK SHEBOYGAN, WISCONSIN

Southwest Pasta Bake

PREP: 20 MIN. ■ **BAKE:** 35 MIN. + STANDING ■ **YIELD:** 8 SERVINGS

8	ounces uncooked penne pasta	1	can (8 ounces) no-salt-added tomato sauce
1	package (8 ounces) fat-free cream cheese, cubed	1	can (6 ounces) no-salt-added tomato paste
1/2	cup fat-free milk	2	teaspoons chili powder
1	package (10 ounces) frozen chopped spinach, thawed and squeezed dry	1	teaspoon ground cumin
1	teaspoon dried oregano	1	cup (4 ounces) shredded reduced-fat cheddar cheese
1	pound lean ground beef (90% lean)	1	can (2-1/4 ounces) sliced ripe olives, drained
2	garlic cloves, minced	1/4	cup sliced green onions
1	jar (16 ounces) picante sauce		

- Cook the pasta according to package directions. Meanwhile, in a small bowl, beat the cream cheese until smooth. Beat in milk. Stir in the spinach and oregano; set aside.

- In a nonstick skillet, cook beef over medium heat until meat is no longer pink. Add garlic; cook 1 minute longer. Drain. Stir in the picante sauce, tomato sauce, tomato paste, chili powder and cumin; bring to a boil. Reduce heat; simmer, uncovered, for 5 minutes. Drain the pasta; stir into the meat mixture.

- In a 13-in. x 9-in. baking dish coated with cooking spray, layer half of the meat mixture and all of the spinach mixture. Top spinach with the remaining meat mixture.

- Cover and bake at 350° for 30 minutes. Uncover; sprinkle with cheese. Bake 5 minutes longer or until cheese is melted. Sprinkle with olives and onions. Let stand for 10 minutes before serving.

➥ **NUTRITION FACTS:** 1 serving equals 328 calories, 9 g fat (4 g saturated fat), 40 mg cholesterol, 855 mg sodium, 36 g carbohydrate, 4 g fiber, 25 g protein. **DIABETIC EXCHANGES:** 3 lean meat, 2 vegetable, 1-1/2 starch.

This recipe, which comes from our family cookbook, is a lot like a lasagna that is made with potatoes. The baked dish is a nice change of pace from pasta. We love casseroles, and this one is truly a cherished favorite.

—SUZETTE JURY
KEENE, CALIFORNIA

POTATO BEEF LASAGNA

Potato Beef Lasagna

PREP: 20 MIN. ■ **BAKE:** 70 MIN. + STANDING ■ **YIELD:** 8 SERVINGS

1 pound lean ground beef	1 medium onion, thinly sliced
1/2 pound bulk Italian sausage	1 cup (4 ounces) shredded part-skim mozzarella cheese
1 can (19 ounces) ready-to-serve tomato-basil soup	1-1/2 cups (6 ounces) shredded Gruyere *or* Swiss cheese
1 can (14-1/2 ounces) Italian diced tomatoes, undrained	3 tablespoons minced fresh parsley
1 package (20 ounces) refrigerated sliced potatoes	

■ In a large skillet, cook beef and sausage over medium heat until no longer pink; drain. Stir in soup and tomatoes; set aside. Place half of the potatoes and onion into a greased 13-in. x 9-in. baking dish. Layer with remaining potatoes and onion. Top with mozzarella cheese and meat mixture.

■ Cover and bake at 350° for 1 hour. Uncover; sprinkle with Gruyere cheese. Bake 10-15 minutes longer or until the potatoes are tender and cheese is melted. Let stand 10 minutes before serving. Sprinkle with the parsley.

Two-Tater Shepherd's Pie

I love shepherd's pie, but our oldest son doesn't like some of the ingredients. So I adjusted the recipe to come up with this version the whole family can enjoy.

—CINDY REBAIN
ROBERTSDALE, ALABAMA

PREP: 20 MIN. ■ **BAKE:** 40 MIN.
YIELD: 8 SERVINGS

1-1/2 pounds ground beef
1 can (10-3/4 ounces) condensed cream of mushroom soup, undiluted
1/2 teaspoon garlic salt
1/4 teaspoon pepper
6 cups frozen Tater Tots
2 cups frozen French-style green beans, thawed
3 cups hot mashed potatoes
1 cup (4 ounces) shredded Colby cheese

■ In a large skillet, cook beef over medium heat until no longer pink; drain. Stir in the soup, garlic salt and pepper.

■ Place Tater Tots in a greased 13-in. x 9-in. baking dish. Top with beef mixture and green beans. Spread mashed potatoes over the top; sprinkle with cheese.

■ Bake, uncovered, at 350° for 40-45 minutes or until casserole is heated through.

Made with only seven simple ingredients, this meaty delight will have the family coming back for seconds! Hearty and filling, it's sure to be a classic with your gang.

—TASTE OF HOME TEST KITCHEN

SOUTHWEST BEEF PIE

Southwest Beef Pie

PREP/TOTAL TIME: 30 MIN. ■ **YIELD:** 6 SERVINGS

- 2 cups coarsely crushed nacho tortilla chips
- 1-1/2 pounds ground beef
- 1 can (8 ounces) tomato sauce
- 1/2 cup water
- 1 envelope taco seasoning
- 1/4 teaspoon pepper
- 1 cup (4 ounces) shredded Monterey Jack cheese

■ Place tortilla chips in an ungreased 9-in. pie plate; set aside. In a large skillet, cook beef over medium heat until no longer pink; drain. Add the tomato sauce, water, taco seasoning and pepper. Bring to a boil; cook and stir for 2 minutes or until thickened.

■ Spoon half of the meat mixture over chips; sprinkle with half of the cheese. Repeat layers.

■ Bake, uncovered, at 375° for 10-15 minutes or until heated through and cheese is melted.

When **buying bulk cheese,** 4 ounces equals 1 cup shredded. Divide and store shredded cheese in airtight containers or resealable plastic bags and **freeze for up to several months.** When ready, thaw the amount of cheese needed and use.

Philly Cheesesteak Pizza

PREP: 30 MIN. ■ **BAKE:** 10 MIN. **YIELD:** 6 SLICES.

- 1 small green pepper, julienned
- 1 small sweet red pepper, julienned
- 1-3/4 cups sliced fresh mushrooms
- 1 small onion, halved and sliced
- 1-1/2 teaspoons canola oil
- 4 garlic cloves, minced
- 1 prebaked 12-inch pizza crust
- 1/2 cup pizza sauce
- 2 ounces cream cheese, cubed
- 2 cups (8 ounces) shredded provolone cheese, *divided*
- 1 cup shredded *or* julienned cooked roast beef
- 1/3 cup pickled pepper rings
- 1/4 cup grated Parmesan cheese
- 1/2 teaspoon dried oregano

■ In a large skillet, saute the peppers, mushrooms and onion in oil until tender. Add garlic; cook 1 minute longer.

■ Place crust on an ungreased 12-in. pizza pan. Spread pizza sauce over crust and dot with cream cheese. Sprinkle with 1 cup provolone cheese. Top with pepper mixture, beef, pepper rings and remaining provolone cheese. Sprinkle with the Parmesan cheese and oregano.

■ Bake at 450° for 10-12 minutes or until cheese is melted.

My convenient recipe has great flavor and is a wonderful way to use up leftover roast beef. The cream cheese makes the sauce extra creamy. Sometimes my family likes their pizza crust extra crispy so I prebake the crust for 5 minutes before adding the toppings. There are never leftovers.

—**LAURA MCDOWELL** LAKE VILLA, ILLINOIS

SPAGHETTI PIE

- In a nonstick skillet, cook the beef, onion and green pepper over medium heat until meat is no longer pink; drain. Stir in the tomatoes, tomato paste, oregano, salt, garlic powder, sugar and pepper; set aside.

- In a large bowl, combine the spaghetti, butter, egg whites and Parmesan cheese. Press onto the bottom and up the sides of a 9-in. deep-dish pie plate coated with cooking spray. Top with cottage cheese and beef mixture.

- Bake, uncovered, at 350° for 20 minutes. Sprinkle with mozzarella cheese. Bake 5-10 minutes longer or until cheese is melted and filling is heated through. Let stand for 5 minutes before cutting.

➥ **NUTRITION FACTS:** 1 serving equals 348 calories, 10 g fat (5 g saturated fat), 52 mg cholesterol, 690 mg sodium, 33 g carbohydrate, 4 g fiber, 29 g protein. **DIABETIC EXCHANGES:** 3 lean meat, 2 vegetable, 1-1/2 starch, 1 fat.

A classic Italian combination is remade into a creamy, family-pleasing casserole in this quick and easy dish. This recipe was given to me several years ago, but my family never grows tired of it.

—ELLEN THOMPSON SPRINGFIELD, OHIO

Spaghetti Pie

PREP: 25 MIN. ■ **BAKE:** 25 MIN. ■ **YIELD:** 6 SERVINGS

1 pound lean ground beef (90% lean)	1/4 teaspoon pepper
1/2 cup finely chopped onion	6 ounces spaghetti, cooked and drained
1/4 cup chopped green pepper	1 tablespoon butter, melted
1 cup canned diced tomatoes, undrained	2 egg whites, lightly beaten
1 can (6 ounces) tomato paste	1/4 cup grated Parmesan cheese
1 teaspoon dried oregano	1 cup (8 ounces) fat-free cottage cheese
3/4 teaspoon salt	1/2 cup shredded part-skim mozzarella cheese
1/2 teaspoon garlic powder	
1/4 teaspoon sugar	

To store **leftover tomato paste,** line a baking sheet with waxed paper. Mound the tomato paste in 1-tablespoon portions **on the waxed paper.** Freeze until firm, then transfer to a resealable freezer bag.

Guests will admire the pretty spiral slices and flavor of this succulent entree. A moist bread stuffing dresses up the tender flank steak.

—ADELAIDE MULDOON
SPRINGFIELD, VIRGINIA

STUFFED FLANK STEAK

Stuffed Flank Steak

PREP: 15 MIN. ■ **BAKE:** 50 MIN. ■ **YIELD:** 6 SERVINGS

1	small onion, finely chopped	1/4	teaspoon pepper, *divided*
1	tablespoon butter	1	beef flank steak (1-1/2 pounds)
3	cups soft bread crumbs	2	teaspoons all-purpose flour
1/2	to 3/4 teaspoon poultry seasoning	1	cup reduced-sodium beef broth
1/2	teaspoon salt		

■ In a small nonstick skillet, saute onion in butter until tender. In a large bowl, combine the bread crumbs, poultry seasoning, salt, 1/8 teaspoon pepper and onion.

■ Flatten steak to 1/2-in. thickness; spread with stuffing to within 1 in. of edges. Roll up jelly-roll style, starting with a long side; tie with kitchen string. Rub with remaining pepper.

■ Place in an 11-in. x 7-in. baking dish coated with cooking spray. Bake, uncovered, at 350° for 50-55 minutes or until meat is tender.

■ Remove meat and discard string. Cut into slices and keep warm. Skim fat from pan juices; pour into a small saucepan. Combine flour and broth until smooth; stir into juices. Bring to a boil; cook and stir for 1-2 minutes or until thickened. Serve with steak.

Mashed Potato Hot Dish

My cousin gave me this simple but savory recipe. Whenever I'm making homemade mashed potatoes, I throw in a few extra spuds so I can make the dish for supper the next night.

—TANYA ABERNATHY
YACOLT, WASHINGTON

PREP: 15 MIN. ■ **BAKE:** 20 MIN.
YIELD: 4 SERVINGS

1	pound ground beef
1	can (10-3/4 ounces) condensed cream of chicken soup, undiluted
2	cups frozen French-style green beans
2	cups hot mashed potatoes (prepared with milk and butter)
1/2	cup shredded cheddar cheese

■ In a large skillet, cook beef over medium heat until no longer pink; drain. Stir in soup and beans.

■ Transfer to a greased 2-qt. baking dish. Top with mashed potatoes; sprinkle with the cheddar cheese. Bake, uncovered, at 350° for 20-25 minutes or until bubbly and the cheese is melted.

If you like stuffed peppers, you'll love this speedy version. It offers all the comforting flavor of the original, but takes just half an hour. Instead of cooking the instant rice, you can use 2 cups leftover cooked rice.

—**BETH DEWYER**
DU BOIS,
PENNSYLVANIA

UNSTUFFED PEPPERS

Unstuffed Peppers

PREP/TOTAL TIME: 30 MIN. ■ YIELD: 6 SERVINGS

1 cup uncooked instant rice	1-1/2 teaspoons salt-free seasoning blend
1 pound ground beef	1/2 cup shredded Italian cheese blend
2 medium green peppers, cut into 1-inch pieces	1/2 cup seasoned bread crumbs
1/2 cup chopped onion	1 tablespoon olive oil
1 jar (26 ounces) marinara sauce	

■ Cook rice according to package directions. Meanwhile, in a large skillet, cook the beef, green peppers and onion over medium-high heat for 10-12 minutes or until meat is no longer pink; drain. Stir in the rice, marinara sauce and seasoning blend. Stir in cheese.

■ Transfer to a greased 2-qt. baking dish. Toss bread crumbs and oil; sprinkle over the top. Bake at 350° for 8-10 minutes or until heated through and topping is golden brown.

An easy way to clean out the insides of **halved green peppers** is to use a melon baller. It works wonders at **scooping out the seeds** and membranes.

Meat Lover's Pizza Bake

This yummy pizza casserole is hearty, made with ground beef and pepperoni. Instead of a typical pizza crust, it features a crust-like topping that's a snap to make with biscuit mix.

—**CAROL OAKES** STURGIS, MICHIGAN

PREP: 20 MIN. ■ BAKE: 25 MIN. + STANDING ■ YIELD: 6 SERVINGS

1 pound ground beef
1/2 cup chopped green pepper
1 can (15 ounces) pizza sauce
1 package (3-1/2 ounces) sliced pepperoni, chopped
1 can (2-1/4 ounces) sliced ripe olives, drained
2 cups (8 ounces) shredded part-skim mozzarella cheese
3/4 cup biscuit/baking mix
2 eggs
3/4 cup milk

■ In a large skillet, cook beef and green pepper over medium heat until meat is no longer pink; drain. Stir in the pizza sauce, pepperoni and olives. Transfer to a greased 11-in. x 7-in. baking dish. Sprinkle with cheese.

■ In a small bowl, combine the biscuit mix, eggs and milk until blended. Pour evenly over cheese. Bake, uncovered, at 400° for 25-30 minutes or until golden brown. Let stand for 10 minutes before serving.

CRANBERRY BRISKET WITH HORSERADISH MASHED POTATOES

- Place brisket in a greased 13-in. x 9-in. baking dish. Combine the cranberry sauce, ginger ale, dried cranberries and soup mix; pour over the meat. Cover and bake at 375° for 2 hours.

- Uncover; bake 1 hour longer or until meat is tender, basting occasionally. Meanwhile, place potatoes in a Dutch oven; cover with water. Bring to a boil. Reduce heat; cover and cook for 15-20 minutes or until tender.

- Drain potatoes; mash with milk, butter and horseradish. Let brisket stand for 5 minutes; thinly slice across the grain. Serve meat and juices with potatoes.

EDITOR'S NOTE: This is a fresh beef brisket, not corned beef.

Sweet and savory brisket is a great complement to the zesty mashed potatoes in my recipe. The rich color of the meat makes it an elegant holiday entree.

—RACELLE SCHAEFER STUDIO CITY, CALIFORNIA

Cranberry Brisket with Horseradish Mashed Potatoes

PREP: 20 MIN. ■ BAKE: 3 HOURS ■ YIELD: 8 SERVINGS (1-2/3 CUPS GRAVY)

1 fresh beef brisket (3 to 4 pounds)

1 can (14 ounces) whole-berry cranberry sauce

1 can (12 ounces) ginger ale

1/2 cup dried cranberries

1 envelope onion soup mix

8 medium potatoes, peeled and quartered

1/3 cup milk

1/4 cup butter, cubed

2 tablespoons prepared horseradish

For a delicious sandwich, take **leftover beef brisket,** sauteed onion and green pepper, and layer them on a toasted sandwich roll. Top with Swiss cheese and **place under the broiler** until the cheese is melted.

Poultry

192

186

186

These **homey casseroles and one-dish meals,** made with chicken and turkey, are perfect for family gatherings, potlucks and weeknight dinners. Full of flavor and wholesome ingredients, the family-friendly recipes include **hot dishes, pizza and roasted or baked entrees**. Add one to your menu tonight!

ROASTED TURKEY BREAST TENDERLOINS AND VEGETABLES

Classic flavors come together quickly in this family-pleasing roasted turkey and gravy. And you won't have to prepare a veggie side dish, because it's all cooked together.

—TASTE OF HOME TEST KITCHEN

Roasted Turkey Breast Tenderloins And Vegetables

PREP: 15 MIN. ■ BAKE: 35 MIN. ■ YIELD: 4 SERVINGS

1 teaspoon dill weed	4 celery ribs, cut into 2-inch pieces
1 teaspoon dried thyme	2 medium onions, cut into wedges
1 teaspoon dried oregano	1 tablespoon olive oil
1 teaspoon dried minced onion	8 turkey breast tenderloins (5 ounces *each*)
3/4 teaspoon salt	2 teaspoons cornstarch
1/4 teaspoon pepper	1/4 cup water
1/4 cup butter, melted	
3 cups fresh baby carrots	

- In a small bowl, combine the first six ingredients. Combine 2 teaspoons of the seasoning mixture with butter; toss with vegetables. Transfer to a roasting pan. Bake, uncovered, at 425° for 15 minutes.

- Meanwhile, rub oil over turkey; sprinkle with remaining seasoning mixture. Move vegetables to edges of pan; place turkey in the center. Bake, uncovered, at 425° for 20-25 minutes or until a thermometer reads 170° and vegetables are tender.

- Save half of the turkey for another use. Remove remaining turkey and vegetables to a serving platter and keep warm.

- Pour cooking juices into a small saucepan. Combine cornstarch and water until smooth; gradually stir into pan. Bring to a boil; cook and stir for 2 minutes or until thickened. Serve with turkey and vegetables.

When roasting different types of vegetables at the same time, be sure to **cut them in uniform pieces** so they cook evenly. Denser vegetables such as carrots can be smaller.

CHICKEN ALFREDO PIZZA

Guests will love my hearty pizza that's loaded with flavorful toppings, such as veggies, chicken and cheese. Serving picky eaters? It can easily be customized and made to order!

—**KRISTIN MCPHERSON** MOULTRIE, GEORGIA

Chicken Alfredo Pizza

PREP: 25 MIN. + MARINATING ■ **BAKE:** 10 MIN. ■ **YIELD:** 6 SLICES.

1	envelope zesty herb marinade mix	3	teaspoons Italian seasoning
1/3	cup water	1	teaspoon garlic powder
3	tablespoons cider vinegar	1	cup (4 ounces) finely shredded pizza cheese blend
3	tablespoons canola oil	1/2	medium green pepper, julienned (about 3/4 cup)
2	boneless skinless chicken breast halves (4 ounces *each*)	1/2	small red onion, thinly sliced and separated into rings (about 1/2 cup)
1	prebaked 12-inch pizza crust	1/2	cup sliced fresh mushrooms
1/2	cup Alfredo sauce		
3	tablespoons grated Parmesan cheese		

■ In a small bowl, combine 2 tablespoons marinade mix, water, vinegar and oil. (Save remaining marinade mix for another use.)

■ Pour 1/3 cup marinade into a large resealable plastic bag; add the chicken. Seal bag and turn to coat; refrigerate for 1 hour. Cover and refrigerate remaining marinade.

■ Drain and discard marinade from chicken. Grill chicken, covered, over medium heat or broil 4 in. from heat for 5-7 minutes on each side or until a thermometer reads 170°, basting occasionally with reserved marinade. Cool. Cube chicken and set aside.

■ Place prebaked crust on an ungreased 12-in. pizza pan. Spread with Alfredo sauce. Sprinkle with the Parmesan cheese, Italian seasoning, garlic powder, 1/2 cup pizza cheese blend, green pepper, onion, mushrooms, cubed chicken and the remaining pizza cheese blend.

■ Bake, uncovered, at 450° for 8-10 minutes or until cheese is melted.

Quick to prepare, this tasty main dish is loaded with turkey flavor and a nice crunch from celery and water chestnuts. Topped with a golden crescent roll crust and a sprinkling of almonds and cheese, it's bound to become a new family favorite.

—BECKY LARSON
MALLARD, IOWA

CRESCENT-TOPPED TURKEY AMANDINE

Crescent-Topped Turkey Amandine

PREP: 20 MIN. ■ **BAKE:** 30 MIN. ■ **YIELD:** 4 SERVINGS

3 cups cubed cooked turkey

1 can (10-3/4 ounces) condensed cream of mushroom soup, undiluted

1 can (8 ounces) sliced water chestnuts, drained

2/3 cup mayonnaise

1/2 cup chopped celery

1/2 cup chopped onion

1 tube (4 ounces) refrigerated crescent rolls

2/3 cup shredded Swiss cheese

1/2 cup sliced almonds

1/4 cup butter, melted

■ In a large saucepan, combine the first six ingredients; heat through. Transfer to a greased 2-qt. baking dish. Unroll crescent dough and place over turkey mixture.

■ In a small bowl, combine the cheese, almonds and butter. Spoon over dough. Bake, uncovered, at 375° for 30-35 minutes or until crust is golden brown and filling is bubbly.

Reduced-fat and **fat-free mayonnaise can break down** when heated, so it's best to use regular mayonnaise in dishes that are baked. **Whipped salad dressing** that contains eggs and fat can be used in equal amounts for mayonnaise.

Bacon-Chicken Crescent Ring

This ring is very easy to put together. It's so good that people always ask for the recipe.

—MICHELE MCWHORTER
JACKSONVILLE, NORTH CAROLINA

PREP: 25 MIN. ■ **BAKE:** 20 MIN.
YIELD: 8 SERVINGS

2 tubes (8 ounces *each*) refrigerated crescent rolls

1 can (10 ounces) chunk white chicken, drained and flaked

1-1/2 cups (6 ounces) shredded Swiss cheese

3/4 cup mayonnaise

1/2 cup finely chopped sweet red pepper

1/4 cup finely chopped onion

6 bacon strips, cooked and crumbled

2 tablespoons Dijon mustard

1 tablespoon Italian salad dressing mix

■ Grease a 14-in. pizza pan. Unroll crescent roll dough; separate into 16 triangles. Place wide end of one triangle 3 in. from edge of prepared pan with point overhanging edge of pan. Repeat with remaining triangles along outer edge of pan, overlapping the wide ends (dough will look like a sun when complete). Lightly press wide ends together.

■ In a small bowl, combine the remaining ingredients. Spoon over wide ends of dough. Fold points of triangles over filling and tuck under wide ends (filling will be visible). Bake at 375° for 20-25 minutes or until golden brown.

I get many requests for this juicy chicken dish. I love the recipe because it's so simple and delicious, but looks like I spent the whole day preparing it.

—SANDI GUETTLER
BAY CITY, MICHIGAN

BACON CHICKEN ROLL-UPS

Bacon Chicken Roll-Ups

PREP: 20 MIN. ■ **BAKE:** 35 MIN. ■ **YIELD:** 6 SERVINGS

12	bacon strips
6	boneless skinless chicken breast halves (4 ounces *each*)
1	package (8 ounces) cream cheese, softened
1	medium sweet onion, halved and cut into slices
	Dash salt and pepper

■ In a large skillet, cook bacon over medium heat until cooked but not crisp. Remove to paper towels to drain.

■ Meanwhile, flatten chicken to 1/8-in. thickness. Spread cream cheese down the center of each chicken breast; top with onion. Roll up from a long side; tuck ends in. Sprinkle with salt and pepper. Wrap two bacon strips around each piece of chicken; secure with toothpicks.

■ Place in a greased 13-in. x 9-in. baking dish. Bake at 350° for 35-40 minutes or until a thermometer reads 170°. Discard toothpicks.

It's okay to use **Neufchatel cheese,** which is **slightly lower in calories** than regular cream cheese, in the above recipe.

Best Chicken 'n' Biscuits

Quick and comforting, this delicious dish is filled with chunky chicken, colorful veggies and spoonfuls of creamy flavor. It's guaranteed to warm your family to their toes!

—JUDITH WHITFORD
EAST AURORA, NEW YORK

PREP/TOTAL TIME: 30 MIN.
YIELD: 6 SERVINGS

6	individually frozen biscuits
1	can (49-1/2 ounces) chicken broth, *divided*
1-1/2	pounds boneless skinless chicken breasts, cubed
5	medium carrots, coarsely chopped
2	celery ribs, chopped
1/2	cup chopped onion
1/2	cup frozen corn
3	teaspoons dried basil
1/4	teaspoon pepper
1	cup all-purpose flour
3/4	teaspoon browning sauce, optional

■ Bake biscuits according to package directions. Meanwhile, in a Dutch oven, combine 4 cups broth, chicken, carrots, celery, onion, corn, basil and pepper. Bring to a boil. Reduce heat; cover and simmer for 7-10 minutes or until vegetables are tender.

■ In a small bowl, combine flour and remaining broth until smooth. Stir into chicken mixture. Bring to a boil; cook and stir for 2 minutes or until thickened. Stir in browning sauce if desired. Split biscuits; top with chicken mixture.

TURKEY CABBAGE BAKE

- Unroll one tube of the crescent dough into one long rectangle; seal seams and perforations. Press onto the bottom of a greased 13-in. x 9-in. baking dish. Bake at 425° for 6-8 minutes or until golden brown.

- Meanwhile, in a large skillet, cook the turkey, onion and carrot over medium heat until meat is no longer pink. Add garlic; cook 1 minute longer. Drain. Add the cabbage, soup and thyme. Pour over crust; sprinkle with cheese.

- On a lightly floured surface, press the second tube of crescent dough into a 13-in. x 9-in. rectangle, sealing the seams and perforations. Place over the casserole.

- Bake, uncovered, at 375° for 14-16 minutes or until crust is golden brown.

I revised this old recipe by using ground turkey instead of ground beef (to make it healthier), by finely chopping the cabbage to improve texture and by adding thyme. Crescent rolls help it go together quickly.

—IRENE GUTZ FORT DODGE, IOWA

Turkey Cabbage Bake

PREP: 30 MIN. ■ BAKE: 15 MIN. ■ YIELD: 6 SERVINGS

- 2 tubes (8 ounces *each*) refrigerated crescent rolls
- 1-1/2 pounds ground turkey
- 1/2 cup chopped onion
- 1/2 cup finely chopped carrot
- 1 teaspoon minced garlic

- 2 cups finely chopped cabbage
- 1 can (10-3/4 ounces) condensed cream of mushroom soup, undiluted
- 1/2 teaspoon dried thyme
- 1 cup (4 ounces) shredded part-skim mozzarella cheese

When **buying cabbage,** look for heads that are heavy with firmly packed, crisp-looking leaves. **Store cabbage** in a tightly wrapped plastic bag in the refrigerator up to 2 weeks.

CHICKEN ROLLS WITH RASPBERRY SAUCE

Give that weeknight meal an elegant feel with this impressive (but easy!) blue-cheese stuffed chicken. The raspberry sauce is also great on grilled pork tenderloin.

—TASTE OF HOME TEST KITCHEN

Chicken Rolls with Raspberry Sauce

PREP: 25 MIN. ■ BAKE: 35 MIN. ■ YIELD: 4 SERVINGS

4 boneless skinless chicken breast halves (6 ounces *each*)

1/2 cup crumbled blue cheese

4 strips ready-to-serve fully cooked bacon, crumbled

2 tablespoons butter, melted, *divided*

Salt and pepper to taste

2 cups fresh raspberries

1/4 cup chicken broth

4 teaspoons brown sugar

1 tablespoon balsamic vinegar

1/2 teaspoon minced garlic

1/4 teaspoon dried oregano

■ Flatten chicken to 1/4-in. thickness; sprinkle with the blue cheese and crumbled bacon to within 1/2 in. of edges. Roll up each jelly-roll style, starting with a short side; secure with toothpicks.

■ Place in a greased 8-in. square baking dish. Brush with 1 tablespoon butter; sprinkle with salt and pepper. Bake, uncovered, at 375° for 35-40 minutes or until meat is no longer pink.

■ Meanwhile, in a small saucepan, combine the raspberries, broth, brown sugar, vinegar, garlic and oregano. Bring to a boil. Reduce heat; simmer, uncovered, for 5 minutes or until thickened.

■ Press through a sieve; discard seeds. Stir in remaining butter until smooth. Discard toothpicks. Serve with raspberry sauce.

When **flattening tender cuts of chicken,** place the meat inside a heavy-duty resealable plastic bag or between two sheets of heavy plastic wrap to **prevent messy splatters.** Use the smooth side of the meat mallet.

My husband loves this recipe, especially when he has a craving for hot wings. If you don't have blue cheese dressing available, ranch works great, too!

—DANIELLE WEETS
GRANDVIEW, WASHINGTON

HOT WING PIZZA

Hot Wing Pizza

PREP/TOTAL TIME: 30 MIN. ■ **YIELD:** 6 SLICES.

- 3 boneless skinless chicken breast halves (5 ounces *each*)
- 1 tablespoon steak seasoning
- 1/2 cup tomato sauce
- 2 tablespoons butter
- 2 tablespoons Louisiana-style hot sauce
- 1 tablespoon hot pepper sauce
- 1 prebaked 12-inch pizza crust
- 1/3 cup blue cheese salad dressing
- 1/2 cup shredded part-skim mozzarella cheese
- 3 green onions, thinly sliced

■ Sprinkle chicken with steak seasoning on both sides. Moisten a paper towel with cooking oil; using long-handled tongs, lightly coat the grill rack. Grill chicken, covered, over medium heat or broil 4 in. from the heat for 4-7 minutes on each side or until a thermometer reads 170°. Cool slightly; cut into strips.

■ In a small saucepan, bring the tomato sauce, butter, hot sauce and pepper sauce to a boil. Reduce heat; simmer, uncovered, for 10-15 minutes or until slightly thickened. Add chicken; heat through.

■ Place crust on a 12-in. pizza pan; spread with salad dressing. Top with chicken mixture, cheese and onions.

■ Bake at 450° for 8-10 minutes or until cheese is melted.

EDITOR'S NOTE: This recipe was tested with McCormick's Montreal Steak Seasoning. Look for it in the spice aisle.

Chicken Artichoke Bake

The first time I tasted this creamy casserole at a friend's get-together, I noted how much everyone loved it. All of the party guests went for seconds...and thirds. I can't believe how easy it was to prepare. It's perfect on a buffet.

—TODD RICHARDS
WEST ALLIS, WISCONSIN

PREP: 15 MIN. ■ **BAKE:** 55 MIN.
YIELD: 6 SERVINGS

- 2 cans (10-3/4 ounces *each*) condensed cream of celery soup, undiluted
- 1 cup mayonnaise
- 3 cups cubed cooked chicken
- 1 can (14 ounces) water-packed artichoke hearts, rinsed, drained and chopped
- 1 can (8 ounces) sliced water chestnuts, drained
- 1 package (6 ounces) long grain and wild rice mix
- 1 cup sliced fresh mushrooms
- 1 medium onion, finely chopped
- 1 jar (2 ounces) diced pimientos, drained
- 1/4 teaspoon pepper
- 1 cup seasoned stuffing cubes

■ In a large bowl, combine soup and mayonnaise. Stir in the chicken, artichokes, water chestnuts, rice mix with contents of seasoning packet, mushrooms, onion, pimientos and pepper.

■ Spoon into a greased 2-1/2-qt. baking dish. Sprinkle with stuffing cubes. Bake, uncovered, at 350° for 55-65 minutes or until edges are bubbly and rice is tender.

Roasting simply seasoned Cornish game hens and vegetables in the same pan results in a full-flavored meal-in-one that's easy and elegant.

—LILY JULOW
GAINESVILLE, FLORIDA

ROASTED CORNISH HENS WITH VEGETABLES

Roasted Cornish Hens with Vegetables

PREP: 20 MIN. ■ BAKE: 1-1/2 HOURS ■ YIELD: 6 SERVINGS

6 medium potatoes, quartered	1-1/2 teaspoons garlic salt
6 medium carrots, cut in half lengthwise and cut into chunks	6 Cornish game hens (20 to 24 ounces *each*)
1 large sweet onion, cut into wedges	1 tablespoon olive oil
1/2 cup butter, melted	1/4 teaspoon salt
2 teaspoons dried oregano	1/4 teaspoon pepper
2 teaspoons dried rosemary, crushed	6 bacon strips

■ In a large bowl, combine the first seven ingredients. Transfer to a shallow roasting pan.

■ Brush hens with oil; sprinkle with salt and pepper. Wrap a bacon strip around each hen; secure with a wooden toothpick. Tie legs together. Place, breast side up, over vegetables.

■ Bake, uncovered, at 350° for 1-1/2 to 2 hours or until a thermometer reads 180° and vegetables are tender. Remove hens to a serving platter; serve with vegetables.

Oregano Roasting Chicken

This is a fantastic five-ingredient recipe that takes almost no time to prep for the oven.

—TASTE OF HOME TEST KITCHEN

PREP: 10 MIN.
BAKE: 2-1/4 HOURS
YIELD: 6 SERVINGS

1/4 cup butter, melted
1 envelope Italian salad dressing mix
2 tablespoons lemon juice
1 roasting chicken (6 to 7 pounds)
2 teaspoons dried oregano

■ In a small bowl, combine the butter, salad dressing mix and lemon juice. Place chicken on a rack in an ungreased roasting pan. Spoon butter mixture over chicken.

■ Cover and bake at 350° for 45 minutes. Uncover; sprinkle with oregano. Bake, uncovered, for 1-1/2 to 1-3/4 hours or until a thermometer reads 180°.

Fresh-squeezed lemon juice can easily be frozen in ice cube trays, and the cubes transferred to a resealable plastic bag. This is a great way to have fresh **lemon juice on hand.**

POTATO-CRUSTED CHICKEN CASSEROLE

An herby, comforting filling is surrounded by a sliced potato "crust" in this unique casserole that tastes anything but healthy! No one will know that the hot dish fits in the "calorie-friendly" category.

—**BECKY MATHENY** STRASBURG, VIRGINIA

Potato-Crusted Chicken Casserole

PREP: 30 MIN. ■ BAKE: 40 MIN. ■ YIELD: 6 SERVINGS

- 1   large potato, thinly sliced
- 1   tablespoon olive oil
- 1/2 teaspoon salt
- 1/4 teaspoon pepper

FILLING:

- 1-1/2 pounds chicken tenderloins, cut into 1/2-inch cubes
- 2   teaspoons olive oil
- 1   medium onion, chopped
- 1   tablespoon butter
- 2   tablespoons all-purpose flour
- 1-1/2 cups fat-free milk
- 1/4 cup shredded part-skim mozzarella cheese
- 1/4 cup grated Parmesan cheese
- 2   tablespoons shredded reduced-fat cheddar cheese
- 2   cups frozen peas and carrots
- 1/2 teaspoon salt
- 1/2 teaspoon dried thyme
- 1/4 teaspoon dried basil

Dash rubbed sage

CRUMB TOPPING:

- 1   cup soft bread crumbs
- 1   tablespoon butter, melted
- 1/2 teaspoon garlic powder

- ■ In a large bowl, toss potato slices with oil, salt and pepper. Arrange slices onto the bottom and sides of an 11-in. x 7-in. baking dish coated with cooking spray. Bake at 400° for 20-25 minutes or until potato is tender. Reduce heat to 350°.

- ■ Meanwhile, for filling, in a large skillet over medium heat, cook the chicken in oil until no longer pink. Remove from skillet. In the same skillet, saute the onion in butter. Stir in flour until blended; gradually add milk. Bring to a boil; cook and stir for 2 minutes or until thickened. Reduce heat; stir in cheeses until melted. Stir in vegetables, seasonings and chicken. Spoon into potato crust.

- ■ Combine topping ingredients; sprinkle over chicken mixture. Bake, uncovered, for 40-45 minutes or until bubbly and topping is golden brown.

➤➤ **NUTRITION FACTS:** 1 serving equals 340 calories, 11 g fat (4 g saturated fat), 85 mg cholesterol, 674 mg sodium, 28 g carbohydrate, 3 g fiber, 35 g protein. **DIABETIC EXCHANGES:** 4 lean meat, 2 starch, 1 fat.

This recipe comes with lots of mass appeal, thanks to its cheesy sauce. Pasta, veggies and leftover turkey combine to create a filling meal.

—STEVE FOY
KIRKWOOD, MISSOURI

CHEDDAR TURKEY CASSEROLE

Cheddar Turkey Casserole

PREP: 20 MIN. ■ **BAKE:** 35 MIN. ■ **YIELD:** 6 SERVINGS

4 cups uncooked spiral pasta	1/4 teaspoon pepper
1 garlic clove, minced	2 cups 2% milk
3 tablespoons butter	1-1/2 cups (6 ounces) shredded cheddar cheese
3 tablespoons all-purpose flour	2 cups cubed cooked turkey
1 teaspoon salt	2 cups frozen mixed vegetables, thawed
1/4 teaspoon prepared mustard	1/2 cup slivered almonds
1/4 teaspoon dried thyme	

■ Cook pasta according to package directions.

■ Meanwhile, in a large saucepan, saute garlic in butter until tender. Stir in the flour, salt, mustard, thyme and pepper. Gradually stir in milk. Bring to a boil; cook and stir for 2 minutes or until thickened. Remove from the heat; stir in cheese until melted. Drain pasta; place in a large bowl. Toss with turkey, vegetables and cheese sauce.

■ Transfer to a greased 13-in. x 9-in. baking dish. Sprinkle with slivered almonds. Bake, uncovered, at 350° for 35-40 minutes or until heated through.

Chicken Rice Dinner

PREP: 20 MIN. ■ **BAKE:** 1 HOUR
YIELD: 5 SERVINGS

1/2 cup all-purpose flour
1 teaspoon salt
1/2 teaspoon pepper
10 bone-in chicken thighs (about 3-3/4 pounds)
3 tablespoons canola oil
1 cup uncooked long grain rice
1/4 cup chopped onion
2 garlic cloves, minced
1 can (4 ounces) mushroom stems and pieces, undrained
2 teaspoons chicken bouillon granules
2 cups boiling water

Minced fresh parsley, optional

■ In a large resealable plastic bag, combine the flour, salt and pepper; add chicken thighs, one at a time, and shake to coat. In a large skillet over medium heat, brown chicken in oil.

■ Place rice in an ungreased 13-in. x 9-in. baking dish. Sprinkle with onion and garlic; top with mushrooms. Dissolve bouillon in boiling water; pour over all. Place chicken on top.

■ Cover and bake at 350° for 1 hour or until a thermometer reads 180° and the rice is tender. Sprinkle with parsley if desired.

Everyone enjoys the classic country-style combination of chicken, rice and mushrooms. This recipe uses affordable chicken thighs as the main ingredient, with chicken bouillon, which adds wonderful flavor. The dish is hearty enough on its own, but it pairs well with a crisp, green salad.

—JUDITH ANGLEN RIVERTON, WYOMING

Holiday-special in every way, this moist chicken is coated with pecans and drizzled with a rich blue cheese sauce. It's easy and delicious...a real winner in my book. You can also use turkey breast and simply adjust the cook time.

—MAGGIE RUDDY
ALTOONA, IOWA

PECAN CHICKEN WITH BLUE CHEESE SAUCE

Pecan Chicken With Blue Cheese Sauce

PREP: 15 MIN. ■ **BAKE:** 20 MIN. ■ **YIELD:** 4 SERVINGS

4 boneless skinless chicken breast halves (5 ounces *each*)

1/4 teaspoon salt

1/8 teaspoon pepper

1/4 cup all-purpose flour

1 tablespoon minced fresh rosemary *or* 1 teaspoon dried rosemary, crushed

1/4 cup butter, melted

1 tablespoon brown sugar

3/4 cup finely chopped pecans

SAUCE:

1 cup heavy whipping cream

1/3 cup crumbled blue cheese

1 tablespoon finely chopped green onion

1/4 teaspoon salt

1/4 teaspoon pepper

■ Sprinkle chicken with salt and pepper. In a shallow bowl, combine flour and rosemary; in a separate shallow bowl, combine butter and brown sugar. Place pecans in another shallow bowl. Coat chicken with flour mixture, then dip in butter mixture and coat with pecans.

■ Transfer to a greased baking sheet. Bake at 375° for 20-25 minutes or until a thermometer reads 170°.

■ Meanwhile, place cream in a small saucepan. Bring to a boil; cook and stir for 8-10 minutes or until thickened. Stir in the cheese, onion, salt and pepper. Serve with chicken.

Taco Chicken Wraps

The flavorful filling in these wraps has a definite kick, but you can adjust the chilies and peppers to suit your taste. I like to serve them alongside Spanish rice.

—MELISSA GREEN
LOUISVILLE, KENTUCKY

PREP/TOTAL TIME: 30 MIN.
YIELD: 6 SERVINGS

1 can (10 ounces) diced tomatoes and green chilies, drained

1 can (9-3/4 ounces) chunk white chicken, drained

1 cup (4 ounces) shredded cheddar-Monterey Jack cheese

2 tablespoons diced jalapeno pepper

2 teaspoons taco seasoning

6 flour tortillas (6 inches), warmed

Taco sauce and sour cream, optional

■ In a small bowl, combine the tomatoes, chicken, cheese, jalapeno and taco seasoning. Place about 1/3 cupful down the center of each tortilla. Roll up and place seam side down in a greased 11-in. x 7-in. baking dish.

■ Bake, uncovered, at 350° for 10-15 minutes or until heated through. Serve with the taco sauce and the sour cream if desired.

EDITOR'S NOTE: Wear disposable gloves when cutting hot peppers; the oils can burn skin. Avoid touching your face.

MEXICAN CORN BREAD PIZZA

- In a small bowl, combine the corn bread mix, milk and egg. Stir in corn just until blended. Spread evenly into a 10-in. ovenproof skillet coated with cooking spray. Bake at 400° for 14-18 minutes or until a toothpick inserted near the center comes out clean.

- Meanwhile, in a large nonstick skillet, cook the turkey, onion, red pepper and jalapenos over medium heat until meat is no longer pink; drain. Stir in taco seasoning and water; bring to a boil. Reduce heat; simmer, uncovered, for 5 minutes.

- Spoon the turkey mixture over corn bread; sprinkle with cheese. Bake for 5-10 minutes or until cheese is melted. Sprinkle with tomato, olives and green onions. Cut into six wedges and top each with sour cream.

EDITOR'S NOTE: Wear disposable gloves when cutting hot peppers; the oils can burn skin. Avoid touching your face.

➤➤ **NUTRITION FACTS:** 1 wedge equals 354 calories, 11 g fat (4 g saturated fat), 82 mg cholesterol, 793 mg sodium, 43 g carbohydrate, 2 g fiber, 25 g protein. **DIABETIC EXCHANGES:** 3 starch, 2 lean meat.

The combination of sweet corn bread and spicy taco flavors really livens up a meal. Using ground turkey instead of beef cuts the fat and makes a delicious dinner guilt-free.

—**CHRISTY WEST** GREENFIELD, INDIANA

Mexican Corn Bread Pizza

PREP: 25 MIN. ■ **BAKE:** 20 MIN. ■ **YIELD:** 6 SERVINGS

1 package (8-1/2 ounces) corn bread/muffin mix	3 tablespoons reduced-sodium taco seasoning
1/3 cup fat-free milk	1/2 cup water
1 egg, lightly beaten	3/4 cup shredded reduced-fat Mexican cheese blend
1 cup frozen corn, thawed	1 small tomato, chopped
3/4 pound extra-lean ground turkey	1/4 cup sliced ripe olives
1 small onion, chopped	2 green onions, chopped
1 small sweet red pepper, chopped	6 tablespoons reduced-fat sour cream
2 jalapeno peppers, seeded and chopped	

CHICKEN 'N' DRESSING CASSEROLE

This casserole is a real favorite in our area and in my family, too. It's a great way to use leftover chicken or turkey, and so easy that even beginner cooks will have success making it.

—BILLIE BLANTON KINGSPORT, TENNESSEE

Chicken 'n' Dressing Casserole

PREP: 1 HOUR ■ BAKE: 35 MIN. ■ YIELD: 8 SERVINGS

4 cups cubed cooked chicken
2 tablespoons all-purpose flour
1/2 cup chicken broth
1/2 cup milk
Salt and pepper to taste

DRESSING:
2 celery ribs, chopped
1 small onion, finely chopped
1 tablespoon butter
1 teaspoon rubbed sage
1/2 teaspoon poultry seasoning
1/4 teaspoon salt
1/8 teaspoon pepper
2 cups unseasoned stuffing cubes, crushed
2 cups coarsely crumbled corn bread
1/2 cup chicken broth
1 egg, beaten

GRAVY:
1/4 cup butter
6 tablespoons all-purpose flour
2 cups chicken broth
1/2 cup milk

■ Place chicken in a greased 2-qt. baking dish; set aside. In a small saucepan, combine the flour, broth and milk until smooth. Bring to a boil; cook and stir for 2 minutes. Season with salt and pepper. Spoon over chicken.

■ In a large skillet, saute celery and onion in butter until tender. Stir in seasonings. Remove from the heat; add the stuffing cubes, corn bread, broth and egg. Mix well. Spoon over chicken mixture. Cover and bake at 350° for 35-40 minutes or until a thermometer inserted near the center reads 160°.

■ For gravy, melt butter in a small saucepan. Stir in flour until smooth; gradually add broth and milk. Bring to a boil; cook and stir for 2 minutes or until thickened. Serve with chicken and dressing.

A great way to have **cooked chicken on hand** is to buy chicken on sale, then bake it all at once skin-side up on foil-lined pans. When cool, remove the skin and bones, **cube the meat and freeze** in measured portions.

A friend served this one night, and I just had to try it at home. It's quick, easy and oh-so delicious! I love to serve it to guests with a Caesar salad and warm rolls. Also, it can be frozen and saved for a busy night.

—JANELLE RUTROUGH
ROCKY MOUNT, VIRGINIA

CHICKEN LASAGNA

Chicken Lasagna

PREP: 25 MIN. ■ BAKE: 30 MIN. + STANDING ■ YIELD: 8 SERVINGS

- 2 cups (16 ounces) 2% cottage cheese
- 1 package (3 ounces) cream cheese, softened
- 4 cups cubed cooked chicken
- 1 can (10-3/4 ounces) condensed cream of chicken soup, undiluted
- 1 can (10-3/4 ounces) condensed cream of celery soup, undiluted
- 2/3 cup 2% milk
- 1/2 cup chopped onion
- 1/2 teaspoon salt
- 6 lasagna noodles, cooked and drained
- 1 package (6 ounces) stuffing mix
- 1/2 cup butter, melted

- ■ In a small bowl, combine cottage cheese and cream cheese. In a large bowl, combine the chicken, soups, milk, onion and salt.

- ■ Spread half of the chicken mixture into a greased 13-in. x 9-in. baking dish. Top with three noodles. Spread with half of the cheese mixture. Repeat layers. Toss the stuffing mix with butter; sprinkle over casserole.

- ■ Bake, uncovered, at 350° for 30-40 minutes or until bubbly and golden brown. Let stand for 10 minutes before cutting.

Golden Cornish Hens

I clipped this recipe out of a newspaper years ago. This is an easy entree with old-fashioned flavor—perfect for the holidays!
—MARY LEE ALLRED PARIS, IDAHO

PREP: 30 MIN. ■ BAKE: 2 HOURS
YIELD: 6 SERVINGS

- 1 package (6 ounces) long grain and wild rice mix
- 1 can (8 ounces) unsweetened crushed pineapple
- 1/2 cup raisins
- 6 Cornish game hens (20 to 24 ounces *each*)
- 2 tablespoons butter, melted
- 1/4 teaspoon salt
- 1/4 teaspoon pepper
- 3 tablespoons honey

- ■ Prepare rice mix according to package directions. Drain pineapple, reserving juice; set aside. Stir pineapple and raisins into rice.

- ■ Just before baking, loosely stuff each hen with 3/4 cup rice mixture; tie legs together with kitchen string. Place hens, breast side up, on a rack in a shallow roasting pan. Brush with butter; sprinkle with salt and pepper.

- ■ Bake, uncovered, at 350° for 1-3/4 to 2 hours or until a thermometer reads 180° for hens and 165° for stuffing.

- ■ In a small saucepan, bring honey and reserved pineapple juice to a boil. Remove from the heat. Baste over hens. Bake 15 minutes longer or until golden brown.

With chunks of chicken, veggies and a golden biscuit topping, this makes a hearty meal that will rival homey dishes from Mom.

—SALA HOUTZER
GOLDSBORO, NORTH CAROLINA

CHICKEN POTPIE WITH CHEDDAR BISCUIT TOPPING

Chicken Potpie with Cheddar Biscuit Topping

PREP: 20 MIN. ■ **BAKE:** 45 MIN. ■ **YIELD:** 9 SERVINGS

4 cups cubed cooked chicken

1 package (12 ounces) frozen broccoli and cheese sauce

1 can (10-3/4 ounces) condensed cream of chicken and mushroom soup, undiluted

1 can (10-3/4 ounces) condensed cream of chicken soup, undiluted

2 medium potatoes, cubed

3/4 cup chicken broth

2/3 cup sour cream

1/2 cup frozen peas

1/4 teaspoon pepper

TOPPING:

1-1/2 cups biscuit/baking mix

3/4 cup shredded sharp cheddar cheese

3/4 cup 2% milk

3 tablespoons butter, melted

■ In a Dutch oven, combine the first nine ingredients; bring to a boil. Transfer to a greased 13-in. x 9-in. baking dish.

■ In a small bowl, combine the topping ingredients; spoon over top. Bake, uncovered, at 350° for 40-45 minutes or until bubbly and topping is golden brown. Let stand for 10 minutes before serving.

Crunchy Baked Chicken

PREP: 10 MIN. ■ **BAKE:** 50 MIN.
YIELD: 4-6 SERVINGS

1 egg

1 tablespoon milk

1 can (2.8 ounces) french-fried onions, crushed

3/4 cup grated Parmesan cheese

1/4 cup dry bread crumbs

1 teaspoon paprika

1/2 teaspoon salt

Dash pepper

1 broiler/fryer chicken (3 to 4 pounds), cut up

1/4 cup butter, melted

■ In a shallow bowl, whisk egg and milk. In another shallow bowl, combine the onions, cheese, bread crumbs, paprika, salt and pepper. Dip chicken in egg mixture, then roll in onion mixture.

■ Place in a greased 13-in. x 9-in. baking dish. Drizzle with butter. Bake, uncovered, at 350° for 50-60 minutes or until juices run clear.

A dash is a very small amount of seasoning added to a recipe with a quick downward stroke of the hand. A dash measures **between 1/16 and 1/8 teaspoon.**

I've fixed this dish many times for company, and I've never had anyone fail to ask for the recipe. The leftovers—if there are any—are very good heated up in the microwave. It's a great alternative for people who love fried chicken, but who don't want to deal with the messy frying process.

—ELVA JEAN CRISWELL CHARLESTON, MISSISSIPPI

Pork

198

208

197

The rich taste of **pork, ham and sausage** takes center stage in the entrees featured in this chapter. From lip-smacking **ribs to juicy pork roasts,** these family-pleasing recipes are tasty and versatile enough to be popular at picnics, buffets, everyday meals or special Sunday dinners.

MACARONI & CHEESE PIZZA

- Prepare macaroni and cheese according to package directions; stir in eggs. Spread onto a greased 12-in. pizza pan. Bake at 375° for 10 minutes or until a thermometer reads 160°.

- Meanwhile, in a large skillet, cook sausage and onion over medium heat until meat is no longer pink; drain.

- In a small bowl, combine the tomato sauce, basil and oregano. Spread over macaroni mixture. Layer with sausage mixture, mushrooms and cheese. Bake for 10 minutes or until the cheese is melted.

Kids love this recipe! What could be better than pizza and mac 'n' cheese all in one meal? To simplify things, use a can of pizza sauce instead of the tomato sauce, oregano and basil.

—**JENNY STANIEC** OAK GROVE, MINNESOTA

Macaroni & Cheese Pizza

PREP: 30 MIN. ■ BAKE: 10 MIN. ■ YIELD: 8 SERVINGS

- 1 package (7-1/4 ounces) macaroni and cheese dinner mix
- 2 eggs, lightly beaten
- 1/2 pound bulk Italian sausage
- 1/4 cup chopped onion
- 1 can (8 ounces) tomato sauce
- 1 teaspoon dried basil
- 1 teaspoon dried oregano
- 1 can (4 ounces) mushroom stems and pieces, drained
- 1 cup (4 ounces) shredded part-skim mozzarella cheese

To add **fresh and zesty crunch** to the pizza, sprinkle on **sliced green onions** and/or **chopped celery.** They add a more dimensional flavor and texture.

- Place ribs, meaty side up, on a rack in a greased 13-in. x 9-in. baking pan. Cover pan tightly with foil. Bake at 350° for 1-1/4 hours.

- Meanwhile, combine the next nine ingredients in a saucepan. Bring to a boil over medium heat. Reduce heat; simmer for 15 minutes, stirring occasionally.

- Drain ribs; remove rack and return ribs to pan. Cover with sauce. Bake, uncovered, for 35 minutes or until meat is tender, basting occasionally. Sprinkle with sesame seeds just before serving.

MAPLE GLAZED RIBS

I love maple syrup, and so does my family, so I gave this recipe a try. It's well worth the effort! I make these ribs often, and I never have leftovers. With two teenage boys who like to eat, this main dish is a real winner.

—**LINDA KOBELUCK** ARDROSSAN, ALBERTA

Maple Glazed Ribs

PREP: 30 MIN. ■ BAKE: 1 HOUR 50 MIN. ■ YIELD: 6 SERVINGS

- 3 pounds pork spareribs, cut into serving-size pieces
- 1 cup maple syrup
- 3 tablespoons orange juice concentrate
- 3 tablespoons ketchup
- 2 tablespoons soy sauce
- 1 tablespoon Dijon mustard
- 1 tablespoon Worcestershire sauce
- 1 teaspoon curry powder
- 1 garlic clove, minced
- 2 green onions, minced
- 1 tablespoon sesame seeds, toasted

Toast seeds in a dry skillet over medium heat for 3-5 minutes or until lightly browned, stirring occasionally. Or **bake on an ungreased baking sheet** at 350° for 8-10 minutes or until lightly browned. Watch the seeds to avoid scorching.

This tender roast is my husband's favorite meal. He even asks for it on his birthday! The recipe comes together easily but tastes like it was a labor of love.

—CAMIE HEWITT REDMOND, OREGON

GERMAN PORK ROAST

German Pork Roast

PREP: 20 MIN. ■ **BAKE:** 1-3/4 HOURS + STANDING ■ **YIELD:** 8 SERVINGS

- 3 tablespoons olive oil
- 4 garlic cloves, minced
- 1 teaspoon lemon juice
- 1 teaspoon stone-ground mustard
- 1 teaspoon salt
- 1/2 teaspoon *each* dried oregano, thyme and rosemary, crushed
- 1/4 teaspoon pepper
- 1 boneless whole pork loin roast (3 to 4 pounds)
- 4 medium potatoes, peeled and cut into wedges
- 3 medium onions, cut into wedges
- 1 medium yellow tomato, cut into wedges

- In a small bowl, combine the oil, garlic, lemon juice, mustard and seasonings. Rub over roast. Place on a rack in a shallow roasting pan.

- Bake, uncovered, at 350° for 20 minutes. Add the potatoes, onions and tomato to the pan; bake 40-70 minutes longer or until a thermometer reads 160° and vegetables are tender. Let stand for 10 minutes before slicing.

Cutting pork across the grain will produce slices with shorter fibers, **resulting in more tender pieces.** For a crisp surface on your roast, be sure the oven is **fully preheated** before placing the roast in it, and do not cover the meat while you are roasting it.

Roast Pork with Apples & Onions

Here, the sweetness of apples and onions complements roast pork. With its crisp skin and melt-in-your-mouth flavor, it is my family's favorite weekend meal.

—LILY JULOW GAINESVILLE, FLORIDA

PREP: 25 MIN.
BAKE: 45 MIN. + STANDING
YIELD: 8 SERVINGS

- 1 boneless whole pork loin roast (2 pounds)
- 1/4 teaspoon salt
- 1/4 teaspoon pepper
- 1 tablespoon olive oil
- 3 large Golden Delicious apples, cut into wedges
- 2 large onions, cut into wedges
- 5 garlic cloves, peeled
- 1 tablespoon minced fresh rosemary *or* 1 teaspoon dried rosemary, crushed

- Sprinkle roast with salt and pepper. In a large nonstick skillet, brown roast in oil on all sides. Place in a shallow roasting pan coated with cooking spray. Arrange the apples, onions and garlic around roast; sprinkle with the rosemary.

- Bake, uncovered, at 350° for 45-60 minutes or until a thermometer reads 145°, turning the apples, onions and garlic once. Let meat stand for 10 minutes before slicing.

➡ **NUTRITION FACTS:** 3 ounces cooked pork with 1/2 cup apple mixture equals 215 calories, 7 g fat (2 g saturated fat), 56 mg cholesterol, 109 mg sodium, 15 g carbohydrate, 3 g fiber, 23 g protein. **DIABETIC EXCHANGES:** 3 lean meat, 1 fruit.

This dish, made with flavorful smoked sausage, is a hearty meal all by itself. My family thinks it's a fantastic meal. Maybe your family will love it, too!

—CATHERINE O'HARA
BRIDGETON, NEW JERSEY

FARM-STYLE SAUSAGE BAKE

Farm-Style Sausage Bake

PREP: 30 MIN. ■ BAKE: 30 MIN. ■ YIELD: 6 SERVINGS

6 medium potatoes (about 2 pounds), peeled and cubed

3/4 cup milk

2 tablespoons butter

3 to 4 green onions, sliced

2 garlic cloves, minced

2 egg yolks

Dash *each* pepper and ground nutmeg

1 pound smoked sausage, sliced

1/2 cup cubed part-skim mozzarella cheese

2 tablespoons grated Parmesan cheese

2 tablespoons dried parsley flakes

1 teaspoon dried thyme *or* rubbed sage

■ Place potatoes in a large saucepan and cover with water. Bring to a boil. Reduce heat; cover and simmer for 15-20 minutes or until tender. Drain.

■ Transfer to a large bowl; mash the potatoes. Beat in the milk, butter, green onions, garlic, egg yolks, pepper and nutmeg until light and fluffy.

■ Stir in the sausage, cheeses and parsley. Spoon into a greased 2-qt. baking dish. Sprinkle with thyme. Bake, uncovered, at 400° for 30 minutes or until a thermometer reads 160°.

Barbecued Sticky Ribs

PREP: 10 MIN.
BAKE: 1 HOUR 20 MIN.
YIELD: 6-8 SERVINGS

3/4 teaspoon garlic powder

1 teaspoon salt

1/2 teaspoon pepper

3-1/2 to 4-1/2 pounds pork spareribs (2 racks)

SAUCE:

1 can (10-3/4 ounces) condensed tomato soup, undiluted

1 small onion, chopped

1 cup water

1/2 cup light corn syrup

1/2 cup ketchup

1/4 cup cider vinegar

2 tablespoons Worcestershire sauce

2 teaspoons chili powder

1 teaspoon hot pepper sauce

1/2 teaspoon ground cinnamon

■ Combine garlic powder, salt and pepper; rub onto both sides of ribs. Place in a single layer in a 15-in. x 10-in. x 1-in. baking pan.

■ Bake at 325° for 30-35 minutes; drain. Combine sauce ingredients; pour over ribs. Bake 50-60 minutes longer or until meat is tender, basting occasionally. Cut into serving-size pieces.

If you're really hungry, there's nothing like a rack of these ribs! They're a great summertime treat, but our family also traditionally enjoys them with side dishes of coleslaw and beans during the football games on New Year's Day. What's not to like?

—JACKIE REMSBERG LA CANADA, CALIFORNIA

TATER BRAT BAKE

- In a large saucepan, combine bratwurst and beer. Bring to a boil. Reduce heat. Cover and simmer for 10-15 minutes or until a thermometer reads 160°. Drain and cut into 1/4-in. slices. In a large skillet, brown brats in butter over medium-high heat; drain on paper towels.

- Spoon sauerkraut into a greased 13-in. x 9-in. baking dish. Top with brats. Combine soup and milk; drizzle over brats. Top with Tater Tots. Bake at 450° for 20-25 minutes or until potatoes are lightly browned.

- Sprinkle with cheese; bake 5 minutes longer or until cheese is melted.

My husband suggested a brats-and-kraut lunch for friends that were visiting for their high school reunion. Rather than cut his visiting time, I made this. It was so easy!

—**PAULINE LENTZ** MESA, ARIZONA

Tater Brat Bake

PREP: 25 MIN. ■ **BAKE:** 25 MIN. ■ **YIELD:** 6 SERVINGS

- 1 package (1-1/4 pounds) uncooked bratwurst links
- 2 bottles (12 ounces *each*) beer *or* nonalcoholic beer
- 2 tablespoons butter
- 1 can (16 ounces) sauerkraut, rinsed, drained and chopped

- 1 can (10-3/4 ounces) condensed cheddar cheese soup, undiluted
- 1/2 cup milk
- 1 package (32 ounces) frozen Tater Tots
- 1 cup (4 ounces) shredded cheddar cheese

The term "simmer" means to cook liquids alone or a combination of ingredients with liquid just **under the boiling point** (180° to 200°). The surface of the liquid will have some movement and there may be **small bubbles** around the side of the pan.

My husband loves pizza and this is a fast alternative to the real thing. They're a great football game party snack, too, and always a hit. Let the kids select their own ingredients, such as cooked ground beef, ham or black olives.

—MARY ADDY
WEST POINT, NEBRASKA

ZIPPY CALZONES

Zippy Calzones

PREP/TOTAL TIME: 30 MIN. ■ **YIELD:** 4 SERVINGS

- 1 tube (13.8 ounces) refrigerated pizza crust
- 1 cup (4 ounces) shredded part-skim mozzarella cheese
- 32 slices pepperoni
- 3/4 cup 1% cottage cheese
- 3/4 cup julienned green, sweet red *and/or* yellow pepper
- 1/4 cup finely chopped onion

■ Unroll pizza crust; roll into a 12-in. square. Cut into four 6-in. squares. Sprinkle 2 tablespoons mozzarella cheese over half of each square to within 1/2 in. of edges. Top with eight slices pepperoni and 3 tablespoons cottage cheese.

■ Combine pepper and onion; place 1/4 cup mixture on each square; top with 2 tablespoons cottage cheese. Fold dough over filling; press edges with a fork to seal.

■ Transfer to a lightly greased baking sheet. Bake at 400° for 13-18 minutes or until golden brown.

Lemon-Rosemary Pork Tenderloin

This moist, tender pork is seasoned with a wonderful herb and lemon rub I perfected myself. Even my husband, who is a chef, thinks this dish is special enough for company.

—CAROL BIRKEMEIER
NASHVILLE, INDIANA

PREP: 10 MIN.
BAKE: 25 MIN. + STANDING
YIELD: 8 SERVINGS

- 1 medium onion, finely chopped
- 2 tablespoons olive oil
- 1 tablespoon lemon juice
- 1 teaspoon minced fresh rosemary *or* 1/4 teaspoon dried rosemary, crushed
- 1 teaspoon minced fresh thyme *or* 1/4 teaspoon dried thyme
- 1 teaspoon grated lemon peel
- 1 garlic clove, minced
- 1/2 teaspoon salt
- 1/2 teaspoon pepper
- 2 pork tenderloins (1 pound *each*)

■ In a small bowl, combine the first nine ingredients; rub over tenderloins. Place on a rack in a shallow roasting pan.

■ Bake, uncovered, at 400° for 25-35 minutes or until a thermometer reads 160°. Cover with foil; let stand for 10 minutes before slicing.

➤➤ **NUTRITION FACTS:** 1 serving equals 176 calories, 7 g fat (2 g saturated fat), 74 mg cholesterol, 204 mg sodium, 2 g carbohydrate, trace fiber, 24 g protein. **DIABETIC EXCHANGES:** 3 lean meat.

I sometimes make several of these savory loaves to keep in my freezer for weeknight meals. Loaded with ham, broccoli and cheese, the spiral sandwich slices are ideal for folks with lively lifestyles.

—SUSAN BROWN
LITHONIA, GEORGIA

HAM 'N' CHEESE STROMBOLI

Ham 'n' Cheese Stromboli

PREP: 15 MIN. ■ **BAKE:** 35 MIN. + STANDING ■ **YIELD:** 6 SERVINGS

- 1 loaf (1 pound) frozen white bread dough, thawed
- 1/2 pound sliced Swiss cheese
- 1/2 pound thinly sliced deli ham
- 1 cup (4 ounces) shredded cheddar cheese
- 1 cup (4 ounces) shredded Colby cheese
- 1 package (16 ounces) frozen chopped broccoli, thawed and drained
- 1/2 teaspoon garlic powder

■ On a floured surface, roll dough into an 18-in. x 12-in. rectangle. Layer with Swiss cheese, ham, cheddar cheese, Colby cheese and broccoli to within 1 in. of edges; sprinkle with garlic powder. Roll up jelly-roll style, starting with a long side; seal seams and ends.

■ Place seam side down on a greased 15-in. x 10-in. x 1-in. baking pan. Bake, uncovered, at 400° for 20 minutes. Cover loosely with foil; bake 15-20 minutes longer. Let stand for 10 minutes before slicing.

Potato Sausage Casserole

The subtle spices in the pork sausage give this dish a distinctive flavor that my family has loved for years. Not only is this hearty casserole a great main dish on the dinner table, it reheats nicely.

—MRS. FRED OSBORN
THAYER, KANSAS

PREP: 20 MIN. ■ **BAKE:** 70 MIN.
YIELD: 6 SERVINGS

- 1 pound bulk pork sausage
- 1 can (10-3/4 ounces) condensed cream of mushroom soup, undiluted
- 3/4 cup milk
- 1/2 cup chopped onion
- 1/2 teaspoon salt
- 1/4 teaspoon pepper
- 3 cups sliced peeled potatoes
- 2 cups (8 ounces) shredded cheddar cheese

Minced fresh parsley, optional

■ In a large skillet, cook sausage over medium heat until no longer pink; drain and set aside. Combine the soup, milk, onion, salt and pepper.

■ In a greased 2-qt. baking dish, layer half of the potatoes, soup mixture and sausage. Repeat layers.

■ Cover and bake at 350° for 60-65 minutes or until potatoes are tender. Sprinkle with cheese; bake, uncovered, for 2-3 minutes or until the cheese is melted. Garnish with parsley if desired.

- In a large nonstick skillet coated with cooking spray, cook ham over medium heat for 3-5 minutes or until lightly browned. Stir in the carrots, soup, spinach, water, pepper and salt. Bring to a boil. Reduce heat, simmer for 5-10 minutes or until heated through. Pour into a greased 8-in. square baking dish.

- Unroll the crescent roll dough; separate it into two rectangles. Seal seams and perforations. Cut each rectangle lengthwise into four strips; make a lattice crust.

- Bake at 375° for 18-22 minutes or until bubbly and crust is golden brown.

HAM & SPINACH CASSEROLE

This is down-home cooking at its best! Ham and veggies join forces with a creamy sauce and golden topping to create a hearty meal in one. It looks impressive, but it's easy to prepare.

—TASTE OF HOME TEST KITCHEN

Ham & Spinach Casserole

PREP: 25 MIN. ■ **BAKE:** 20 MIN. ■ **YIELD:** 4 SERVINGS

- 3 cups cubed fully cooked ham
- 1 package (16 ounces) frozen sliced carrots, thawed
- 1 can (10-3/4 ounces) condensed cream of potato soup, undiluted
- 1 package (10 ounces) frozen creamed spinach, thawed
- 1/4 cup water
- 1/4 teaspoon pepper
- 1/8 teaspoon salt
- 1 tube (4 ounces) refrigerated crescent rolls

Fully cooked ham is ham **that is cooked and smoked** and/or cured. It can be **eaten without heating** but is generally heated to about 140° for optimal flavor.

1. Sprinkle pork chops with pepper and salt. Place flour in a large resealable plastic bag; add the pork chops, one at a time, and shake to coat.

2. In a large nonstick skillet coated with cooking spray, brown chops on both sides. Transfer to an ungreased 11-in. x 7-in. baking dish. Top with tomatoes, mushrooms, onions and olives. Sprinkle with garlic, basil and oregano.

3. Cover and bake at 350° for 35-40 minutes or until a thermometer reads 160°.

➤ **NUTRITION FACTS:** 1 pork chop equals 251 calories, 10 g fat (3 g saturated fat), 57 mg cholesterol, 670 mg sodium, 15 g carbohydrate, 2 g fiber, 25 g protein. **DIABETIC EXCHANGES:** 3 lean meat, 2 vegetable, 1/2 fat.

ZESTY PORK CHOPS

My own creation, this recipe is light, flavorful and simple to make. I sometimes top these chops with bread crumbs and shredded mozzarella for the last 10 minutes of baking. They're a favorite with family and friends.

—**CHERYL BOAK** ROTHESAY, NEW BRUNSWICK

Zesty Pork Chops

PREP: 25 MIN. ■ BAKE: 35 MIN. ■ YIELD: 4 SERVINGS

4 boneless pork loin chops (4 ounces *each*)
1/4 teaspoon pepper
1/8 teaspoon salt
1/4 cup all-purpose flour
1 can (14-1/2 ounces) diced tomatoes, undrained
1-3/4 cups sliced fresh mushrooms

4 green onions, chopped
1/2 cup pimiento-stuffed olives
1 garlic clove, minced
1 teaspoon minced fresh basil *or* 1/4 teaspoon dried basil
1 teaspoon minced fresh oregano *or* 1/4 teaspoon dried oregano

Remove dirt from mushrooms by wiping with a damp paper towel. Or rinse under cold water, drain and pat dry. Do not peel, but trim stems. Mushrooms can be eaten **raw, grilled, stir-fried, baked, broiled, grilled or marinated.**

A slightly sweet glaze coats these delicious pork chops that have been described as both hearty and homey. We think you'll agree!

—DAWN KLOMAN
WATERTOWN, WISCONSIN

GLAZED PORK CHOPS WITH CORN BREAD DRESSING

Glazed Pork Chops With Corn Bread Dressing

PREP: 10 MIN. ■ **BAKE:** 25 MIN. ■ **YIELD:** 6 SERVINGS

1-1/4 cups reduced-sodium chicken broth

3/4 cup chopped onion

3/4 cup frozen corn

1 celery rib, chopped

Dash cayenne pepper

3 cups crushed corn bread stuffing

6 boneless pork loin chops (6 ounces *each*)

2 tablespoons brown sugar

2 teaspoons spicy brown mustard

■ In a large saucepan, bring the broth, onion, corn, celery and cayenne to a boil. Remove from the heat; stir in stuffing.

■ Transfer to a 13-in. x 9-in. baking dish coated with cooking spray. Top with pork chops. Combine brown sugar and mustard; spread over chops. Bake, uncovered, at 400° for 25-30 minutes or until a thermometer reads 160°.

➥ **NUTRITION FACTS:** 1 serving equals 389 calories, 11 g fat (4 g saturated fat), 82 mg cholesterol, 516 mg sodium, 33 g carbohydrate, 2 g fiber, 37 g protein. **DIABETIC EXCHANGES:** 5 lean meat, 2 starch, 1 fat.

Bavarian Wiener Supper

Here's a family meal that also goes over well at potlucks. The dish is always scraped clean, and I'm asked for the recipe—which my daughter received from a friend.

—HELEN KENDIG
LAWRENCEBURG, KENTUCKY

PREP: 10 MIN. ■ **BAKE:** 35 MIN.
YIELD: 8 SERVINGS

1 can (10-3/4 ounces) condensed cream of mushroom soup, undiluted

1/2 cup mayonnaise

1 jar (16 ounces) sauerkraut, rinsed and well drained

1 package (1 pound) hot dogs, halved lengthwise and cut into bite-size pieces

1 teaspoon caraway seeds

4 cups cubed cooked potatoes

1/4 cup soft bread crumbs

1 tablespoon butter, melted

1/4 teaspoon paprika

■ In a large bowl, combine the soup and the mayonnaise. In another large bowl, combine the sauerkraut, hot dogs, caraway seeds and half of the soup mixture. Spread into a greased shallow 2-qt. baking dish.

■ In a large bowl, combine potatoes and remaining soup mixture. Spoon over sauerkraut mixture.

■ Combine the bread crumbs, butter and paprika; sprinkle over potatoes. Bake, uncovered, at 350° for 35-40 minutes or until heated through.

I learned to make this hearty pork, corn and noodle dish from my grandmother. We never have a family get-together without it. It's a great addition to a buffet and makes a full meal with the addition of warm dinner rolls.

—BARBARA BEYER
TWO RIVERS, WISCONSIN

PORK NOODLE CASSEROLE

Pork Noodle Casserole

PREP: 10 MIN. ■ BAKE: 1 HOUR ■ YIELD: 6 SERVINGS

- 3 cups cubed cooked pork
- 1 can (14-3/4 ounces) cream-style corn
- 1 cup chicken broth
- 4 ounces process cheese (Velveeta), diced
- 2/3 cup chopped green pepper
- 2/3 cup chopped onion
- 1 jar (4-1/2 ounces) whole mushrooms, drained
- 2 tablespoons diced pimientos
- 1/2 teaspoon salt
- 1/4 teaspoon pepper
- 8 ounces uncooked egg noodles

- In a large bowl, combine the first 10 ingredients. Add noodles; gently toss to coat. Transfer to a greased 2-1/2-qt. baking dish.

- Cover and bake at 325° for 1 hour or until noodles are tender, stirring every 20 minutes.

Creamy Spinach Sausage Pasta

PREP: 15 MIN. ■ BAKE: 45 MIN.
YIELD: 5 SERVINGS

- 3 cups uncooked rigatoni *or* large tube pasta
- 1 pound bulk Italian sausage
- 1 cup finely chopped onion
- 1 can (14-1/2 ounces) Italian diced tomatoes, undrained
- 1 package (10 ounces) frozen creamed spinach, thawed
- 1 package (8 ounces) cream cheese, softened
- 2 cups (8 ounces) shredded part-skim mozzarella cheese, *divided*

- Cook pasta according to package directions. Meanwhile, in a Dutch oven, cook sausage and onion over medium heat until sausage is no longer pink; drain. Stir in the tomatoes, spinach, cream cheese and 1 cup mozzarella cheese. Transfer to a greased 11-in. x 7-in. baking dish.

- Cover and bake at 350° for 35 minutes. Uncover; sprinkle with remaining cheese. Bake 10 minutes longer or until cheese is melted.

Process cheese is a **blend of different cheeses** that is similar in flavor to the natural cheese from which it's made. **The most common brand** name of process American cheese is Velveeta.

So rich and creamy, this pasta is wonderfully cheesy and delicious! It comes together with just seven simple yet flavorful ingredients. For time-saving convenience, I like to assemble it the night before, then bake it the next day! It's an all-around great recipe.

—SUSIE SIZEMORE COLLINSVILLE, VIRGINIA

CHILI CHEESE DOG CASSEROLE

- Prepare corn bread batter according to package directions. Spread half the batter into a greased 8-in. square baking dish; set aside.

- In a large skillet, saute the green pepper, onion and celery in oil until crisp-tender. Stir in the hot dogs; saute 3-4 minutes longer or until lightly browned. Stir in the chili with beans, brown sugar, garlic powder and chili powder; heat through. Stir in 3/4 cup cheese.

- Spoon over corn bread batter; top with remaining corn bread batter. Sprinkle remaining cheese over the top.

- Bake, uncovered, at 350° for 28-32 minutes or until a toothpick inserted near the center comes out clean. Let casserole stand for 5 minutes before serving.

Kids and adults alike will dive right into this hearty, comforting dish. With a crispy cheese topping on a warm corn bread crust, this family-pleasing recipe is a keeper.

—TASTE OF HOME TEST KITCHEN

Chili Cheese Dog Casserole

PREP: 20 MIN. ■ BAKE: 30 MIN. ■ YIELD: 6 SERVINGS

- 1 package (8-1/2 ounces) corn bread/muffin mix
- 1 cup chopped green pepper
- 1/2 cup chopped onion
- 1/2 cup chopped celery
- 1 tablespoon olive oil
- 1 package (1 pound) hot dogs, halved lengthwise and cut into bite-size pieces

- 1 can (15 ounces) chili with beans
- 2 tablespoons brown sugar
- 1/2 teaspoon garlic powder
- 1/2 teaspoon chili powder
- 1 cup (4 ounces) shredded cheddar cheese, *divided*

Garlic and onion powders tend to absorb moisture from the air, especially during warm weather months. **Store them in airtight spice jars** to keep them as free from moisture and humidity as possible.

Many pork recipes were too spicy for me, so I decided to try this sweeter alternative. That was 18 years ago, and it became a family favorite. It tastes great the day after in a cold sandwich, too.

—MADELINE STRAUSS
CLINTON TOWNSHIP, MICHIGAN

CRANBERRY GLAZED PORK ROAST

Cranberry Glazed Pork Roast

PREP: 15 MIN. ■ **BAKE:** 1 HOUR + STANDING ■ **YIELD:** 6-8 SERVINGS

1 teaspoon salt	1 cup jellied cranberry sauce
1/2 teaspoon pepper	1/2 cup orange juice
1 boneless rolled pork loin roast (3 pounds)	1/4 cup packed brown sugar

- Combine the salt and pepper; rub over the roast. Place roast, fat side up, on a rack in a greased roasting pan. Bake, uncovered, at 350° for 40 minutes.

- Meanwhile, combine the cranberry sauce, orange juice and brown sugar in a saucepan; cook over medium heat until cranberry sauce is melted. Drizzle a fourth of the glaze over roast.

- Bake 20 minutes longer; or until a thermometer reads 145°, basting frequently with remaining glaze. Let stand for 10 minutes before slicing. Warm remaining glaze; serve with roast.

Ham 'n' Tater Bake

This casserole reminds me of a loaded baked potato. I usually make it several times a month—I've even served it to company. I'm always asked for the recipe, which I got from my sister.

—PEGGY GRIEME
PINEHURST, NORTH CAROLINA

PREP: 10 MIN. ■ **BAKE:** 40 MIN.
YIELD: 6-8 SERVINGS

- 1 package (28 ounces) frozen steak fries
- 3 cups frozen chopped broccoli, thawed and drained
- 1-1/2 cups diced fully cooked ham
- 1 can (10-3/4 ounces) condensed cream of broccoli soup, undiluted
- 3/4 cup milk
- 1/2 cup mayonnaise
- 1 cup (4 ounces) shredded cheddar cheese

- Arrange the fries in a greased 3-qt. baking dish; layer with broccoli and then ham. Combine the soup, milk and mayonnaise until smooth; pour over ham.

- Cover and bake at 350° for 20 minutes. Sprinkle casserole with cheese; bake, uncovered, 20-25 minutes longer or until it is bubbly.

I'm a home health nurse and got this recipe from one of my elderly clients, who had used it for years. Now it's one of my family's favorites. It will never curdle, thanks to the secret ingredient which is powdered creamer.

—KATHY JOHNSON
LAKE CITY,
SOUTH DAKOTA

SCALLOPED POTATOES 'N' HAM CASSEROLE

Scalloped Potatoes 'n' Ham Casserole

PREP: 25 MIN. ■ **BAKE:** 1 HOUR ■ **YIELD:** 6 SERVINGS

3/4	cup powdered nondairy creamer	3/4	teaspoon paprika
1-3/4	cups water	6	large potatoes, peeled and thinly sliced
3	tablespoons butter	2	cups diced fully cooked ham
3	tablespoons all-purpose flour	1	cup (4 ounces) shredded cheddar cheese
2	tablespoons dried minced onion		
1	teaspoon salt		

■ In a small bowl, combine creamer and water until smooth. In a small saucepan, melt butter. Stir in the flour, onion, salt and paprika until smooth; gradually add creamer mixture. Bring to a boil; cook and stir for 1-2 minutes or until thickened.

■ In a greased shallow 2-1/2-qt. baking dish, combine potatoes and ham. Pour sauce over the top.

■ Cover and bake at 350° for 15 minutes. Uncover; bake 40-50 minutes longer or until potatoes are tender. Sprinkle with cheese; bake for 5-10 minutes or until edges are bubbly and cheese is melted.

Beer-Glazed Ham

Here's a fuss-free way to "fancy up" your Easter ham that everyone will love. My motto is: Anything with brown sugar has to be good. And this ham really is!

—KIM RYON
FACTORYVILLE, PENNSYLVANIA

PREP: 5 MIN.
BAKE: 1 HOUR 40 MIN.
YIELD: 8 SERVINGS

- 1 boneless fully cooked ham (3 pounds)
- 1 can (12 ounces) beer *or* nonalcoholic beer
- 1 cup packed brown sugar
- 2 tablespoons balsamic vinegar
- 2 teaspoons ground mustard

■ Place ham on a rack in a shallow roasting pan. Score the surface of the ham, making diamond shapes 1/2 in. deep. Set aside 2 tablespoons beer. Pour remaining beer over the ham. Bake, uncovered, at 350° for 1 hour.

■ In a small bowl, combine the brown sugar, vinegar, mustard and reserved beer; spread over ham. Bake 40-45 minutes longer or until a thermometer reads 140°, basting occasionally.

- In a large saucepan, melt butter. Stir in flour until smooth; gradually add broth and milk. Bring to a boil; cook and stir for 2 minutes or until thickened. Add the pork, vegetables, cheese, seasoned salt and pepper; heat through.

- Transfer to a greased 11-in. x 7-in. baking dish. On a lightly floured surface, roll pastry into an 11-in. x 7-in. rectangle. Place over pork mixture. Brush with egg.

- Bake, uncovered, at 425° for 18-22 minutes or until golden brown. Let stand for 5 minutes before cutting.

To **ensure that puff pastry rises**, handle it as little as possible to avoid stretching and tearing. Only **brush egg on top** of the dough, not the edges. If the edges are brushed, the layers of dough will stick together, and the pastry won't rise during baking.

This stick-to-your-ribs entree is made for cold weather, so huddle up with the family and enjoy! You might even have enough delicious leftovers for lunch the next day.

—TASTE OF HOME TEST KITCHEN

Creamy Pork Potpie

PREP: 20 MIN. ■ COOK: 20 MIN. ■ YIELD: 6 SERVINGS

1/4 cup butter, cubed	1-1/2 cups (6 ounces) shredded cheddar cheese
1/2 cup all-purpose flour	1/2 teaspoon seasoned salt
1 can (14-1/2 ounces) chicken broth	Dash pepper
3/4 cup milk	1 sheet frozen puff pastry, thawed
2-1/2 cups cubed cooked pork	1 egg, lightly beaten
2-1/2 cups frozen broccoli-cauliflower blend	

Fish & Seafood

217 220 216

For a healthy change of scenery at the dinner table, turn to these **one-dish meals that spotlight fish or seafood** as the main attraction. Friends and family will **welcome a refreshing new twist** on hearty casseroles, classic quiche, pasta bakes and more. Keep an eye out for Nutrition Information.

CHEESY CLAM MANICOTTI

- In a large saucepan, combine spaghetti sauce and hot pepper sauce. Drain one can of clams; add clams to sauce. Stir in clams and juice from second can. Bring to a boil. Reduce heat; simmer, uncovered, for 20 minutes.

- Meanwhile, in a large bowl, beat the ricotta and cream cheeses until smooth. Stir in the cheeses, garlic, pepper and oregano. Stuff into manicotti shells.

- Spread 3/4 cup clam sauce into a greased 11-in. x 7-in. baking dish. Arrange manicotti over sauce; top with remaining sauce.

- Bake, uncovered, at 350° for 25-30 minutes or until bubbly. Let stand for 5 minutes before serving.

I created this recipe when I was having company and couldn't decide between serving seafood or dishing up something Italian. Manicotti was a big hit! I usually add a little extra hot sauce to give it that special kick.

—**KATHY KYSAR** HOMER, ALASKA

Cheesy Clam Manicotti

PREP: 30 MIN. ■ BAKE: 25 MIN. ■ YIELD: 4 SERVINGS

1 jar (24 ounces) meatless spaghetti sauce	2 cups (8 ounces) shredded part-skim mozzarella cheese
1/4 teaspoon hot pepper sauce	1/3 cup grated Parmesan cheese
2 cans (6-1/2 ounces *each*) minced clams	1 teaspoon minced garlic
1 carton (8 ounces) ricotta cheese	1/2 teaspoon pepper
4 ounces cream cheese, softened	1/4 teaspoon dried oregano
1/4 cup spreadable chive and onion cream cheese	8 manicotti shells, cooked and drained

Spooning a cheesy filling into manicotti shells can be time-consuming and messy. To avoid the trouble, put the filling in a cake-decorating bag and easily **pipe it into the pasta** tubes.

APRICOT-GLAZED SALMON WITH HERB RICE

- Place salmon in a 13-in. x 9-in. baking dish coated with cooking spray. Sprinkle with salt and pepper. In a small bowl, combine the wine, spreadable fruit and ginger; spoon over salmon.

- Bake at 375° for 15-20 minutes or until fish flakes easily with a fork.

- Meanwhile, in a small saucepan, bring the broth, rice and butter to a boil. Reduce heat; cover and simmer for 10 minutes. Add apricots; cover and cook 5-8 minutes longer or until liquid is absorbed and rice is tender. Stir in the parsley, chives and thyme. Serve with salmon. Sprinkle each serving with almonds.

Salmon lovers will really enjoy this nice and fruity tasting fish with just the right amount of sweetness. If salmon is new to your family, this is a great way to introduce it to them.

—CHARLENE CHAMBERS ORMOND BEACH, FLORIDA

Apricot-Glazed Salmon With Herb Rice

PREP: 25 MIN. ■ COOK: 20 MIN. ■ YIELD: 6 SERVINGS

6 salmon fillets (4 ounces *each*)	2 teaspoons butter
1/4 teaspoon salt	2 tablespoons chopped dried apricots
1/8 teaspoon pepper	2 tablespoons minced fresh parsley
1/3 cup white wine *or* reduced-sodium chicken broth	1 tablespoon minced chives
1/3 cup apricot spreadable fruit	1 teaspoon minced fresh thyme *or* 1/4 teaspoon dried thyme
1/2 teaspoon grated fresh gingerroot	3 tablespoons sliced almonds, toasted
2 cups reduced-sodium chicken broth	
1 cup uncooked long grain rice	

Fish should smell and look good, whether it is refrigerated or frozen. **Good-quality refrigerated fish** doesn't have a heavy fish odor. **Fillets and steaks** should have a fresh-cut appearance with no discoloration or browning along the edges.

You can toss your other tuna casserole recipes, 'cause this one's the ultimate! You'll love the ease of this tasty dish.

—BONNIE HORD
LEE'S SUMMIT, MISSOURI

TUNA MAC AND CHEESE BAKE

Tuna Mac and Cheese Bake

PREP: 15 MIN. ■ **BAKE:** 30 MIN. ■ **YIELD:** 8 SERVINGS

1 package (7-1/4 ounces) macaroni and cheese dinner mix

1 can (12 ounces) light water-packed tuna, drained and flaked

1 can (10-3/4 ounces) condensed cream of mushroom soup, undiluted

1-1/3 cups 2% milk

2 packages (9 ounces *each*) frozen peas and pearl onions

1 can (4 ounces) mushroom stems and pieces, drained

1 can (2.8 ounces) french-fried onions, *divided*

■ Prepare macaroni and cheese according to package directions. Stir in the tuna, soup, milk, peas, mushrooms and half of the fried onions.

■ Place in a greased 11-in. x 7-in. baking dish. Bake, uncovered, at 325° for 25 minutes. Sprinkle with remaining fried onions; bake 5 minutes longer or until heated through.

Shrimp Rice Casserole

This casserole offers meal-in-one convenience and is practically guaranteed to satisfy your family's cravings for comfort food.

—MARIE ROBERTS
LAKE CHARLES, LOUISIANA

PREP: 30 MIN. ■ **BAKE:** 35 MIN.
YIELD: 6 SERVINGS

1 large green pepper, chopped

1 medium onion, chopped

1/2 cup butter

1 pound uncooked medium shrimp, peeled and deveined

1/2 teaspoon salt

1/4 teaspoon cayenne pepper

3 cups cooked long grain rice

1 can (10-3/4 ounces) condensed cream of mushroom soup, undiluted

2 cups (8 ounces) shredded cheddar cheese, *divided*

■ In a large skillet, saute green pepper and onion in butter until tender. Add the shrimp, salt and cayenne; cook and stir for 2-3 minutes or until shrimp turn pink. Add the rice, soup and 1 cup cheese; stir until combined.

■ Pour into a greased 1-1/2-qt. baking dish. Cover and bake at 325° for 30 minutes. Sprinkle with remaining cheese. Bake, uncovered, for 5 minutes longer or until heated through and cheese is melted.

I created this entree years ago when a friend gave me some fresh-caught mahi mahi. Shortly after, I entered the recipe in a contest and won! I think you'll agree it's a real keeper.

—VIRGINIA ANTHONY
JACKSONVILLE, FLORIDA

MEDITERRANEAN MAHI MAHI

Mediterranean Mahi Mahi

PREP: 30 MIN. ■ BAKE: 10 MIN. ■ YIELD: 4 SERVINGS

1 medium onion, chopped	1/2 teaspoon Greek seasoning
1 medium green pepper, chopped	4 mahi mahi fillets (6 ounces *each*)
4-1/2 teaspoons olive oil, *divided*	1/4 teaspoon salt
1 garlic clove, minced	1/4 teaspoon pepper
3/4 cup salsa	1/4 cup crumbled tomato and basil feta cheese
1/2 cup white wine *or* chicken broth	
1/4 cup halved Greek olives	

■ In a large ovenproof skillet, saute onion and green pepper in 1-1/2 teaspoons oil until tender. Add garlic; saute 1 minute longer.

■ Stir in the salsa, wine, olives and Greek seasoning. Bring to a boil. Reduce heat; simmer, uncovered, for 5 minutes or until slightly thickened. Transfer to a bowl; set aside.

■ Sprinkle mahi mahi with salt and pepper. In the same skillet, lightly brown fillets in remaining oil for 2 minutes on each side. Spoon salsa mixture over fillets.

■ Bake, uncovered, at 425° for 6 minutes. Sprinkle with cheese; bake 2-3 minutes longer or until fish just turns opaque.

Tuna-Chip Casserole

Unlike casseroles that have chips only on top, this one has them on the bottom and in the middle. Cheddar cheese and sliced almonds make a cheesy and crunchy topping.

—JANIS PLOURDE
SMOOTH ROCK FALLS, ONTARIO

PREP: 20 MIN. ■ BAKE: 20 MIN.
YIELD: 6 SERVINGS

1 package (7 ounces) plain potato chips, *divided*

1 can (5 ounces) light water-packed tuna, drained and flaked

1 package (10-1/2 ounces) frozen asparagus tips, thawed and patted dry *or* 1 can (15 ounces) asparagus spears, drained and sliced

SAUCE:

2/3 cup evaporated milk

1 tablespoon lemon juice

1/4 teaspoon ground mustard

1/8 teaspoon white pepper

TOPPING:

1/4 cup shredded cheddar cheese

1/2 cup sliced almonds

■ Crush chips and place half in greased 2-qt. baking dish. Arrange tuna over chips. Top with asparagus and the remaining chips. Combine sauce ingredients and pour over top. Sprinkle with cheese and almonds.

■ Bake, uncovered, at 325° for 20-25 minutes or until heated through. Let stand for 5 minutes before serving.

SPICY SHRIMP PIZZA

- In a large skillet over medium heat, cook shrimp and pepper flakes in oil for 2-3 minutes or until shrimp turn pink. Remove and keep warm.

- In the same skillet, saute onion until tender. Add garlic; cook 1 minute longer. Add the cherry tomatoes, crushed tomatoes, wine, oregano and pepper. Bring to a boil; cook until liquid is reduced, stirring occasionally. Add shrimp and parsley; heat through.

- Place crust on an ungreased pizza pan. Spread shrimp mixture over crust to within 1/2 in. of edges; sprinkle with cheeses.

- Bake at 450° for 8-10 minutes or until cheese is melted and edges are lightly browned.

The sophisticated blend of seasonings, shrimp and a splash of white wine will make my awesome pizza a favorite with your grown-up friends. This recipe is special enough for company but quick enough for weeknights, too.

—**DEBRA UDDEN** COLORADO SPRINGS, COLORADO

Spicy Shrimp Pizza

PREP: 30 MIN. ■ **BAKE:** 10 MIN. ■ **YIELD:** 6 SLICES.

1 pound uncooked medium shrimp, peeled and deveined	1/2 teaspoon dried oregano
1/2 to 3/4 teaspoon crushed red pepper flakes	1/8 teaspoon pepper
	3 tablespoons minced fresh parsley
2 tablespoons olive oil	1 prebaked 12-inch thin pizza crust
1 medium onion, chopped	
5 garlic cloves, minced	1 cup (4 ounces) shredded Italian cheese blend
12 cherry tomatoes, halved	
1 can (15 ounces) crushed tomatoes, undrained	1 cup (4 ounces) shredded Parmesan *or* Parmigiano-Reggiano cheese
1 cup white wine *or* chicken broth	

If garlic cloves start to sprout, **they pick up a strong, bitter taste.** To prevent this flavor from being added to your food, cut the cloves in half before using and **remove the green sprout** in the middle. The garlic will taste fresher.

ASPARAGUS FISH BUNDLES

- Wrap each fillet around five asparagus spears; secure with toothpicks. Place in a 13-in. x 9-in. baking dish coated with cooking spray. Sprinkle with salt and pepper.

- Cover and bake at 350° for 15 minutes. Uncover; sprinkle with onions. Bake, uncovered, 12-15 minutes longer or until fish flakes easily with a fork and asparagus is crisp-tender.

- Meanwhile, in a small saucepan, combine the sauce ingredients until blended. Bring to a boil; cook and stir for 1-2 minutes or until thickened. Discard toothpicks from the bundles; serve with sauce.

➡ **NUTRITION FACTS:** 1 bundle with 2 tablespoons sauce equals 172 calories, 1 g fat (trace saturated fat), 34 mg cholesterol, 414 mg sodium, 6 g carbohydrate, 2 g fiber, 27 g protein. **DIABETIC EXCHANGES:** 5 lean meat, 1 vegetable.

Low-fat food can look just as appealing as heavier entrees. Wrapped around asparagus bundles, these mouthwatering fish fillets are an ideal example. The sauce adds an exceptional touch to any dinner.

—JANE SHAPTON IRVINE, CALIFORNIA

Asparagus Fish Bundles

PREP: 25 MIN. ■ **BAKE:** 30 MIN. ■ **YIELD:** 4 SERVINGS

 4 orange roughy fillets
    (6 ounces *each*)

20 fresh asparagus spears, trimmed

1/2 teaspoon salt

1/4 teaspoon pepper

 2 green onions, chopped

SAUCE:

2/3 cup white wine *or* reduced-
    sodium chicken broth

 2 tablespoons lemon juice

 2 teaspoons cornstarch

 1 teaspoon minced fresh basil *or*
    1/4 teaspoon dried basil

 1 teaspoon minced fresh thyme *or*
    1/4 teaspoon dried thyme

1/8 teaspoon pepper

To prepare asparagus, **rinse stalks well in cold water.** Snap off the stalk ends as far down as they will easily break when gently bent, or cut off the tough white portion. If stalks are large, **gently peel the tough areas** of the stalk from the end to just below the tip.

I first sampled this casserole at a baby shower and found myself going back for more. I was surprised to taste the artichokes with the seafood, but it is fantastic.

—ANGELA SCHWARTZ
MARIETTA, GEORGIA

SPECIAL SEAFOOD CASSEROLE

Special Seafood Casserole

PREP: 25 MIN. ■ **BAKE:** 25 MIN. + STANDING ■ **YIELD:** 6 SERVINGS

1/2 pound sea scallops	1/4 teaspoon cayenne pepper
1 small onion, finely chopped	1 pound cooked medium shrimp, peeled and deveined
1 celery rib, finely chopped	1 can (6 ounces) crab
6 tablespoons butter, cubed	1 can (14 ounces) water-packed artichoke hearts, drained, rinsed, chopped and patted dry
7 tablespoons all-purpose flour	
1-1/2 cups half-and-half cream	
1 cup (4 ounces) shredded sharp cheddar cheese	1 can (8 ounces) sliced water chestnuts, drained
6 tablespoons sherry *or* apple juice	1/2 cup sliced almonds
3/4 teaspoon salt	1/4 cup grated Parmesan cheese

■ In a Dutch oven, saute the scallops, onion and celery in butter until scallops are firm and opaque. Stir in the flour until blended. Add cream. Bring to a boil; cook and stir for 2 minutes or until thickened. Reduce heat; add the cheddar cheese, sherry, salt and cayenne, stirring until cheese is melted. Remove from the heat; set aside.

■ In a greased 11-in. x 7-in. baking dish, layer with shrimp, crab, artichokes and water chestnuts. Top with sauce. Sprinkle with almonds and cheese.

■ Bake, uncovered, at 350° for 25-30 minutes or until heated through. Let stand for 10 minutes before serving.

Easy Haddock Bake

We call this recipe "Mock Lobster Casserole" because it turns haddock into something fancy. The canned soup lends a creamy touch, making the dinner seem indulgent even though it's actually quite light.

—DOROTHY BATEMAN
CARVER, MASSACHUSETTS

PREP: 15 MIN. ■ **BAKE:** 25 MIN.
YIELD: 6 SERVINGS

- 2 pounds haddock fillets
- 1 can (10-3/4 ounces) condensed cream of shrimp soup, undiluted
- 2 tablespoons lemon juice
- 2 tablespoons sherry *or* reduced-sodium chicken broth
- 2 tablespoons finely chopped onion
- 4-1/2 teaspoons butter
- 2 garlic cloves, minced
- 1/4 cup dry bread crumbs
- 1/4 teaspoon Worcestershire sauce

■ Place the fillets in a 13-in. x 9-in. baking dish coated with cooking spray. In a small bowl, combine the soup, lemon juice and sherry or broth. Pour over fillets. Bake, uncovered, at 350° for 20 minutes.

■ In a small nonstick skillet, saute the chopped onion in butter for 2 minutes. Add the garlic; cook 1 minute longer. Stir in bread crumbs and Worcestershire sauce. Sprinkle over fillets. Bake 5-10 minutes longer or until fish flakes easily with a fork.

➡ **NUTRITION FACTS:** 1 serving equals 219 calories, 6 g fat (3 g saturated fat), 102 mg cholesterol, 569 mg sodium, 8 g carbohydrate, trace fiber, 30 g protein. **DIABETIC EXCHANGES:** 4 lean meat, 1 fat, 1/2 starch.

Crabmeat, zucchini, cheddar cheese and green onions flavor this savory crustless quiche. I take this to potlucks and cut it into appetizer-size slices. As a diabetic, I know there will be at least one dish there I can eat guilt-free.

—NANCY ROMERO
CLARKSTON, WASHINGTON

SKINNY CRAB QUICHE

Skinny Crab Quiche

PREP: 15 MIN. ■ **BAKE:** 25 MIN. + STANDING ■ **YIELD:** 6 SERVINGS

1 can (6 ounces) crab	3/4 teaspoon ground mustard
1-1/2 cups (6 ounces) shredded reduced-fat cheddar cheese	1/2 teaspoon salt
1/2 cup shredded zucchini	1/4 teaspoon salt-free lemon-pepper seasoning
1/3 cup chopped green onions	Dash paprika
1-1/2 cups egg substitute	
1 can (12 ounces) fat-free evaporated milk	

■ In a bowl, combine the crab, cheese, zucchini and onions. Press onto the bottom and up the sides of a 9-in. deep-dish pie plate coated with cooking spray. In another bowl, combine the egg substitute, milk, mustard, salt and lemon pepper; mix well. Pour into crust. Sprinkle with paprika.

■ Bake, uncovered, at 400° for 25-30 minutes or until a knife inserted near the center comes out clean. Let quiche stand for 10 minutes before cutting.

➤ **NUTRITION FACTS:** 1 slice equals 223 calories, 9 g fat (5 g saturated fat), 50 mg cholesterol, 736 mg sodium, 10 g carbohydrate, 1 g fiber, 26 g protein. **DIABETIC EXCHANGES:** 3 lean meat, 1/2 fat-free milk.

Pastry-Topped Salmon Casserole

PREP: 20 MIN. ■ **BAKE:** 30 MIN.
YIELD: 6 SERVINGS

1 large onion, chopped
5 tablespoons butter, *divided*
1 garlic clove, minced
1-1/4 cups 2% milk
1 package (8 ounces) cream cheese, softened, cubed
2 cups frozen peas and carrots, thawed
1 can (14-1/2 ounces) diced potatoes, drained
2 pouches (6 ounces *each*) boneless skinless pink salmon, flaked
1/2 teaspoon salt
1/4 teaspoon pepper
10 sheets phyllo dough (14 inches x 9 inches)

■ In a large skillet, saute onion in 2 tablespoons butter for 5 minutes or until crisp-tender. Add garlic; cook 1 minute longer. Stir in milk; heat over medium until bubbles form around side of pan. Add cheese; stir until melted. Remove from heat; stir in peas and carrots, potatoes, salmon, salt and pepper.

■ Melt remaining butter; brush some of the butter over the bottom and sides of a 2-1/2-qt. round baking dish. Line with five sheets of phyllo dough. Pour in salmon mixture. Crimp remaining sheets of dough; place over filling to cover the top. Brush dough with remaining butter.

■ Bake at 375° for 30-35 minutes or until crust is lightly browned.

This costs about the same as an ordinary chicken potpie, but one bite and you'll be amazed at how much the salmon adds. With cream cheese and the flaky crust, this is no ordinary casserole. It works just as well for a special occasion as it does for a weeknight meal.

—TYLER SHERMAN WILLIAMSBURG, VIRGINIA

CRAB MACARONI & CHEESE

Crab and mushrooms put a deliciously different spin on classic macaroni and cheese. It's an upscale casserole for special occasions, but my family could eat it every day!

—ANGELA OCHOA LAKE ELSINORE, CALIFORNIA

Crab Macaroni & Cheese

PREP: 45 MIN. ■ **BAKE:** 15 MIN. ■ **YIELD:** 10 SERVINGS

- 1 package (16 ounces) elbow macaroni
- 6 baby portobello mushrooms
- 2 green onions, sliced
- 1 tablespoon plus 1/4 cup butter, *divided*
- 1/4 cup all-purpose flour
- 1 teaspoon ground mustard
- 1 teaspoon pepper
- 1/2 teaspoon salt
- 1/4 teaspoon paprika
- 2-1/2 cups half-and-half cream
- 1-1/2 cups (6 ounces) shredded part-skim mozzarella cheese, *divided*
- 1-1/2 cups (6 ounces) shredded medium cheddar cheese, *divided*

TOPPING:
- 1/2 cup panko (Japanese) bread crumbs
- 3 tablespoons butter, melted
- 1 tablespoon dried basil
- 1-1/2 pounds cooked snow crab legs, meat removed
- 4 thin slices Swiss cheese
- 1/4 cup grated Parmesan cheese

■ Cook macaroni according to package directions. Drain pasta and rinse in cold water.

■ Meanwhile, in a large skillet, saute mushrooms and onions in 1 tablespoon butter until tender; set aside.

■ In a large saucepan, melt remaining butter. Stir in the flour, mustard, pepper, salt and paprika until smooth; gradually add cream. Bring to a boil; cook and stir for 2 minutes or until thickened. Stir in 3/4 cup each mozzarella and cheddar cheeses until blended. Remove from the heat; fold in macaroni.

■ In a small bowl, combine the bread crumbs, butter and basil. Transfer half of the macaroni mixture into a greased 13-in. x 9-in. baking dish. Layer with: reserved mushroom mixture; remaining macaroni mixture; and remaining mozzarella and cheddar cheeses. Top with crab and Swiss cheese. Sprinkle with crumb mixture and Parmesan cheese.

■ Bake at 350° for 15-20 minutes or until golden brown. Let stand for 5 minutes before serving.

My husband had high cholesterol so I created this heart-healthy recipe. Now I serve it to guests all the time—even fish-haters rave and ask for the recipe!

—SUSAN ROBENSON HOT SPRINGS, ARKANSAS

COMPANY-READY CRUSTED SALMON

Company-Ready Crusted Salmon

PREP: 20 MIN. ■ **BAKE:** 20 MIN. ■ **YIELD:** 6 SERVINGS

- 2 packages (6 ounces *each*) fresh baby spinach
- 1 salmon fillet (1-1/2 pounds)
- 1 teaspoon olive oil
- 3 tablespoons honey
- 3 tablespoons Dijon mustard
- 1/4 cup cornflakes
- 2 tablespoons sliced almonds
- 2 tablespoons chopped pecans
- 1/4 cup fat-free mayonnaise

Hot cooked couscous, optional

- Place spinach in a 13-in. x 9-in. baking dish coated with cooking spray; top with salmon. Drizzle oil over spinach.

- Combine honey and mustard. Remove 2 tablespoons mixture; brush over salmon. Place the cornflakes, almonds and pecans in a small food processor; cover and process until ground. Press onto salmon. Stir the mayonnaise into the remaining honey mixture; refrigerate until serving.

- Bake, uncovered, at 450° for 18-22 minutes or until the fish flakes easily with a fork. Drizzle with reserved sauce. Serve with couscous if desired.

Couscous is a commercially produced grain product usually **made from semolina and shaped into tiny beads.** Found in the rice or pasta section of the grocery store, it's available in **regular or quick-cooking** forms.

Bayou Casserole

Seafood is popular in our area and is a typical ingredient in recipes.

—ETHEL MILLER EUNICE, LOUISIANA

PREP: 35 MIN. ■ **BAKE:** 30 MIN.
YIELD: 8 SERVINGS

- 1 medium onion, chopped
- 1 medium green pepper, chopped
- 1 celery rib, chopped
- 8 tablespoons butter, *divided*
- 1 garlic clove, minced
- 1 can (10-3/4 ounces) condensed cream of mushroom soup, undiluted
- 1 pound uncooked shrimp, peeled and deveined
- 1-1/2 cups cooked rice
- 2 cans (6 ounces *each*) crabmeat, drained, flaked, cartilage removed
- 4 slices day-old bread, cubed
- 3/4 cup half-and-half cream
- 1/4 cup chopped green onion tops
- 1/2 teaspoon salt
- 1/4 teaspoon pepper

Dash cayenne pepper

- 1/3 cup dry bread crumbs
- 2 tablespoons snipped fresh parsley

- In a large skillet, saute onion, green pepper and celery in 6 tablespoons butter until tender. Add garlic; cook 1 minute longer. Add soup and shrimp; cook and stir over medium heat 10 minutes or until shrimp turn pink. Stir in rice, crab, bread cubes, cream, onion tops and seasonings.

- Spoon into a greased 2-qt. baking dish. Melt remaining butter; combine with crumbs and parsley. Sprinkle over casserole. Bake uncovered at 375° for 25-30 minutes or until heated through.

I used salmon, imagination and my taste buds to come up with a smart twist on an Italian classic. This healthy indulgence makes a pretty dish that's fit for company.

—**PAT PATTY**
SPRING, TEXAS

SALMON WITH FETTUCCINE ALFREDO

Salmon with Fettuccine Alfredo

PREP/TOTAL TIME: 30 MIN. ■ **YIELD:** 4 SERVINGS

4 salmon fillets (4 ounces *each*)
1/4 teaspoon coarsely ground pepper, *divided*
4 ounces uncooked fettuccine
2 garlic cloves, minced
1 tablespoon reduced-fat margarine
1 tablespoon all-purpose flour
1/8 teaspoon salt
1 cup fat-free milk
4 tablespoons grated Parmesan cheese, *divided*

■ Place salmon, skin side down, on a broiler rack coated with cooking spray. Sprinkle with 1/8 teaspoon pepper. Broil 4-6 in. from the heat for 10-12 minutes or until fish flakes easily with a fork. Meanwhile, cook fettuccine according to package directions.

■ In a small saucepan, cook garlic in margarine for 1 minute or until tender. Stir in the flour, salt and remaining pepper; gradually stir in milk. Bring to a boil; cook and stir for 2 minutes or until thickened. Remove from the heat. Stir in 3 tablespoons cheese.

■ Drain fettuccine; toss with sauce. Serve with salmon. Sprinkle with remaining cheese.

EDITOR'S NOTE: This recipe was tested with Parkay Light stick margarine.

➤ **NUTRITION FACTS:** 1 fillet with 1/2 cup fettuccine equals 372 calories, 16 g fat (4 g saturated fat), 72 mg cholesterol, 294 mg sodium, 25 g carbohydrate, 1 g fiber, 31 g protein. **DIABETIC EXCHANGES:** 3 lean meat, 1-1/2 starch, 1-1/2 fat.

Angel Hair Shrimp Bake

Shrimp and pasta blend beautifully with the herbs, salsa and cheeses in my hearty layered casserole.
—**SUSAN DAVIDSON**
ELM GROVE, WISCONSIN

PREP: 25 MIN. ■ **BAKE:** 25 MIN.
YIELD: 12 SERVINGS

1 package (9 ounces) refrigerated angel hair pasta
1-1/2 pounds uncooked medium shrimp, peeled and deveined
3/4 cup crumbled feta cheese
1/2 cup shredded Swiss cheese
1 jar (16 ounces) chunky salsa
1/2 cup shredded Monterey Jack cheese
3/4 cup minced fresh parsley
1 teaspoon dried basil
1 teaspoon dried oregano
2 eggs
1 cup half-and-half cream
1 cup (8 ounces) plain yogurt

■ In a greased 13-in. x 9-in. baking dish, layer half of the pasta, shrimp, feta cheese, Swiss cheese and salsa. Repeat layers. Sprinkle with the Monterey Jack cheese, parsley, basil and oregano.

■ In a small bowl, whisk the eggs, cream and yogurt; pour over casserole. Bake, uncovered, at 350° for 25-30 minutes or until a thermometer reads 160°. Let stand for 5 minutes before serving.

➤ **NUTRITION FACTS:** 1 cup equals 220 calories, 8 g fat (5 g saturated fat), 144 mg cholesterol, 452 mg sodium, 15 g carbohydrate, 2 g fiber, 17 g protein. **DIABETIC EXCHANGES:** 2-1/2 lean meat, 1-1/2 starch.

MAKEOVER CREAMY HALIBUT ENCHILADAS

Our Test Kitchen reeled in a winner with this pared-down entree. The makeover recipe has 256 fewer calories, one-third of the fat, one-fourth of the saturated fat and 93 milligrams less sodium than the original.

—TASTE OF HOME TEST KITCHEN

Makeover Creamy Halibut Enchiladas

PREP: 15 MIN. ■ **BAKE:** 25 MIN. ■ **YIELD:** 8 SERVINGS

4 cups water	2 jalapeno peppers, seeded and chopped
2 pounds halibut, cut into 1-inch cubes	1-1/2 teaspoons ground cumin
6 ounces reduced-fat cream cheese	8 flour tortillas (8 inches)
2/3 cup fat-free sour cream	4-1/2 teaspoons all-purpose flour
4 green onions, chopped	1-1/2 cups fat-free half-and-half
2 cans (4 ounces *each*) chopped green chilies	1-1/4 cups shredded reduced-fat Monterey Jack *or* part-skim mozzarella cheese
1 can (4-1/4 ounces) chopped ripe olives, drained	1/3 cup shredded Parmesan cheese
	1/2 cup salsa

- In a large saucepan, bring water to a boil. Carefully add fish; reduce heat. Cover and simmer for 5 minutes or until fish flakes easily with a fork; drain well. In a large bowl, combine the cream cheese, sour cream, onions, chilies, olives, jalapenos and cumin. Fold in fish.

- Place generous 1/2 cup down the center of each tortilla; roll up. Place enchiladas in a 13-in. x 9-in. baking dish coated with cooking spray. Combine flour and cream until smooth; pour over enchiladas.

- Cover and bake at 350° for 20-25 minutes or until heated through. Uncover; sprinkle with cheeses. Broil 4 in. from the heat for 2 minutes or until lightly browned. Serve with the salsa.

EDITOR'S NOTE: Wear disposable gloves when cutting hot peppers; the oils can burn skin. Avoid touching your face.

➤ **NUTRITION FACTS:** 1 enchilada with 1 tablespoon salsa equals 464 calories, 16 g fat (6 g saturated fat), 66 mg cholesterol, 948 mg sodium, 40 g carbohydrate, 1 g fiber, 39 g protein. **DIABETIC EXCHANGES:** 3 lean meat, 2 starch, 1 fat, 1/2 fat-free milk.

Breads & Salads

230

236

229

Creating a hearty, well-rounded meal using the recipes in this book just got easier with this beautiful bonus chapter. It features **fresh-from-the-oven breads and potluck-friendly salads** that are delicious accompaniments to any slow cooker, stovetop or oven entree.

- Cook quinoa according to package directions. Transfer to a large bowl; cool completely.

- In a small bowl, combine water and tomatoes; let stand for 5 minutes. Drain and chop tomatoes; add to quinoa. Stir in the cucumber, peppers, onions, cheese and 1/4 cup salad dressing.

- Cover and refrigerate for 2 hours. Just before serving, stir in remaining salad dressing.

EDITOR'S NOTE: Look for quinoa in the cereal, rice or organic food aisle.

➤➤ **NUTRITION FACTS:** 3/4 cup equals 148 calories, 4 g fat (1 g saturated fat), 6 mg cholesterol, 248 mg sodium, 22 g carbohydrate, 2 g fiber, 5 g protein. **DIABETIC EXCHANGES:** 1-1/2 starch, 1 fat.

SUMMER-FRESH QUINOA SALAD

This light and refreshing salad is easy to prepare and perfect for hot summer days. I often add zucchini or summer squash and use fresh tomatoes instead of sun-dried.

—LIZ GADBOIS WOODVILLE, WISCONSIN

Summer-Fresh Quinoa Salad

PREP: 25 MIN. + CHILLING ■ **YIELD:** 14 SERVINGS

- 2 cups quinoa, rinsed
- 1 cup boiling water
- 1/2 cup sun-dried tomatoes (not packed in oil)
- 1 medium cucumber, peeled, seeded and chopped

- 1 *each* medium green, sweet red and yellow pepper, chopped
- 6 green onions, thinly sliced
- 1 package (4 ounces) crumbled garlic and herb feta cheese
- 1/2 cup reduced-fat sun-dried tomato salad dressing, *divided*

Quinoa, pronounced KEEN-wah, is a grain-like crop with **origins in South America.** Although quinoa is technically not a grain, it is **cooked like rice or couscous.**

- Divide dough into 24 pieces. In a small bowl, combine the onion, butter, garlic, parsley and salt. Dip each piece of dough into butter mixture; place in a 10-in. fluted tube pan coated with cooking spray. Cover and let rise in a warm place until doubled, about 1 hour.

- Bake at 375° for 20-25 minutes or until golden brown. Serve warm with olive oil if desired.

Here's a quick and simple way to remove the skin from fresh garlic cloves. Use the blade of a chef's knife and **crush the garlic clove. Peel the skin** away, then chop or mince as directed in the recipe.

ONION-GARLIC BUBBLE BREAD

This lovely, golden loaf has great garlic goodness in every bite. Guests will go wild over its savory flavor. Try dipping bite-size pieces in herb-seasoned olive oil or dunking in warm pasta sauce for a unique appetizer.

—TASTE OF HOME TEST KITCHEN

Onion-Garlic Bubble Bread

PREP/TOTAL TIME: 30 MIN. ■ YIELD: 1 LOAF (24 PIECES)

- 2 loaves (1 pound each) frozen bread dough or 24 frozen unbaked white dinner rolls, thawed
- 1/2 cup finely chopped sweet onion
- 1/2 cup butter, melted

- 2 garlic cloves, minced
- 1 teaspoon dried parsley flakes
- 1/4 teaspoon salt

Herb-seasoned olive oil, optional

This festive salad features some of my favorite fruits, complemented by a creamy vanilla pudding mix. It even works as a dessert.

—PRISCILLA GILBERT
INDIAN HARBOR BEACH, FLORIDA

ORZO CHEESECAKE FRUIT SALAD

Orzo Cheesecake Fruit Salad

PREP: 30 MIN. + CHILLING ■ **YIELD:** 16 SERVINGS

1 cup uncooked orzo pasta

1 package (3.4 ounces) instant cheesecake *or* vanilla pudding mix

1/3 cup sour cream

1 can (20 ounces) crushed pineapple, undrained

1 large banana, sliced

2 teaspoons lemon juice

2 cans (11 ounces *each*) mandarin oranges, drained

2 cups miniature marshmallows

1 cup chopped pecans, toasted

1 cup canned sliced peaches, drained and chopped

1/2 cup maraschino cherries, drained and quartered

1 carton (8 ounces) frozen whipped topping, thawed

1/2 cup flaked coconut, toasted

■ Cook orzo according to package directions. Drain and rinse in cold water; set aside.

■ In a large bowl, combine the pudding mix, sour cream and pineapple. Toss banana with lemon juice; stir into pudding mixture. Stir in the oranges, marshmallows, pecans, peaches, cherries and orzo. Fold in whipped topping. Sprinkle with coconut. Cover and refrigerate for 2 hours or until chilled.

Mixed Fruit With Lemon-Basil Dressing

A slightly savory dressing really complements the sweet fruit in this recipe. I also use the dressing on salad greens.

—DIXIE TERRY
GOREVILLE, ILLINOIS

PREP/TOTAL TIME: 15 MIN.
YIELD: 8 SERVINGS

2 tablespoons lemon juice

1/2 teaspoon sugar

1/4 teaspoon salt

1/4 teaspoon ground mustard

1/8 teaspoon onion powder

Dash pepper

6 tablespoons olive oil

4-1/2 teaspoons minced fresh basil

1 cup cubed fresh pineapple

1 cup sliced fresh strawberries

1 cup sliced peeled kiwifruit

1 cup cubed seedless watermelon

1 cup fresh blueberries

1 cup fresh raspberries

■ In a blender, combine the lemon juice, sugar, salt, mustard, onion powder and pepper; cover and process for 5 seconds. While processing, gradually add oil in a steady stream. Stir in basil.

■ In a large bowl, combine the fruit. Drizzle with dressing and toss to coat. Refrigerate until serving.

GREEN SALAD WITH HERB VINAIGRETTE

My mother-in-law regularly makes this crisp and refreshing starter for birthdays and holiday dinners. It is best in the summer when fresh, locally grown tomatoes are available.

—AMY SAUSER OMAHA, NEBRASKA

Green Salad with Herb Vinaigrette

PREP: 15 MIN. + CHILLING ■ **YIELD:** 8 SERVINGS

2/3	cup canola oil		1	teaspoon dill weed
1/4	cup red wine vinegar		1/4	teaspoon pepper
1/4	cup minced fresh parsley		6	cups torn mixed salad greens
2	green onions, chopped		6	medium tomatoes, cut into wedges
1	garlic clove, minced		6	large fresh mushrooms, sliced
1	teaspoon salt			
1	teaspoon dried basil			

- In a small bowl, whisk the first nine ingredients. Cover and refrigerate for at least 8 hours.

- Divide the salad greens, tomatoes and mushrooms among eight salad plates. Whisk dressing; drizzle over salads.

Fresh Tomato Flatbread

PREP/TOTAL TIME: 25 MIN.
YIELD: 12 SERVINGS

2	plum tomatoes
1	tube (8 ounces) refrigerated crescent rolls
1	small onion, thinly sliced
2	tablespoons olive oil
1	teaspoon Italian seasoning
1	garlic clove, minced
1/4	teaspoon salt
1/8	teaspoon pepper
1	tablespoon grated Parmesan cheese

- Thinly slice the tomatoes; place on paper towels to drain. Unroll crescent dough; place on an ungreased baking sheet. Roll into a 14-in. x 10-in. rectangle; seal seams and perforations.

- Arrange tomatoes and onion over crust. In a small bowl, combine the oil, Italian seasoning, garlic, salt and pepper; brush over top. Sprinkle with cheese.

- Bake at 375° for 10-14 minutes or until lightly browned. Cut into squares.

➤■ **NUTRITION FACTS:** 1 piece equals 101 calories, 6 g fat (1 g saturated fat), trace cholesterol, 205 mg sodium, 9 g carbohydrate, trace fiber, 2 g protein. **DIABETIC EXCHANGES:** 1 fat, 1/2 starch.

Looking for an easy side dish or appetizer? All you need is a can of refrigerated crescent rolls, fresh tomatoes, a sprinkle of flavorful cheese, olive oil and Italian seasoning. Preparing this delicious recipe is as easy as ordering takeout, and it's more affordable, too.

—MARLENE MOHR CINCINNATI, OHIO

MINI TOFFEE ROLLS

- In a small bowl, cream the butter, brown sugar and cinnamon until light and fluffy. Stir in toffee bits.

- Separate each tube of crescent dough into four rectangles; seal perforations. Spread evenly with butter mixture. Roll up each rectangle jelly-roll style, starting with a long side.

- Cut each into six 1-in. slices; place cut side down into two greased 8-in. square baking dishes. Bake at 375° for 14-16 minutes or until golden brown.

- In a small bowl, combine the confectioners' sugar, milk and vanilla until smooth. Drizzle over warm rolls.

I found this delicious recipe in a magazine years ago and adapted the original to make it my own. The rich, bite-size treats are full of cinnamon flavor and great with coffee!

—**CAROL GILLESPIE** CHAMBERSBURG, PENNSYLVANIA

Mini Toffee Rolls

PREP: 20 MIN. ■ BAKE: 15 MIN. ■ YIELD: 4 DOZEN.

6	tablespoons butter, softened	2	tubes (8 ounces *each*) refrigerated crescent rolls
1/2	cup packed brown sugar		
1	teaspoon ground cinnamon	1	cup confectioners' sugar
1/3	cup milk chocolate English toffee bits	4-1/2	teaspoons 2% milk
		1/4	teaspoon vanilla extract

In the case of **light brown vs. dark brown sugar,** the choice is yours! But keep in mind that light brown sugar has a **subtle, delicate flavor.** If you like a more **intense molasses flavor** in baked goods, use dark brown instead.

This easy salad with its crowd-pleasing flavors makes a wonderful addition to cookouts and picnics. It's a favorite with folks of all ages.

—MARY WILT
IPSWICH, MASSACHUSETTS

PARTY TORTELLINI SALAD

Party Tortellini Salad

PREP/TOTAL TIME: 25 MIN. ■ **YIELD:** 10 SERVINGS

1 package (19 ounces) frozen cheese tortellini	1/2 cup pimiento-stuffed olives, halved
2 cups fresh broccoli florets	3/4 cup reduced-fat red wine vinaigrette
1 medium sweet red pepper, chopped	1/2 teaspoon salt

■ Cook tortellini according to package directions; drain and rinse in cold water.

■ In a large bowl, combine the tortellini, broccoli, red pepper and olives. Drizzle with dressing and sprinkle with salt; toss to coat. Cover and refrigerate until serving.

➥ **NUTRITION FACTS:** 3/4 cup equals 156 calories, 7 g fat (2 g saturated fat), 8 mg cholesterol, 596 mg sodium, 19 g carbohydrate, 1 g fiber, 6 g protein. **DIABETIC EXCHANGES:** 1 starch, 1 lean meat, 1/2 fat.

Celery Seed Slaw

A simple cooked dressing gives this crisp cabbage mixture a delightful sweet-and-sour flavor my family absolutely savors. When I was a child, my mother used the recipe often, too. It's perfect for potlucks since you make it ahead then chill it before serving.

—RONNIE STONE
ARAPAHOE, NORTH CAROLINA

PREP: 10 MIN. + CHILLING
YIELD: 12-16 SERVINGS

3	pounds medium head cabbage, coarsely shredded
1/2	cup finely shredded carrot
1/2	cup chopped green pepper
1	cup sugar
1	cup white vinegar
3	teaspoons salt
1	teaspoon celery seed

■ In a large bowl, combine the cabbage, carrot and green pepper; set aside. In a small saucepan, combine the sugar, vinegar, salt and celery seed; bring to a boil. Pour over cabbage mixture; toss to coat. Cover and refrigerate for 4 hours or overnight. Serve with a slotted spoon.

To shred cabbage, first cut it in half or quarters, then make a **V-shaped cut around the core** and remove it. **Cut the cabbage into wedges,** and with a sharp knife, slice as directed by the recipe.

Tender and moist, these easy whole wheat rolls boast great herb flavor as well as a hint of sweetness from the honey.

—DEBORAH PATRAUCHUK
SICAMOUS, BRITISH COLUMBIA

NO-KNEAD WHOLE WHEAT ROLLS

No-Knead Whole Wheat Rolls

PREP: 15 MIN. + RISING ■ **BAKE:** 10 MIN. ■ **YIELD:** 1 DOZEN

- 1 package (1/4 ounce) active dry yeast
- 1-1/4 cups warm water (110° to 115°)
- 2 cups all-purpose flour
- 1 cup whole wheat flour
- 2 tablespoons butter, softened
- 1 tablespoon honey
- 1 tablespoon molasses
- 1 teaspoon salt
- 1 teaspoon Italian seasoning

- In a large bowl, dissolve yeast in warm water. Add the remaining ingredients. Beat on medium speed for 3 minutes (dough will be sticky). Do not knead. Cover and let rise in a warm place until doubled, about 30 minutes.

- Stir dough down. Set aside 1/4 cup batter. Fill muffin cups coated with nonstick cooking spray half full. Top each with 1 teaspoon reserved batter. Cover and let rise until doubled, about 8-12 minutes.

- Bake at 375° for 10-15 minutes or until golden brown. Cool for 1 minute before removing from pan to a wire rack.

➡ **NUTRITION FACTS:** 1 roll equals 139 calories, 2 g fat (1 g saturated fat), 5 mg cholesterol, 212 mg sodium, 26 g carbohydrate, 2 g fiber, 4 g protein. **DIABETIC EXCHANGE:** 1-1/2 starch.

Garlic-Cheese Crescent Rolls

PREP/TOTAL TIME: 20 MIN.
YIELD: 8 SERVINGS

- 1 tube (8 ounces) refrigerated crescent rolls
- 3 tablespoons butter, melted
- 1-1/2 teaspoons garlic powder
- 1 teaspoon dried oregano
- 2 tablespoons grated Parmesan cheese

- Separate crescent dough into eight triangles. Roll up from the wide end and place point side down 2 in. apart on an ungreased baking sheet. Curve ends to form a crescent.

- Combine the butter, garlic powder and oregano; brush over rolls. Sprinkle with the cheese.

- Bake at 375° for 10-12 minutes or until golden brown. Serve warm.

Here's a recipe that couldn't be much quicker or easier and is sure to add a nice touch to any meal. The garlic and Parmesan flavors really come through, and the butteriness is just right. The light brown, golden color of these tender rolls will add a festive flair to your dinner table. Enjoy!

—LORI ABAD EAST HAVEN, CONNECTICUT

PULL-APART STICKY BUN RING

- Cut cream cheese into 20 cubes; roll in sugar mixture. Place one cube in the center of each piece of dough. Fold dough over cheese cube; pinch edges to seal tightly. Dip one side of each biscuit in butter, then sugar mixture.

- Arrange biscuits in prepared pan, sugar side up. Pour remaining butter over top; sprinkle with remaining sugar mixture. Bake at 375° for 25-30 minutes or until golden brown. Immediately invert onto a serving platter. Serve warm. Refrigerate leftovers.

Moist, sticky and filled with rich maple flavor, this treat tastes as delicious as it looks. Whether you serve it after dinner or as a wonderful brunch treat, the gooey cream cheese inside is sure to get mouths watering.

—**DOREEN WRIGHT-LAUKAITIS** OXFORD, MASSACHUSETTS

Pull-Apart Sticky Bun Ring

PREP: 25 MIN. ■ **BAKE:** 25 MIN. ■ **YIELD:** 20 SERVINGS

3/4 cup chopped pecans	1/2 cup sugar
1/2 cup butter, melted, *divided*	1 teaspoon ground cinnamon
1/3 cup maple syrup	1 package (8 ounces) cream cheese
2 tubes (6 ounces *each*) refrigerated flaky buttermilk biscuits	

- Sprinkle pecans into a greased 10-in. fluted tube pan. In a small bowl, combine 2 tablespoons butter and maple syrup; pour over pecans. Set aside.

- Separate biscuits; split each in half horizontally. Place the remaining butter in a shallow bowl. In another shallow bowl, combine the sugar and cinnamon.

An **easy way to chop nuts** is to put them in a plastic bag and crush them with a rolling pin to the desired fineness. **It's quick,** plus it saves even more time since there's no chopper to clean.

These rolls make an elegant accent to any meal. They also freeze well or can be made ahead of time and heated just before serving.

LOIS GALLUP EDWARDS, WOODLAND, CALIFORNIA

HERB-SWIRLED ROLLS

Herb-Swirled Rolls

PREP: 20 MIN. + RISING ■ **BAKE:** 15 MIN. + COOLING

- 1 loaf (1 pound) frozen bread dough, thawed
- 3 tablespoons butter, melted
- 2 tablespoons minced chives
- 2 tablespoons dried parsley flakes
- 1/2 teaspoon dill weed *or* dried thyme
- 1/4 teaspoon salt
- 1/8 teaspoon pepper
- 1 egg
- 2 tablespoons water
- Sesame *and/or* poppy seeds

- On a floured surface, roll dough into a 14-in. x 12-in. rectangle; brush with butter. Sprinkle with chives, parsley, dill, salt and pepper. Roll up jelly-roll style, starting with a long side; pinch seam to seal. Cut into 12 slices.

- Place cut side down in greased muffin cups. Cover and let rise until doubled, about 45 minutes.

- Combine egg and water; brush over tops. Sprinkle with seeds. Bake at 375° for 12-15 minutes or until golden brown. Remove from pan to a wire rack to cool.

➤➤ **NUTRITION FACTS:** 1 roll equals 133 calories, 4 g fat (2 g saturated fat), 13 mg cholesterol, 284 mg sodium, 18 g carbohydrate, 2 g fiber, 4 g protein. **DIABETIC EXCHANGES:** 1 starch, 1/2 fat.

Apple Walnut Slaw

A coworker shared this recipe with me. Now it's a family favorite. Apples, walnuts and raisins are a fun way to dress up coleslaw.

—JOAN HALLFORD
NORTH RICHLAND HILLS, TEXAS

PREP/TOTAL TIME: 15 MIN.
YIELD: 12 SERVINGS

- 6 cups shredded cabbage
- 1-1/2 cups shredded carrot
- 1 cup coarsely chopped walnuts, toasted
- 3/4 cup raisins
- 1/3 cup finely chopped red onion
- 3/4 cup mayonnaise
- 3/4 cup buttermilk
- 4 to 5 tablespoons sugar
- 4-1/2 teaspoons lemon juice
- 3/4 teaspoon salt
- 1/4 to 1/2 teaspoon pepper
- 2 medium apples, chopped

- In a large salad bowl, toss the cabbage, carrots, walnuts, raisins and onion. In a small bowl, combine the mayonnaise, buttermilk, sugar, lemon juice, salt and pepper. Pour over cabbage mixture and toss to coat. Gently fold in apples. Cover and refrigerate until serving.

Since I grow so many herbs, I always look for opportunities to use them in my cooking. This recipe uses two of my favorites, but it's also delicious with other combinations. Try thyme and marjoram or oregano and basil.

—BEV CREDLE
HAMPTON, VIRGINIA

FRESH HERB FLATBREAD

Fresh Herb Flatbread

PREP/TOTAL TIME: 25 MIN. ■ YIELD: 10 SERVINGS

- 1 tube (8 ounces) refrigerated crescent rolls
- 1/4 cup fresh basil leaves, thinly sliced
- 1-1/2 teaspoons minced fresh rosemary
- 1 egg, lightly beaten
- 1 tablespoon grated Parmesan cheese

- Unroll crescent dough and separate into two rectangles. On a lightly floured surface, roll each into a 10-in. x 7-in. rectangle, sealing seams and perforations.

- Place one rectangle on an ungreased baking sheet. Sprinkle basil and rosemary to within 1/2 in. of edges. Top with remaining dough; pinch edges to seal. Brush with egg; sprinkle with cheese.

- Bake at 375° 10-12 minutes or until golden brown. Cut into slices. Serve warm.

➡➡ NUTRITION FACTS: 1 slice equals 99 calories, 6 g fat (1 g saturated fat), 22 mg cholesterol, 193 mg sodium, 9 g carbohydrate, trace fiber, 2 g protein. DIABETIC EXCHANGES: 1 fat, 1/2 starch.

Marinated Salad

PREP: 25 MIN. + MARINATING
YIELD: 16 SERVINGS
(3/4 CUP EACH)

- 4 cups fresh cauliflowerets
- 4 cups fresh broccoli florets
- 1 medium red onion, halved and sliced
- 1 can (8 ounces) sliced water chestnuts, drained
- 1 can (6 ounces) pitted ripe olives, drained
- 1 jar (4-1/2 ounces) sliced mushrooms, drained
- 1 bottle (16 ounces) Italian salad dressing

- In a large bowl, combine the first six ingredients. Drizzle with dressing and toss to coat. Cover and refrigerate overnight.

It's easy to **store cauliflower.** Simply wrap an unwashed head tightly and **refrigerate for up to 5 days.** Before using, wash and remove the leaves at the base; trim the stem.

This is a delicious salad that is both easy to prepare and able to be made ahead of time. The fresh, crisp cauliflower and broccoli give the dish a festive look that is appropriate for holiday meals, and the marinating gives it a lot of flavor. Your family will be sure to love it.

—MARTY RUMMEL TROUT LAKE, WASHINGTON

Classic Macaroni Salad

Here's a refreshingly light take on an all-time favorite. It's perfect for a fast weeknight dinner or festive weekend barbecue.

—**DOROTHY BAYES** SARDIS, OHIO

PREP/TOTAL TIME: 30 MIN.
YIELD: 8 SERVINGS

    2 cups uncooked elbow macaroni
    1 cup fat-free mayonnaise
    2 tablespoons sweet pickle relish
Sugar substitute equivalent to
    2 teaspoons sugar
  3/4 teaspoon ground mustard
  1/4 teaspoon salt
  1/8 teaspoon pepper
  1/2 cup chopped celery
  1/3 cup chopped carrot
  1/4 cup chopped onion
    1 hard-cooked egg, sliced
Dash paprika

- Cook the macaroni according to package directions; drain and rinse with cold water. Cool completely.

- For dressing, in a small bowl, combine the mayonnaise, pickle relish, sugar substitute, mustard, salt and pepper. In a large bowl, combine the macaroni, celery, carrot and onion. Add dressing and toss gently to coat.

- Refrigerate until serving. Garnish with egg and paprika.

EDITOR'S NOTE: This recipe was tested with Splenda no-calorie sweetener.

➡ **NUTRITION FACTS:** 3/4 cup equals 111 calories, 2 g fat (trace saturated fat), 30 mg cholesterol, 362 mg sodium, 20 g carbohydrate, 2 g fiber, 4 g protein. **DIABETIC EXCHANGES:** 1-1/2 starch.

FESTIVE PEA SALAD

Colorful and dressed up enough for Christmas, here's an easy-to-make salad that is wonderful all year round. The green peas and red onion make it especially festive-looking.

—**J. O'NEALL** WESTMINSTER, COLORADO

Festive Pea Salad

PREP: 15 MIN. + CHILLING ■ **YIELD:** 8 SERVINGS

    1 package (16 ounces) frozen petite peas, thawed
1-1/2 cups fresh snow peas, trimmed and halved
    1 cup halved thinly sliced red onion
    1 jar (2 ounces) diced pimientos, drained
  1/3 cup mayonnaise
  1/3 cup sour cream
    1 teaspoon minced fresh mint
  1/4 teaspoon salt
  1/8 teaspoon white pepper
Dash to 1/8 teaspoon ground nutmeg
    5 bacon strips, cooked and crumbled

- In a large bowl, combine the peas, onion and pimientos. In a small bowl, combine the mayonnaise, sour cream, mint, salt, pepper and nutmeg.

- Pour over pea mixture; toss to coat. Cover and refrigerate for at least 1 hour. Just before serving, stir in the bacon.

We guarantee you'll enjoy our Test Kitchen's take on this classic salad. The dressing can be prepared up to 3 days in advance.

—TASTE OF HOME TEST KITCHEN

COLORFUL CAESAR SALAD

Colorful Caesar Salad

PREP/TOTAL TIME: 25 MIN. ■ **YIELD:** 12 SERVINGS

12 cups torn romaine

3 medium tomatoes, cut into wedges

1 medium cucumber, halved and sliced

3 hard-cooked eggs

6 anchovy fillets

1/4 cup red wine vinegar

2 tablespoons lemon juice

2 tablespoons Dijon mustard

1 tablespoon Worcestershire sauce

4 garlic cloves, minced

1 teaspoon sugar

1/2 teaspoon pepper

3/4 cup olive oil

1-1/2 cups Caesar salad croutons

3/4 cup shredded Parmesan cheese

■ In a large salad bowl, combine the romaine, tomatoes and cucumber. Slice eggs in half; remove yolks. (Refrigerate whites for another use.)

■ In a blender, combine the anchovies, vinegar, lemon juice, mustard, Worcestershire sauce, garlic, sugar, pepper and egg yolks; cover and process until smooth. While processing, gradually add the oil in a steady stream.

■ Drizzle desired amount of dressing over salad and toss to coat. Sprinkle with croutons and cheese. Refrigerate any leftover dressing for up to 3 days.

Blue Cheese Herb Loaf

This is delicious, goes with everything and makes a rather elegant-looking loaf.

—JANET ALLEN SARASOTA, FLORIDA

PREP: 15 MIN. ■ **BAKE:** 20 MIN.
YIELD: 1 LOAF

1 tube (12 ounces) refrigerated flaky buttermilk biscuits

2 tablespoons butter, melted

2 tablespoons crumbled blue cheese

1 tablespoon dried minced onion

2 teaspoons dried parsley flakes

1 garlic clove, minced

1 teaspoon dried tarragon

1 teaspoon minced chives

1/2 teaspoon celery seed

1/2 teaspoon dried oregano

■ Separate biscuits; cut each into quarters. Arrange into an 11-in. long loaf on a greased baking sheet. In a small bowl, combine the remaining ingredients; brush over loaf.

■ Bake at 375° for 18-20 minutes or until golden brown.

➡ **NUTRITION FACTS:** 1 slice equals 111 calories, 4 g fat (2 g saturated fat), 7 mg cholesterol, 331 mg sodium, 17 g carbohydrate, trace fiber, 3 g protein. **DIABETIC EXCHANGES:** 1 starch, 1/2 fat.

My family enjoys this salad. If strawberries are not available, you can easily swap them with dried cranberries and mandarin oranges.

—IRENE KELLER
KALAMAZOO, MICHIGAN

STRAWBERRY ROMAINE SALAD

Strawberry Romaine Salad

PREP/TOTAL TIME: 30 MIN. ■ **YIELD:** 10 SERVINGS

1/4	cup sugar
1/3	cup slivered almonds
1	bunch romaine, torn
1	small onion, halved and thinly sliced
2	cups halved fresh strawberries

CREAMY POPPY SEED DRESSING:

1/4	cup mayonnaise
2	tablespoons sugar
1	tablespoon sour cream
1	tablespoon milk
2-1/4	teaspoons cider vinegar
1-1/2	teaspoons poppy seeds

■ In a small heavy skillet over medium-low heat, cook and stir the sugar until melted and caramel in color, about 10 minutes. Stir in almonds until coated. Spread on foil to cool; break into small pieces.

■ In a large bowl, combine the romaine, onion and strawberries. Combine the dressing ingredients; drizzle over salad and toss to coat. Sprinkle with coated almonds.

➡ **NUTRITION FACTS:** 3/4 cup equals 112 calories, 7 g fat (1 g saturated fat), 2 mg cholesterol, 35 mg sodium, 12 g carbohydrate, 2 g fiber, 2 g protein. **DIABETIC EXCHANGES:** 1 vegetable, 1 fat, 1/2 starch.

Refreshing Cucumber Salad

This refreshing salad from our home economists can be prepared days in advance.
—TASTE OF HOME TEST KITCHEN

PREP: 15 MIN. + CHILLING
YIELD: 6-8 SERVINGS

3	medium cucumbers, thinly sliced
1	medium onion, thinly sliced
1/3	cup lemon juice
3/4	teaspoon salt

■ In a large bowl, combine the cucumbers and onion. Stir in lemon juice and salt. Cover and refrigerate for 1-2 days, stirring occasionally. Serve with a slotted spoon.

➡ **NUTRITION FACTS:** 3/4 cup equals 27 calories, 0 fat (0 saturated fat), 0 cholesterol, 222 mg sodium, 6 g carbohydrate, 2 g fiber, 1 g protein. **DIABETIC EXCHANGES:** 1 vegetable.

To **remove seeds from a cucumber,** cut it in half lengthwise and run a melon baller down the length of both halves, scooping out the seeds. This is **faster than using a knife** and wastes little of the cucumber.

ONION SWISS LOAF

Here is one of our favorite bread recipes—onion and cheese lovers will really enjoy it. I hope you like the savory treat just as much as our family and friends do.

—PAT BREMSON KANSAS CITY, MISSOURI

Onion Swiss Loaf

PREP: 20 MIN. ■ BAKE: 15 MIN. ■ YIELD: 8 SERVINGS

1/2 cup butter, cubed	1/4 teaspoon lemon juice
1 large sweet *or* yellow onion, halved and thinly sliced	1 loaf (1 pound) French bread, halved lengthwise
1/2 teaspoon prepared mustard	12 slices Swiss cheese

■ Melt butter in a large skillet over medium heat. Add the onion, mustard and lemon juice; cook and stir for 10-12 minutes or until tender. Remove from the heat.

■ Brush cut sides of bread with some of the butter from the pan. Spoon the onion mixture onto bread bottom; top with the Swiss cheese. Replace bread top.

■ Wrap loaf in foil; place on a baking sheet. Bake at 350° for 15 minutes or until cheese is melted. Slice and serve warm.

Mediterranean Potato Salad

I use Greek olives and feta cheese to bring Mediterranean flavors to an all-American classic.

—JENNY HAEN
RED WING, MINNESOTA

PREP: 25 MIN. + STANDING
YIELD: 10 SERVINGS

- 2 pounds small red potatoes, cut into 1/4-inch slices
- 3 cups water
- 1 small red onion, thinly sliced and separated into rings
- 1/2 cup pitted Greek olives
- 1/2 cup oil-packed sun-dried tomatoes, undrained, chopped
- 1/2 cup minced fresh parsley
- 1/3 cup pine nuts, toasted
- 1/8 teaspoon salt
- 1/8 teaspoon pepper
- 1/2 cup sun-dried tomato salad dressing
- 1 package (4 ounces) crumbled tomato and basil feta cheese

■ Place potatoes in a 3-qt. microwave-safe dish; add water. Cover and microwave on high for 10-15 minutes or until tender, stirring once. Drain; rinse in cold water.

■ In a large bowl, combine the potatoes, onion, olives, tomatoes, parsley, pine nuts, salt and pepper. Drizzle with dressing; toss to coat.

■ Let stand at room temperature for 1 hour before serving. Sprinkle with feta cheese. Refrigerate leftovers.

EDITOR'S NOTE: This recipe was tested in a 1,100-watt microwave.

- In a large bowl, combine the flour, sugar, baking powder, onion powder, garlic powder, salt and baking soda. Cut in butter until mixture resembles coarse crumbs. Stir in 1-1/4 cups cheddar-Monterey Jack cheese and the Parmesan cheese. Stir in the buttermilk just until mixture is moistened.

- Turn onto a lightly floured surface; knead 6-8 times. Pat or roll out to 1/2-in. thickness; cut with a floured 2-1/2-in. biscuit cutter. Place 2 in. apart on a greased baking sheet. Sprinkle with remaining cheddar-Monterey Jack cheese. Bake at 400° for 10-15 minutes or until golden brown. Serve warm.

Laced with garlicky goodness, melted cheese and a lick of onion, these quick, buttery muffins from our Test Kitchen are easy enough for weekday suppers but special enough for any company dinner.

—TASTE OF HOME TEST KITCHEN

Onion Cheese Biscuits

PREP/TOTAL TIME: 30 MIN. ■ YIELD: 1 DOZEN

2	cups all-purpose flour	
1	tablespoon sugar	
2	teaspoons baking powder	
1	teaspoon onion powder	
1	teaspoon garlic powder	
1/4	teaspoon salt	
1/4	teaspoon baking soda	

- 1/4 cup cold butter, cubed
- 2 cups (8 ounces) shredded cheddar-Monterey Jack cheese, *divided*
- 1/2 cup grated Parmesan cheese
- 1 cup buttermilk

For a more tender biscuit, be careful not to overmix or overknead the dough. Dip the biscuit cutter in flour after each cut to prevent sticking. Biscuits are done when they're **golden brown on the top and bottom.**

Buffet Rice Salad

This chilled rice and ham salad goes well with barbecue dinners. The green pepper, radishes and cucumber add color and crunch while complementing the herbed vinaigrette.

—JOSIE VARRO COQUITLAM, BRITISH COLUMBIA

PREP: 30 MIN. + COOLING ■ YIELD: 12 SERVINGS

1	cup uncooked instant rice	1-1/2	cups frozen peas, thawed
1/3	cup canola oil	1	cup cubed fully cooked lean ham
3	tablespoons white vinegar	1	cup sliced radishes
1/2	teaspoon dried oregano	1	small green pepper, diced
1/2	teaspoon Dijon mustard	1/2	cup chopped cucumber
1	garlic clove, minced	1/2	cup chopped green onions
1/4	teaspoon salt	1/4	cup minced fresh parsley
1/8	teaspoon pepper	10	cherry tomatoes, halved
1	can (16 ounces) kidney beans, rinsed and drained		

■ Cook rice according to package directions. Cool to room temperature. For dressing, in a small bowl, combine the oil, vinegar, oregano, mustard, garlic, salt and pepper.

■ In a large bowl, combine the rice, beans, peas, ham, radishes, green pepper, cucumber, onions and parsley. Just before serving, add dressing and toss to coat. Top with tomatoes.

➡➡ **NUTRITION FACTS:** 2/3 cup equals 155 calories, 7 g fat (1 g saturated fat), 4 mg cholesterol, 287 mg sodium, 17 g carbohydrate, 3 g fiber, 6 g protein. **DIABETIC EXCHANGES:** 1-1/2 fat, 1 starch.

Wheely-Good Pasta Salad

Red pepper pieces accent this yummy side dish, and the pasta wheels really "drive" the theme.

—AMBER KIMMICH POWHATAN, VIRGINIA

PREP/TOTAL TIME: 25 MIN. ■ YIELD: 12 SERVINGS

1	package (16 ounces) wagon wheel pasta	1	can (3.8 ounces) sliced ripe olives, drained
8	ounces cheddar cheese, cut into small cubes	2	teaspoons minced fresh oregano
1	medium sweet red pepper, diced	1	bottle (16 ounces) creamy Parmesan Romano salad dressing

■ Cook pasta according to package directions; drain and rinse in cold water. In a large serving bowl, combine the pasta, cheese, red pepper, olives and oregano. Drizzle with dressing and toss to coat. Cover and refrigerate until serving.

Tangy Potato Salad

My potato salad is so easy, I can quickly put it together in the kitchen of our trailer home on the lake. I've shared the recipe with our three daughters, and it's become a signature dish with all of them. Our grandchildren eat it up.

—MARILYN VAN SCYOC CARTHAGE, INDIANA

PREP: 15 MIN. + CHILLING
YIELD: 10-12 SERVINGS

8	cups cubed peeled cooked potatoes (about 11 medium)
10	bacon strips, cooked and crumbled
3	hard-cooked eggs, chopped
1	carton (8 ounces) French onion dip
1/2	cup dill pickle relish
1/2	teaspoon salt
1/2	teaspoon pepper

Leaf lettuce, optional

■ In a large bowl, combine the potatoes, bacon and eggs. In a small bowl, combine the dip, relish, salt and pepper. Stir into potato mixture. Cover and refrigerate for at least 2 hours. Serve in a lettuce-lined bowl if desired.

APPETIZERS & SNACKS

Buffet Meatballs, 86
Creamy Onion Dip, 82
Hawaiian Kielbasa, 88
Loaded Veggie Dip, 81
Mini Hot Dogs 'n' Meatballs, 92
Reuben Spread, 82
Slow Cooker Mexican Dip, 90
Sweet-and-Sour Chicken Wings, 90
Sweet-and-Sour Smokies, 82

APPLES

Apple Chicken Stew, 32
Apple Comfort, 92
Apple-Dijon Pork Roast, 46
Apple Walnut Slaw, 237
Blue Cheese and Apple
 Pork Chops, 56
Butterscotch Apple Crisp, 85
Cran-Apple Turkey Skillet, 127
Cranberry Apple Topping, 70
Fruit Dessert Topping, 88
Harvest Stew, 143
Pork and Apple Supper, 132
Roast Pork with Apples & Onions, 197

APRICOTS

Apricot Beef Stir-Fry, 108
Apricot-Glazed Salmon with
 Herb Rice, 214

ARTICHOKES

Chicken Artichoke Bake, 183
Loaded Veggie Dip, 81
Pork with Artichokes and Capers, 136
Special Seafood Casserole, 219

ASPARAGUS

Asparagus Beef Stir-Fry, 97
Asparagus Fish Bundles, 218
Asparagus Scallop Stir-Fry, 154
Caribbean Chicken Tenderloins, 120
Tuna-Chip Casserole, 216

AVOCADOS

Open-Faced Chicken Avocado
 Burgers, 122

BACON

Bacon Cheeseburger Spaghetti, 111
Bacon-Chicken Crescent Ring, 179
Bacon Chicken Roll-Ups, 180
Buffalo Chicken Wraps, 119
Pasta Carbonara, 131

BARLEY

Vegetable Barley Soup, 59

BEANS & LEGUMES
(ALSO SEE LENTILS)

Beef 'n' Chili Beans, 26
Black Bean Stuffed Peppers, 57
Brown-Bag Burritos, 99
Creole Black Beans 'n' Sausage, 55
Favorite Jiffy Jambalaya, 148
Fiesta Chicken Burritos, 42
Fiesta Corn and Beans, 60
Georgian Bay Baked Beans, 70
Hearty Beans with Beef, 21
Posole Verde, 63
Ranch Beans, 69
Slow-Cooked Chili, 63
Slow-Cooked White Chili, 65
Slow Cooker Mexican Dip, 90
Taco Salad, 106
Zesty Garbanzo Sausage Soup, 73

BEEF (ALSO SEE GROUND BEEF)

OVEN

Asian Barbecued Short Ribs, 162
Beef Spinach Hot Dish, 162
Cranberry Brisket with Horseradish Mashed Potatoes, 175
Homemade Italian Pot Roast, 166
Pepper-Crusted Beef Tenderloin, 165
Philly Cheesesteak Pizza, 170
Reuben Crescent Bake, 161
Steak over Potatoes, 160
Tender Stuffed Flank Steak, 173

SLOW COOKER

Barbecued Beef Brisket, 21
Coffee-Flavored Beef Roast, 17
Corned Beef Dinner, 20
Favorite Beef Chimichangas, 19
Gone-All-Day Goulash, 19
Herbed Beef with Noodles, 26
Italian Beef Hoagies, 77
Italian Pot Roast, 24
Italian Roast with Alfredo Potatoes, 27
Reuben Spread, 82
Slow Cooker Fajitas, 14
Slow Cooker Shredded Beef, 78
Sweet Chili Short Ribs, 13
Swiss Steak Supper, 16
Tangy Beef and Vegetable Stew, 22
Thai-Style Beef, 27
Zesty Orange Beef, 16

STOVETOP

Apricot Beef Stir-Fry, 108
Asparagus Beef Stir-Fry, 97
Bohemian Beef Dinner, 104
Hearty Beef and Noodles, 102
Italian Strip Steaks with Focaccia, 101
Loaded Vegetable Beef Stew, 103
Mom's Pot Roast, 104
Mushroom Steak 'n' Linguine, 100
Teriyaki Steak, 99

BEVERAGES

Caramel Hot Chocolate, 93
Mocha Mint Coffee, 84
Mulled Grape Cider, 93
Spiced Cranberry Punch, 85
Sweet Kahlua Coffee, 89

BREADS & ROLLS

(INCLUDES RECIPES THAT CALL FOR BREAD; ALSO SEE PIZZA)

Best Chicken 'n' Biscuits, 180
Blue Cheese Herb Loaf, 241
Caribbean Bread Pudding, 83
Fresh Herb Flatbread, 238
Fresh Tomato Flatbread, 230
Garlic-Cheese Crescent Rolls, 234
Herb-Swirled Rolls, 237
Italian Strip Steaks with Focaccia, 101
Mini Toffee Rolls, 232
Moist Poultry Dressing, 62
No-Knead Whole Wheat Rolls, 234
Onion Cheese Biscuits, 244
Onion-Garlic Bubble Bread, 228
Onion Swiss Loaf, 243
Pull-Apart Sticky Bun Ring, 236

BROCCOLI

Broccoli-Cheddar Hash Browns, 72
Casserole in the Cooker, 54
Ham 'n' Cheese Stromboli, 202
Ham 'n' Tater Bake, 209
Marinated Salad, 239
Party Tortellini Salad, 233
Pork Ribs Lo Mein, 52
Salmon with Broccoli and Pasta, 151

CABBAGE & SAUERKRAUT

(ALSO SEE COLE SLAW)

Bavarian Wiener Supper, 205
Bohemian Beef Dinner, 104
Celery Seed Slaw, 233
Corned Beef Dinner, 20
Grandma's Cabbage Rolls, 23
Reuben Crescent Bake, 161
Reuben Spread, 82
Tater Brat Bake, 200
Turkey Cabbage Bake, 181

CAPERS

Healthy Shrimp Piccata Pasta, 152
Pork with Artichokes and Capers, 136

CASSEROLES, POTPIES & QUICHES (ALSO SEE LASAGNA)

OVEN

Angel Hair Shrimp Bake, 224
Bavarian Wiener Supper, 205
Bayou Casserole, 223
Beef Spinach Hot Dish, 162
Cheddar Turkey Casserole, 186
Cheesy Clam Manicotti, 213
Chicken 'n' Dressing Casserole, 190
Chicken Artichoke Bake, 183
Chicken Potpie with Cheddar Biscuit Topping, 192
Chili Cheese Dog Casserole, 208
Chinese Beef Casserole, 166
Crab Macaroni & Cheese, 222
Creamy Pork Potpie, 211
Creamy Spinach Sausage Pasta, 206
Crescent-Topped Casserole, 163
Crescent-Topped Turkey Amandine, 179
Farm-Style Sausage Bake, 198
Ham & Spinach Casserole, 203
Ham 'n' Tater Bake, 209
Loaded Spaghetti Bake, 159
Mashed Potato Hot Dish, 173
Meat Lover's Pizza Bake, 174
Meaty Noodle Casserole, 161
Pastry-Topped Salmon Casserole, 220
Pork Noodle Casserole, 206
Potato-Crusted Chicken Casserole, 185
Potato Sausage Casserole, 202
Reuben Crescent Bake, 161
Scalloped Potatoes 'n' Ham Casserole, 210
Shrimp Rice Casserole, 215
Skinny Crab Quiche, 220
Southwest Beef Pie, 170
Southwest Pasta Bake, 168
Spaghetti Pie, 172
Special Seafood Casserole, 219
Taco Pie, 160
Tater Brat Bake, 200
Tuna-Chip Casserole, 216
Tuna Mac and Cheese Bake, 215
Turkey Cabbage Bake, 181
Two-Tater Shepherd's Pie, 169
Unstuffed Peppers, 174

CASSEROLES, POTPIES & QUICHES (CONTINUED)

SLOW COOKER
California Tamale Pie, 15
Casserole in the Cooker, 54

STOVETOP
Nacho Mac 'n' Cheese, 103

CAULIFLOWER
Cheesy Cauliflower Soup, 74
Marinated Salad, 239

CHEESE (ALSO SEE PIZZA)
Bacon Cheeseburger Spaghetti, 111
Blue Cheese and Apple
 Pork Chops, 56
Broccoli-Cheddar Hash Browns, 72
Cheddar Turkey Casserole, 186
Cheesy Cauliflower Soup, 74
Cheesy Clam Manicotti, 213
Chicken Potpie with Cheddar Biscuit
 Topping, 192
Chili Cheese Dog Casserole, 208
Crab Macaroni & Cheese, 222
Creamy Onion Dip, 82
Ham 'n' Cheese Stromboli, 202
Loaded Veggie Dip, 81
Makeover Slow-Cooked
 Mac 'n' Cheese, 61
Nacho Mac 'n' Cheese, 103
Onion Swiss Loaf, 243
Pecan Chicken with Blue Cheese
 Sauce, 188
Penne Gorgonzola with Chicken, 123
Reuben Spread, 82
Tuna Mac and Cheese Bake, 215

CHICKEN
(ALSO SEE CORNISH HENS)

OVEN
Bacon-Chicken Crescent Ring, 179
Bacon Chicken Roll-Ups, 180
Best Chicken 'n' Biscuits, 180
Chicken Alfredo Pizza, 178
Chicken 'n' Dressing Casserole, 190
Chicken Artichoke Bake, 183
Chicken Lasagna, 191
Chicken Potpie with Cheddar Biscuit
 Topping, 192

Chicken Rice Dinner, 186
Chicken Rolls with Raspberry
 Sauce, 182
Crunchy Baked Chicken, 192
Hot Wing Pizza, 183
Oregano Roasting Chicken, 184
Pecan Chicken with Blue Cheese
 Sauce, 188
Potato-Crusted Chicken
 Casserole, 185
Taco Chicken Wraps, 188

SLOW COOKER
Apple Chicken Stew, 32
Buffalo Chicken Wing Soup, 73
Cajun Chicken Lasagna, 36
Chicken Chop Suey with a Twist, 36
Chicken in Sour Cream Sauce, 43
Chicken Stew with Gnocchi, 67
Fiesta Chicken Burritos, 42
Forgotten Jambalaya, 40
Greek Orzo Chicken, 30
Harvest Chicken with Walnut
 Gremolata, 34
Hearty Chicken Enchiladas, 35
Herbed Chicken and Shrimp, 40
Mushroom Chicken Florentine, 31
Pepper Jack Chicken, 35
Posole Verde, 63
Satisfying Chicken and Veggies, 33
Saucy Raspberry Chicken, 33
Slow-Cooked Italian Chicken, 38
Slow-Cooked White Chili, 65
So-Easy Coq Au Vin, 31
Southwestern Chicken Soup, 75
Sweet-and-Sour Chicken Wings, 90
Sunday Chicken Stew, 41
Tangy Tropical Chicken, 39
Tasty Chicken Marsala, 30
Tropical BBQ Chicken, 43

STOVETOP
Buffalo Chicken Wraps, 119
Caribbean Chicken Tenderloins, 120
Chicken Saltimbocca, 123
Chicken Veronique, 114
Citrus Chicken with Peppers, 126
Creamy Chicken Angel Hair, 113
Fried Chicken with Pan Gravy, 115
Italian Chicken, 121
Mexican Chicken Penne for Kids, 116

Open-Faced Chicken Avocado
 Burgers, 122
Pasta Primavera with Shrimp, 152
Penne Gorgonzola with Chicken, 123
Prosciutto Chicken in Wine
 Sauce, 124
Roasted Pepper Chicken Penne, 120
Spicy Chicken Lettuce Wraps, 124
Spinach-Stuffed Chicken Pockets, 127
Thai Portobello Chicken Stir-Fry, 117

CHILI (ALSO SEE SOUPS; STEWS)
Slow-Cooked Chili, 63
Slow-Cooked White Chili, 65

CHOCOLATE
Caramel Hot Chocolate, 93
Chocolate Malt Pudding Cake, 86
Mocha Mint Coffee, 84

COFFEE
Coffee-Flavored Beef Roast, 17
Mocha Mint Coffee, 84
Sweet Kahlua Coffee, 89

COLE SLAW
Apple Walnut Slaw, 237
Celery Seed Slaw, 233

CORN & CORN BREAD
Chili Cheese Dog Casserole, 208
Fiesta Corn and Beans, 60
Glazed Pork Chops with Corn Bread
 Dressing, 205
Mexican Corn Bread Pizza, 189

CORNISH HENS
Cornish Game Hens with
 Couscous, 29
Golden Cornish Hens, 191
Roasted Cornish Hens with
 Vegetables, 184

CRANBERRIES
Cran-Apple Turkey Skillet, 127
Cranberry Apple Topping, 70
Cranberry Brisket with Horseradish
 Mashed Potatoes, 175
Cranberry Glazed Pork Roast, 209
Spiced Cranberry Punch, 85
Winter Fruit Compote, 84

CUCUMBERS

Refreshing Cucumber Salad, 242

DESSERTS

Apple Comfort, 92
Burgundy Pears, 90
Butterscotch Apple Crisp, 85
Caribbean Bread Pudding, 83
Chocolate Malt Pudding Cake, 86
Fruit Dessert Topping, 88
Hot Fruit Salad, 89
Spiced Sweet Potato Pudding, 93
Warm Strawberry Fondue, 86

FISH & SEAFOOD

OVEN

Angel Hair Shrimp Bake, 224
Apricot-Glazed Salmon with
  Herb Rice, 214
Asparagus Fish Bundles, 218
Bayou Casserole, 223
Cheesy Clam Manicotti, 213
Company-Ready Crusted
  Salmon, 223
Crab Macaroni & Cheese, 222
Easy Haddock Bake, 219
Makeover Creamy Halibut
  Enchiladas, 225
Mediterranean Mahi Mahi, 216
Pastry-Topped Salmon
  Casserole, 220
Salmon with Fettuccine
  Alfredo, 224
Shrimp Rice Casserole, 215
Skinny Crab Quiche, 220
Special Seafood Casserole, 219
Spicy Shrimp Pizza, 217
Tuna-Chip Casserole, 216
Tuna Mac and Cheese Bake, 215

SLOW COOKER

Bayou Gulf Shrimp Gumbo, 50
Forgotten Jambalaya, 40
Greek Shrimp Orzo, 56
Herbed Chicken and Shrimp, 40
Trout Chowder, 6

STOVETOP

Asparagus Scallop Stir-Fry, 154
Cod & Vegetable Skillet, 155
Easy Crab Lo Mein, 147

Favorite Jiffy Jambalaya, 148
Healthy Shrimp Piccata Pasta, 152
Paella, 146
Pasta Primavera with Shrimp, 152
Peppered Sole, 151
Red Snapper Vera Cruz, 148
Salmon with Broccoli and Pasta, 151
Scallops in Sage Cream, 155
Sesame Shrimp & Rice, 152
Shrimp Gumbo, 150
Tilapia with Sauteed Spinach, 145
Tilapia Wraps, 147
Veggie Tuna Burgers, 153

FRUIT (ALSO SEE SPECIFIC KINDS)

Fruit Dessert Topping, 88
Hot Fruit Salad, 89
Mixed Fruit with Lemon-Basil
  Dressing, 229
Orzo Cheesecake Fruit Salad, 229
Winter Fruit Compote, 84

GRAPES

Chicken Veronique, 114

GROUND BEEF

OVEN

Beef Spinach Hot Dish, 162
Chinese Beef Casserole, 166
Crescent-Topped Casserole, 163
Enchiladas Verdes, 167
Loaded Spaghetti Bake, 159
Mashed Potato Hot Dish, 173
Meat Lover's Pizza Bake, 174
Meaty Noodle Casserole, 161
Potato Beef Lasagna, 169
Southwest Beef Pie, 170
Southwest Pasta Bake, 168
Spaghetti Pie, 172
Taco Pie, 160
Traditional Meat Loaf, 165
Two-Tater Shepherd's Pie, 169
Unstuffed Peppers, 174

SLOW COOKER

Bavarian Meatballs, 62
Beef 'n' Chili Beans, 26
Buffet Meatballs, 86
California Tamale Pie, 15
Easy-Does-It Spaghetti, 20

Family-Style Meat Loaf Dinner, 24
Grandma's Cabbage Rolls, 23
Ground Beef Stew, 16
Hamburger Vegetable Soup, 76
Hearty Beans with Beef, 21
Hearty Hash Brown Dinner, 15
Mini Hot Dogs 'n' Meatballs, 92
Simple Swedish Meatballs, 23
Slow-Cooked Chili, 63
Slow Cooker Mexican Dip, 90

STOVETOP

Bacon Cheeseburger
  Spaghetti, 111
Brown-Bag Burritos, 99
Easy Beef Taco Skillet, 108
Hamburger Goulash, 100
Hearty Beef Ravioli, 97
Meatball Stew, 111
Nacho Mac 'n' Cheese, 103
Onion Loose-Meat
  Sandwiches, 110
Pepperoni Pizza Skillet, 106
Pizza Joes, 107
Skillet Beef Tamales, 110
Spaghetti with Italian
  Meatballs, 109
Taco Macaroni, 107
Taco Salad, 106

HAM & PROSCIUTTO

Beer-Glazed Ham, 210
Casserole in the Cooker, 54
Chicken Saltimbocca, 123
Christmas Carol Ham, 56
Ham 'n' Cheese Stromboli, 202
Ham and Hash Browns, 52
Ham & Spinach Casserole, 203
Ham 'n' Tater Bake, 209
Ham Barbecue, 69
Ham Fettuccine, 142
Ham Fried Rice, 131
Harvest Ham Steak, 139
Hearty Split Pea Soup, 66
His Favorite Ravioli, 135
Muffuletta Pasta, 135
Prosciutto Chicken in Wine
  Sauce, 124
Scalloped Potatoes 'n' Ham
  Casserole, 210
Tropical Triple Pork, 45

HOT DOGS

Bavarian Wiener Supper, 205
Chili Cheese Dog Casserole, 208
Mini Hot Dogs 'n' Meatballs, 92
Skillet Franks, 143

LAMB

Glazed Lamb Shanks, 49
Gyro Soup, 65
Mint Lamb Stew, 52

LASAGNA

Cajun Chicken Lasagna, 36
Chicken Lasagna, 191
Favorite Skillet Lasagna, 115
Potato Beef Lasagna, 169

LEMON & LIME

Citrus Chicken with Peppers, 126
Lemon Pork Chops, 51
Lemon-Rosemary Pork
 Tenderloin, 201
Mixed Fruit with Lemon-Basil
 Dressing, 22
Refreshing Cucumber Salad, 242

LENTILS

Southwest Vegetarian Lentil
 Soup, 61

MANGOES

Tangy Tropical Chicken, 39
Tropical Triple Pork, 45

MAPLE

Fruit Dessert Topping, 88
Maple-Almond Butternut
 Squash, 68
Maple Glazed Ribs, 196
Pull-Apart Sticky Bun Ring, 236

MEATBALLS & MEAT LOAF

Bavarian Meatballs, 62
Buffet Meatballs, 86
Family-Style Meat Loaf Dinner, 24
Mini Hot Dogs 'n' Meatballs, 92
Simple Swedish Meatballs, 23
Spaghetti with Italian Meatballs, 109
Traditional Meat Loaf, 165

MUSHROOMS

His Favorite Ravioli, 135
Mushroom Chicken Florentine, 31
Mushroom Steak 'n' Linguine, 100
Peppered Sole, 151
Tasty Chicken Marsala, 30
Thai Portobello Chicken Stir-Fry, 117
Zesty Orange Beef, 16
Zesty Pork Chops, 204

OKRA

Bayou Gulf Shrimp Gumbo, 50
Shrimp Gumbo, 150
Zesty Garbanzo Sausage Soup, 73

ONIONS

Creamy Onion Dip, 82
Onion Cheese Biscuits, 244
Onion-Garlic Bubble Bread, 228
Onion Loose-Meat Sandwiches, 110
Onion Swiss Loaf, 243
Roast Pork with Apples &
 Onions, 197

ORANGE

Pork in Orange Sauce, 134
Zesty Orange Beef, 16

PASTA & NOODLES

(ALSO SEE LASAGNA)

CASSEROLES

Angel Hair Shrimp Bake, 224
Cheesy Clam Manicotti, 213
Crab Macaroni & Cheese, 222
Creamy Spinach Sausage Pasta, 206
Meaty Noodle Casserole, 161
Loaded Spaghetti Bake, 159
Pork Noodle Casserole, 206
Tuna Mac and Cheese Bake, 215
Southwest Pasta Bake, 168
Spaghetti Pie, 172

OVEN

Cornish Game Hens with
 Couscous, 29
Macaroni & Cheese Pizza, 195

SALADS

Classic Macaroni Salad, 240
Orzo Cheesecake Fruit Salad, 229
Party Tortellini Salad, 233
Wheely-Good Pasta Salad, 245

SLOW COOKER

Easy-Does-It Spaghetti, 20
Greek Orzo Chicken, 30
Greek Shrimp Orzo, 56
Herbed Beef with Noodles, 26
Makeover Slow-Cooked
 Mac 'n' Cheese, 61
Pork Ribs Lo Mein, 52
Ratatouille with a Twist, 45
Sausage-Veggie Pasta Sauce, 47
Slow-Cooked Italian Chicken, 38

SOUPS & STEWS

Chicken Stew with Gnocchi, 67
Hearty Pasta Tomato Soup, 73

STOVETOP

Bacon Cheeseburger Spaghetti, 111
Creamy Chicken Angel Hair, 113
Easy Crab Lo Mein, 147
Ham Fettuccine, 142
Healthy Shrimp Piccata Pasta, 152
Hearty Beef and Noodles, 102
Hearty Beef Ravioli, 97
His Favorite Ravioli, 135
Italian Pork Skillet, 133
Mexican Chicken Penne for Kids, 116
Muffuletta Pasta, 135
Mushroom Steak 'n' Linguine, 100
Nacho Mac 'n' Cheese, 103
Pasta Carbonara, 131
Pasta Primavera with Shrimp, 152
Penne Gorgonzola with Chicken, 123
Pepperoni Pizza Skillet, 106
Peppy Parmesan Pasta, 143
Pronto Penne Pasta, 119
Roasted Pepper Chicken Penne, 120
Salmon with Broccoli and Pasta, 151
Salmon with Fettuccine Alfredo, 224
Sausage Macaroni Supper, 132
Skillet Franks, 143
Spaghetti with Italian Meatballs, 109
Taco Macaroni, 107

PEANUT BUTTER

Thai Portobello Chicken Stir-Fry, 117
Thai-Style Beef, 27
Turkey Fried Rice, 116

PEARS

Burgundy Pears, 90
Fruit Dessert Topping, 88

PEAS

Festive Pea Salad, 240
Hearty Split Pea Soup, 66

PEPPERONI

Meat Lover's Pizza Bake, 174
Mini Hot Dogs 'n' Meatballs, 92
Muffuletta Pasta, 135
Pepperoni Pizza Skillet, 106
Peppy Parmesan Pasta, 143
Pizza Joes, 107
Zippy Calzones, 201

PEPPERS

Best Italian Sausage Sandwiches, 69
Black Bean Stuffed Peppers, 57
Citrus Chicken with Peppers, 126
Favorite Beef Chimichangas, 19
Fiesta Chicken Burritos, 42
Pepper Jack Chicken, 35
Pork Chops Creole, 130
Roasted Pepper Chicken Penne, 120
Slow Cooker Fajitas, 14
Slow Cooker Shredded Beef, 78
Unstuffed Peppers, 174
Zesty Orange Beef, 16

PINEAPPLE

Caribbean Bread Pudding, 83
Caribbean Chicken Tenderloins, 120
Hawaiian Kielbasa, 88
Hawaiian Pork Roast, 51
Slow-Cooked Sweet 'n' Sour Pork, 55
Sweet-and-Sour Pork, 140
Sweet 'n' Sour Sausage, 48
Sweet-and-Sour Smokies, 82

PIZZA

Chicken Alfredo Pizza, 178
Hot Wing Pizza, 183
Macaroni & Cheese Pizza, 195
Meat Lover's Pizza Bake, 174
Mexican Corn Bread Pizza, 189
Pepperoni Pizza Skillet, 106
Philly Cheesesteak Pizza, 170

Pizza Joes, 107
Spicy Shrimp Pizza, 217

PLUMS

Spiced Pork Loin with Plums, 138

POMEGRANATE

Pomegranate Pork Tenderloin, 141

PORK (ALSO SEE BACON; HAM & PROSCIUTTO; PEPPERONI; SAUSAGE)

OVEN

Barbecued Sticky Ribs, 198
Cranberry Glazed Pork Roast, 209
Creamy Pork Potpie, 211
German Pork Roast, 197
Glazed Pork Chops with Corn Bread Dressing, 205
Lemon-Rosemary Pork Tenderloin, 201
Maple Glazed Ribs, 196
Pork Noodle Casserole, 206
Roast Pork with Apples & Onions, 197
Zesty Pork Chops, 204

SLOW COOKER

Apple-Dijon Pork Roast, 46
Blue Cheese and Apple Pork Chops, 56
Country Pork Chop Supper, 48
Hawaiian Pork Roast, 51
Hearty Pork Stew, 51
Lemon Pork Chops, 51
Pork Chops & Potatoes in Mushroom Sauce, 46
Pork Ribs Lo Mein, 52
Posole Verde, 63
Sesame Pork Ribs, 54
Slow-Cooked Sweet 'n' Sour Pork, 55
Slow Cooker Pulled Pork Sandwiches, 74
Slow Cooker Ribs, 47
Tropical Triple Pork, 45

STOVETOP

Cherry-Stuffed Pork Chops, 129
Harvest Stew, 143
Hash Brown Pork Skillet, 140
Italian Pork Skillet, 133
Pomegranate Pork Tenderloin, 141

Pork and Apple Supper, 132
Pork Chops Creole, 130
Pork in Orange Sauce, 134
Pork Medallions with Asian Flair, 139
Pork with Artichokes and Capers, 136
Spiced Pork Loin with Plums, 138
Sweet-and-Sour Pork, 140

POTATOES & SWEET POTATOES

Broccoli-Cheddar Hash Browns, 72
Cranberry Brisket with Horseradish Mashed Potatoes, 175
Creamy Red Potatoes, 68
Farm-Style Sausage Bake, 198
Ham and Hash Browns, 52
Ham 'n' Tater Bake, 209
Hash Brown Pork Skillet, 140
Hearty Hash Brown Dinner, 15
Hot German Potato Salad, 77
Italian Roast with Alfredo Potatoes, 27
Mashed Potato Hot Dish, 173
Mediterranean Potato Salad, 243
Pork Chops & Potatoes in Mushroom Sauce, 46
Potato Beef Lasagna, 169
Potato-Crusted Chicken Casserole, 185
Potato Kielbasa Skillet, 136
Potato Sausage Casserole, 202
Scalloped Potatoes 'n' Ham Casserole, 210
Spiced Sweet Potato Pudding, 93
Steak over Potatoes, 160
Tangy Potato Salad, 245
Tater Brat Bake, 200
Two-Tater Shepherd's Pie, 169

PUMPKIN

His Favorite Ravioli, 135
Sausage Pumpkin Soup, 78

RASPBERRIES

Chicken Rolls with Raspberry Sauce, 182
Mixed Fruit with Lemon-Basil Dressing, 229
Saucy Raspberry Chicken, 33

RICE

Apricot-Glazed Salmon with
 Herb Rice, 214
Bayou Casserole, 223
Bayou Gulf Shrimp Gumbo, 50
Buffet Rice Salad, 245
Casserole in the Cooker, 54
Chicken Artichoke Bake, 183
Chicken Chop Suey with a Twist, 36
Chicken Rice Dinner, 186
Chinese Beef Casserole, 166
Favorite Jiffy Jambalaya, 148
Forgotten Jambalaya, 40
Grandma's Cabbage Rolls, 23
Ham Fried Rice, 131
Paella, 146
Sesame Shrimp & Rice, 152
Shrimp Gumbo, 150
Shrimp Rice Casserole, 215
Teriyaki Steak, 99
Turkey Fried Rice, 116
Unstuffed Peppers, 174

SALADS (ALSO SEE COLE SLAW)

Buffet Rice Salad, 245
Classic Macaroni Salad, 240
Colorful Caesar Salad, 241
Festive Pea Salad, 240
Green Salad with Herb
 Vinaigrette, 230
Hot Fruit Salad, 89
Hot German Potato Salad, 77
Marinated Salad, 239
Mediterranean Potato Salad, 243
Mixed Fruit with Lemon-Basil
 Dressing, 229
Orzo Cheesecake Fruit Salad, 229
Party Tortellini Salad, 233
Refreshing Cucumber Salad, 242
Strawberry Romaine Salad, 242
Summer-Fresh Quinoa Salad, 227
Taco Salad, 106
Tangy Potato Salad, 245
Wheely-Good Pasta Salad, 245

SANDWICHES & WRAPS

Bacon-Chicken Crescent Ring, 179
Bavarian Meatballs, 62
Best Italian Sausage Sandwiches, 69
Buffalo Chicken Wraps, 119
Ham 'n' Cheese Stromboli, 202
Ham Barbecue, 69
Italian Beef Hoagies, 77
Melt-in-Your-Mouth Sausages, 66
Onion Loose-Meat Sandwiches, 110
Open-Faced Chicken Avocado
 Burgers, 122
Pizza Joes, 107
Pulled Turkey Tenderloin, 39
Slow Cooker Pulled Pork
 Sandwiches, 74
Slow Cooker Shredded Beef, 78
Spicy Chicken Lettuce Wraps, 124
Taco Chicken Wraps, 188
Tilapia Wraps, 147
Turkey Sloppy Joes, 76
Veggie Tuna Burgers, 153
Zippy Calzones, 201

SAUCES

Cranberry Apple Topping, 70
Easy-Does-It Spaghetti, 20
Fruit Dessert Topping, 88
Sausage-Veggie Pasta Sauce, 47
Warm Strawberry Fondue, 86
Winter Fruit Compote, 84

SAUSAGE (ALSO SEE HOT DOGS)

OVEN

Creamy Spinach Sausage Pasta, 206
Farm-Style Sausage Bake, 198
Macaroni & Cheese Pizza, 195
Meaty Noodle Casserole, 161
Potato Sausage Casserole, 202
Tater Brat Bake, 200

SLOW COOKER

Best Italian Sausage Sandwiches, 69
Creole Black Beans 'n' Sausage, 55
Favorite Skillet Lasagna, 115
Forgotten Jambalaya, 40
Hawaiian Kielbasa, 88
Hearty Pasta Tomato Soup, 73
Melt-in-Your-Mouth Sausages, 66
Posole Verde, 63
Pronto Penne Pasta, 119
Ratatouille with a Twist, 45
Sausage Macaroni Supper, 132
Sausage Pumpkin Soup, 78
Sausage-Veggie Pasta Sauce, 47
Slow Cooker Mexican Dip, 90
Sweet 'n' Sour Sausage, 48
Sweet-and-Sour Smokies, 82
Tropical Triple Pork, 45
Zesty Garbanzo Sausage Soup, 73

STOVETOP

Forgotten Jambalaya, 40
Paella, 146
Potato Kielbasa Skillet, 136

SIDE DISHES

Broccoli-Cheddar Hash Browns, 72
Creamy Red Potatoes, 68
Fiesta Corn and Beans, 60
Georgian Bay Baked Beans, 70
Ham Fried Rice, 131
Hot German Potato Salad, 77
Makeover Slow-Cooked
 Mac 'n' Cheese, 61
Maple-Almond Butternut Squash, 68
Moist Poultry Dressing, 62
Ranch Beans, 69
Stewed Zucchini and Tomatoes, 78

SOUPS (ALSO SEE CHILI; STEWS)

Buffalo Chicken Wing Soup, 73
Cheesy Cauliflower Soup, 74
Gyro Soup, 65
Hamburger Vegetable Soup, 76
Hearty Pasta Tomato Soup, 73
Hearty Split Pea Soup, 66
Posole Verde, 63
Sausage Pumpkin Soup, 78
Southwest Vegetarian Lentil
 Soup, 61
Southwestern Chicken Soup, 75
Trout Chowder, 65
Vegetable Barley Soup, 59
Zesty Garbanzo Sausage Soup, 73

SPINACH

Beef Spinach Hot Dish, 162
Company-Ready Crusted
 Salmon, 223
Creamy Spinach Sausage Pasta, 206
Ham & Spinach Casserole, 203
Mushroom Chicken Florentine, 31
Potato Kielbasa Skillet, 136
Spinach-Stuffed Chicken Pockets, 127
Tilapia with Sauteed Spinach, 145

STEWS

Beef 'n' Chili Beans, 26
Chicken Stew with Gnocchi, 67
Creole Black Beans 'n' Sausage, 55
Gone-All-Day Goulash, 19
Ground Beef Stew, 16
Harvest Stew, 143
Hearty Pork Stew, 51
Loaded Vegetable Beef Stew, 103
Meatball Stew, 111
Mint Lamb Stew, 52
Sunday Chicken Stew, 41
Tangy Beef and Vegetable Stew, 22

STRAWBERRIES

Strawberry Romaine Salad, 242
Warm Strawberry Fondue, 86

TOMATOES & TOMATILLOS

Fresh Tomato Flatbread, 230
Hearty Pasta Tomato Soup, 73
Posole Verde, 63
Red Snapper Vera Cruz, 148
Salmon with Broccoli and Pasta, 151
Stewed Zucchini and Tomatoes, 78

TURKEY

OVEN
Cheddar Turkey Casserole, 186
Crescent-Topped Turkey
  Amandine, 179
Mexican Corn Bread Pizza, 189
Roasted Turkey Breast Tenderloins
  and Vegetables, 177
Turkey Cabbage Bake, 181

SLOW COOKER
Moist & Tender Turkey Breast, 36
Moist Italian Turkey Breast, 39
Pulled Turkey Tenderloin, 39
Turkey in Cream Sauce, 32
Turkey Sloppy Joes, 76

STOVETOP
Cran-Apple Turkey Skillet, 127
Favorite Skillet Lasagna, 115
Pronto Penne Pasta, 119
Turkey Fried Rice, 116

VEGETABLES
(ALSO SEE SPECIFIC KINDS; SALADS)
Chicken Chop Suey with a Twist, 36

Cod & Vegetable Skillet, 155
Hamburger Vegetable Soup, 76
Loaded Vegetable Beef Stew, 103
Loaded Veggie Dip, 81
Pasta Primavera with Shrimp, 152
Roasted Cornish Hens with
  Vegetables, 184
Roasted Turkey Breast Tenderloins
  and Vegetables, 177
Satisfying Chicken and Veggies, 33
Sausage-Veggie Pasta Sauce, 47
Tangy Beef and Vegetable Stew, 22
Vegetable Barley Soup, 59
Veggie Tuna Burgers, 153

WINTER SQUASH

Harvest Chicken with Walnut
  Gremolata, 34
Harvest Stew, 143
Loaded Vegetable Beef Stew, 103
Maple-Almond Butternut
  Squash, 68

ZUCCHINI

Ratatouille with a Twist, 45
Stewed Zucchini and Tomatoes, 78

Alphabetical Recipe Index

A

Angel Hair Shrimp Bake, 224
Apple Chicken Stew, 32
Apple Comfort, 92
Apple-Dijon Pork Roast, 46
Apple Walnut Slaw, 237
Apricot Beef Stir-Fry, 108
Apricot-Glazed Salmon with Herb Rice, 214
Asian Barbecued Short Ribs, 162
Asparagus Beef Stir-Fry, 97
Asparagus Fish Bundles, 218
Asparagus Scallop Stir-Fry, 154

B

Bacon Cheeseburger Spaghetti, 111
Bacon-Chicken Crescent Ring, 179
Bacon Chicken Roll-Ups, 180
Barbecued Beef Brisket, 21
Barbecued Sticky Ribs, 198
Bavarian Meatballs, 62
Bavarian Wiener Supper, 205
Bayou Casserole, 223
Bayou Gulf Shrimp Gumbo, 50
Beef 'n' Chili Beans, 26
Beef Spinach Hot Dish, 162
Beer-Glazed Ham, 210

Best Chicken 'n' Biscuits, 180
Best Italian Sausage Sandwiches, 69
Black Bean Stuffed Peppers, 57
Blue Cheese and Apple Pork Chops, 56
Blue Cheese Herb Loaf, 241
Bohemian Beef Dinner, 104
Broccoli-Cheddar Hash Browns, 72
Brown-Bag Burritos, 99
Buffalo Chicken Wing Soup, 73
Buffalo Chicken Wraps, 119
Buffet Meatballs, 86
Buffet Rice Salad, 245
Burgundy Pears, 90
Butterscotch Apple Crisp, 85

C

Cajun Chicken Lasagna, 36
California Tamale Pie, 15
Caramel Hot Chocolate, 93
Caribbean Bread Pudding, 83
Caribbean Chicken Tenderloins, 120
Casserole in the Cooker, 54
Celery Seed Slaw, 233
Cheddar Turkey Casserole, 186
Cheesy Cauliflower Soup, 74
Cheesy Clam Manicotti, 213
Cherry-Stuffed Pork Chops, 129

Chicken Alfredo Pizza, 178
Chicken 'n' Dressing Casserole, 190
Chicken Artichoke Bake, 183
Chicken Chop Suey with a Twist, 36
Chicken in Sour Cream Sauce, 43
Chicken Lasagna, 191
Chicken Potpie with Cheddar Biscuit Topping, 192
Chicken Rice Dinner, 186
Chicken Rolls with Raspberry Sauce, 182
Chicken Saltimbocca, 123
Chicken Stew with Gnocchi, 67
Chicken Veronique, 114
Chili Cheese Dog Casserole, 208
Chinese Beef Casserole, 166
Chocolate Malt Pudding Cake, 86
Christmas Carol Ham, 56
Citrus Chicken with Peppers, 126
Classic Macaroni Salad, 240
Cod & Vegetable Skillet, 155
Coffee-Flavored Beef Roast, 17
Colorful Caesar Salad, 241
Company-Ready Crusted Salmon, 223
Corned Beef Dinner, 20

Cornish Game Hens with Couscous, 29
Country Pork Chop Supper, 48
Crab Macaroni & Cheese, 222
Cran-Apple Turkey Skillet, 127
Cranberry Apple Topping, 70
Cranberry Brisket with Horseradish Mashed Potatoes, 175
Cranberry Glazed Pork Roast, 209
Creamy Chicken Angel Hair, 113
Creamy Onion Dip, 82
Creamy Pork Potpie, 211
Creamy Red Potatoes, 68
Creamy Spinach Sausage Pasta, 206
Creole Black Beans 'n' Sausage, 55
Crescent-Topped Casserole, 163
Crescent-Topped Turkey Amandine, 179
Crunchy Baked Chicken, 192

E

Easy Beef Taco Skillet, 108
Easy Crab Lo Mein, 147
Easy-Does-It Spaghetti, 20
Easy Haddock Bake, 219
Enchiladas Verdes, 167

F

Family-Style Meat Loaf Dinner, 24
Farm-Style Sausage Bake, 198
Favorite Beef Chimichangas, 19
Favorite Jiffy Jambalaya, 148
Favorite Skillet Lasagna, 115
Festive Pea Salad, 240
Fiesta Chicken Burritos, 42
Fiesta Corn and Beans, 60
Forgotten Jambalaya, 40
Fresh Herb Flatbread, 238
Fresh Tomato Flatbread, 230
Fried Chicken with Pan Gravy, 115
Fruit Dessert Topping, 88

G

Garlic-Cheese Crescent Rolls, 234
Georgian Bay Baked Beans, 70
German Pork Roast, 197
Glazed Lamb Shanks, 49
Glazed Pork Chops with Corn Bread Dressing, 205
Golden Cornish Hens, 191
Gone-All-Day Goulash, 19

Grandma's Cabbage Rolls, 23
Greek Orzo Chicken, 30
Greek Shrimp Orzo, 56
Green Salad with Herb Vinaigrette, 230
Ground Beef Stew, 16
Gyro Soup, 65

H

Ham 'n' Cheese Stromboli, 202
Ham and Hash Browns, 52
Ham & Spinach Casserole, 203
Ham 'n' Tater Bake, 209
Ham Barbecue, 69
Ham Fettuccine, 142
Ham Fried Rice, 131
Hamburger Goulash, 100
Hamburger Vegetable Soup, 76
Harvest Chicken with Walnut Gremolata, 34
Harvest Ham Steak, 139
Harvest Stew, 143
Hash Brown Pork Skillet, 140
Hawaiian Kielbasa, 88
Hawaiian Pork Roast, 51
Healthy Shrimp Piccata Pasta, 152
Hearty Beans with Beef, 21
Hearty Beef and Noodles, 102
Hearty Beef Ravioli, 97
Hearty Chicken Enchiladas, 35
Hearty Hash Brown Dinner, 15
Hearty Pasta Tomato Soup, 73
Hearty Pork Stew, 51
Hearty Split Pea Soup, 66
Herb-Swirled Rolls, 237
Herbed Beef with Noodles, 26
Herbed Chicken and Shrimp, 40
His Favorite Ravioli, 135
Homemade Italian Pot Roast , 166
Hot Fruit Salad, 89
Hot German Potato Salad, 77
Hot Wing Pizza, 183

I

Italian Beef Hoagies, 77
Italian Chicken, 121
Italian Pork Skillet, 133
Italian Pot Roast, 24
Italian Roast with Alfredo Potatoes, 27
Italian Strip Steaks with Focaccia, 101

L

Lemon Pork Chops, 51
Lemon-Rosemary Pork Tenderloin, 201
Loaded Spaghetti Bake, 159
Loaded Vegetable Beef Stew, 103
Loaded Veggie Dip, 81

M

Macaroni & Cheese Pizza, 195
Makeover Creamy Halibut Enchiladas, 225
Makeover Slow-Cooked Mac 'n' Cheese, 61
Maple-Almond Butternut Squash, 68
Maple Glazed Ribs, 196
Marinated Salad, 239
Mashed Potato Hot Dish, 173
Meat Lover's Pizza Bake, 174
Meatball Stew, 111
Meaty Noodle Casserole, 161
Mediterranean Mahi Mahi, 216
Mediterranean Potato Salad, 243
Melt-in-Your-Mouth Sausages, 66
Mexican Chicken Penne for Kids, 116
Mexican Corn Bread Pizza, 189
Mini Hot Dogs 'n' Meatballs, 92
Mini Toffee Rolls, 232
Mint Lamb Stew, 52
Mixed Fruit with Lemon-Basil Dressing, 229
Mocha Mint Coffee, 84
Moist & Tender Turkey Breast, 36
Moist Italian Turkey Breast, 39
Moist Poultry Dressing, 62
Mom's Pot Roast, 104
Muffuletta Pasta, 135
Mulled Grape Cider, 93
Mushroom Chicken Florentine, 31
Mushroom Steak 'n' Linguine, 100

N

Nacho Mac 'n' Cheese, 103
No-Knead Whole Wheat Rolls, 234

O

Onion Cheese Biscuits, 244
Onion-Garlic Bubble Bread, 228
Onion Loose-Meat Sandwiches, 110
Onion Swiss Loaf, 243

Open-Faced Chicken Avocado
  Burgers, 122
Oregano Roasting Chicken, 184
Orzo Cheesecake Fruit Salad, 229

P
Paella, 146
Party Tortellini Salad, 233
Pasta Carbonara, 131
Pasta Primavera with Shrimp, 152
Pastry-Topped Salmon
  Casserole, 220
Pecan Chicken with Blue Cheese
  Sauce, 188
Penne Gorgonzola with Chicken, 123
Pepper-Crusted Beef Tenderloin, 165
Pepper Jack Chicken, 35
Peppered Sole, 151
Pepperoni Pizza Skillet, 106
Peppy Parmesan Pasta, 143
Philly Cheesesteak Pizza, 170
Pizza Joes, 107
Pomegranate Pork Tenderloin, 141
Pork and Apple Supper, 132
Pork Chops & Potatoes in Mushroom
  Sauce, 46
Pork Chops Creole, 130
Pork in Orange Sauce, 134
Pork Medallions with Asian
  Flair, 139
Pork Noodle Casserole, 206
Pork Ribs Lo Mein, 52
Pork with Artichokes and
  Capers, 136
Posole Verde, 63
Potato Beef Lasagna, 169
Potato-Crusted Chicken
  Casserole, 185
Potato Kielbasa Skillet, 136
Potato Sausage Casserole, 202
Pronto Penne Pasta, 119
Prosciutto Chicken in Wine
  Sauce, 124
Pull-Apart Sticky Bun Ring, 236
Pulled Turkey Tenderloin, 39

R
Ranch Beans, 69
Ratatouille with a Twist, 45
Red Snapper Vera Cruz, 148
Refreshing Cucumber Salad, 242
Reuben Crescent Bake, 161
Reuben Spread, 82

Roast Pork with Apples & Onions, 197
Roasted Cornish Hens with
  Vegetables, 184
Roasted Pepper Chicken Penne, 120
Roasted Turkey Breast Tenderloins
  and Vegetables, 177

S
Salmon with Broccoli and Pasta, 151
Salmon with Fettuccine Alfredo, 224
Satisfying Chicken and Veggies, 33
Saucy Raspberry Chicken , 33
Sausage Macaroni Supper, 132
Sausage Pumpkin Soup, 78
Sausage-Veggie Pasta Sauce, 47
Scalloped Potatoes 'n' Ham
  Casserole, 210
Scallops in Sage Cream, 155
Sesame Pork Ribs, 54
Sesame Shrimp & Rice, 152
Shrimp Gumbo, 150
Shrimp Rice Casserole, 215
Simple Swedish Meatballs, 23
Skillet Beef Tamales, 110
Skillet Franks, 143
Skinny Crab Quiche, 220
Slow-Cooked Chili, 63
Slow-Cooked Italian Chicken, 38
Slow-Cooked Sweet 'n' Sour Pork, 55
Slow-Cooked White Chili, 65
Slow Cooker Fajitas, 14
Slow Cooker Mexican Dip, 90
Slow Cooker Pulled Pork
  Sandwiches, 74
Slow Cooker Ribs, 47
Slow Cooker Shredded Beef, 78
So-Easy Coq Au Vin, 31
Southwest Beef Pie, 170
Southwest Pasta Bake, 168
Southwest Vegetarian Lentil Soup, 61
Southwestern Chicken Soup, 75
Spaghetti Pie, 172
Spaghetti with Italian Meatballs, 109
Special Seafood Casserole, 219
Spiced Cranberry Punch, 85
Spiced Pork Loin with Plums, 138
Spiced Sweet Potato Pudding, 93
Spicy Chicken Lettuce Wraps, 124
Spicy Shrimp Pizza, 217
Spinach-Stuffed Chicken Pockets, 127
Steak over Potatoes, 160
Stewed Zucchini and Tomatoes, 78
Strawberry Romaine Salad, 242
Stuffed Flank Steak, 173

Summer-Fresh Quinoa Salad, 227
Sunday Chicken Stew, 41
Sweet-and-Sour Chicken Wings, 90
Sweet-and-Sour Pork, 140
Sweet 'n' Sour Sausage, 48
Sweet-and-Sour Smokies, 82
Sweet Chili Short Ribs, 13
Sweet Kahlua Coffee, 89
Swiss Steak Supper, 16

T
Taco Chicken Wraps, 188
Taco Macaroni, 107
Taco Pie, 160
Taco Salad, 106
Tangy Beef and Vegetable Stew, 22
Tangy Potato Salad, 245
Tangy Tropical Chicken, 39
Tasty Chicken Marsala, 30
Tater Brat Bake, 200
Teriyaki Steak, 99
Thai Portobello Chicken Stir-Fry, 117
Thai-Style Beef, 27
Tilapia with Sauteed Spinach, 145
Tilapia Wraps, 147
Traditional Meat Loaf, 165
Tropical BBQ Chicken, 43
Tropical Triple Pork, 45
Trout Chowder, 65
Tuna-Chip Casserole, 216
Tuna Mac and Cheese Bake, 215
Turkey Cabbage Bake, 181
Turkey Fried Rice, 116
Turkey in Cream Sauce, 32
Turkey Sloppy Joes, 76
Two-Tater Shepherd's Pie, 169

U
Unstuffed Peppers, 174

V
Vegetable Barley Soup, 59
Veggie Tuna Burgers, 153

W
Warm Strawberry Fondue, 86
Wheely-Good Pasta Salad, 245
Winter Fruit Compote, 84

Z
Zesty Garbanzo Sausage Soup, 73
Zesty Orange Beef, 16
Zesty Pork Chops, 204
Zippy Calzones, 201